D1452383

studies in jazz

Institute of Jazz Studies
Rutgers—The State University of New Jersey
General Editors: *Dan Morgenstern & Edward Berger*

The *Annual Review of Jazz Studies* is published yearly by Scarecrow Press for the Institute of Jazz Studies at Rutgers, The State University of New Jersey.

Authors should address manuscripts and editorial correspondence to:

> The Editors
> *Annual Review of Jazz Studies*
> Institute of Jazz Studies
> Bradley Hall 135
> Rutgers, The State University of New Jersey
> Newark, New Jersey 07102

Review copies of books should be sent to this address by publishers and marked to the attention of the Book Review Editor.

Authors preparing manuscripts for consideration should follow *The Chicago Manual of Style*. In particular: (1) manuscripts should be original typed or word-processed copies; (2) except for foreign-language quotations, manuscripts must be in English; (3) *all* material (text, quotations, endnotes, author's biographical note) must be neat, double-spaced, and with adequate margins; (4) notes must be grouped together on separate pages at the end of the manuscript and should be complete references following the samples in *A Manual of Style;* (5) on a separate sheet, authors should provide a one- or two-sentence biographical note, including current affiliation; and (6) musical examples should be on separate sheets in camera-ready form; they must be clear enough to be legible if reduction is required to fit the *ARJS* format.

Authors alone are responsible for the contents of their articles.

ANNUAL REVIEW OF JAZZ STUDIES 6 1993

edited by
Edward Berger
David Cayer
Dan Morgenstern
Lewis Porter

Institute of Jazz Studies
Rutgers—The State University
of New Jersey
and
The Scarecrow Press, Inc.
Metuchen, N.J., & London
1993

British Library Cataloguing-in-Publication data available

ISBN 0-8108-2478-7 (ARJS 5)
ISBN 0-8108-2727-1

82-644466

CONTENTS

BOOK REVIEWS

PREFACE

The sixth volume of the *Annual Review of Jazz Studies* is the second to appear in a hardcover format and to be published by Scarecrow Press, which is also the publisher of the Studies in Jazz monograph series which, like *ARJS,* is sponsored by the Institute of Jazz Studies, a unit of Rutgers, The State University of New Jersey.

Two articles in this volume represent innovations for *ARJS.* As a frontispiece illustrating our lead article, "Anatomy of a Cover" by Charles H. Waters, Jr., we offer the first full-color illustration ever to appear in *ARJS—Time* magazine's August 20, 1956, cover portrait of Duke Ellington by painter Peter Hurd. Through the courtesy of *Time,* the cover, as well as the article and photographs which accompanied it, are reproduced in full as an appendix to Mr. Waters's article.

William Bauer's detailed analysis of the singing styles of Billie Holiday and Betty Carter is the first *ARJS* article based on research supported in part by a grant from the Morroe Berger-Benny Carter Jazz Research Fund at the Institute of Jazz Studies. The editors and publisher of *ARJS* recognized that Mr. Bauer's transcriptions of each artist's performance of "I Didn't Know What Time It Was" would prove hard to decipher if greatly reduced to our format. Furthermore, spreading the music over many pages would make it difficult to follow his detailed comparisons between the two singers. We have therefore reproduced these transcriptions in a larger format and included them in this volume as inserts which can be removed for easy study and comparison.

The introduction of a photographic gallery in *ARJS 5* proved a popular innovation among both readers and reviewers, and this volume includes a gallery of Mitchell Seidel's photos—formal portraits, performance pictures, and backstage or studio candids.

As always, the range of jazz scholarship in *ARJS* remains diverse, both in methodology and in the styles and artists examined.

The current debate in higher education concerning "canons" in the arts and humanities is extended to jazz by a critic with parallel expertise in film and other genres, while another writer ponders the role of Latin influences in defining jazz styles.

Detailed studies of individual jazz artists include two articles on the seminal guitarist Charlie Christian, one presenting a detailed bibliography of his transcribed solos, the other exploring his legacy of after-hours, noncommercial recordings at Minton's. Other articles are devoted to the music of Ornette Coleman, Arthur Taylor, and a proposed standard method of notating melodic elements of jazz performance which are inadequately represented by standard notation.

This volume's book review section examines recent publications ranging from autobiography and biography (including lives of Benny Goodman and Billie Holiday) to a number of reference works.

Publications submitted for review, or for a forthcoming list of newly published works, should be addressed to:

Review Editor
Annual Review of Jazz Studies
Institute of Jazz Studies
135 Bradley Hall
Rutgers, The State University
Newark, NJ 07102

While an annual publication cannot serve as a medium for general correspondence in the manner of a daily or weekly, the editors invite concise commentary on articles and reviews from readers and will publish, as space permits, appropriate correspondence at their discretion and with permission of the writer.

The Editors

Copyright 1956 Time Warner Inc. Reprinted by permission. (The *Time* cover article of August 20, 1956, is reproduced in full on pp. 54–64.)

ANATOMY OF A COVER: THE STORY OF DUKE ELLINGTON'S APPEARANCE ON THE COVER OF *TIME* MAGAZINE

By Charles H. Waters, Jr.

INTRODUCTION

In the summer of 1956, the fortunes of the Duke Ellington orchestra underwent a dramatic reversal as the result of two events which have since become benchmarks in its history. On the evening of Saturday, 7 July, the orchestra appeared at the Newport Jazz Festival in Rhode Island. During that appearance, the rendition of "Diminuendo and Crescendo in Blue," featuring an extended solo by Paul Gonsalves on tenor saxophone, caused a widely publicized sensation.[1] Shortly thereafter, Ellington was the subject of the cover story of the 20 August 1956 issue of *Time* magazine.[2] The immediate effect of these two events was a rebirth in popularity for the Ellington orchestra, which had endured a period of eclipse during the first half of the decade. In the long term, their positive effects would remain with and benefit Ellington for the remainder of his life.

In his autobiography, *Music Is My Mistress*,[3] Ellington formalized a position he had long espoused about the relationship of the two events: that the Newport success resulted in the *Time* cover story. Subsequent literature repeated and reinforced the proposition that preparation of the cover story began only after Newport and solely in response to it. However, closer examination of the circumstances has demonstrated that the decision to put Ellington on the cover of *Time* resulted from different and far-reaching considerations. Ellington's publicist, Joe Morgen, began efforts to secure the *Time* cover months before Newport. His work came to fruition through an editorial climate as remarkable as it was receptive.

The cover portrait was painted by the noted Southwestern artist, Peter Hurd. His correspondence clearly established that *Time* began to prepare the Ellington cover story prior to the Newport appearance. The portrait also subsumed a meeting between two great American artists from very different backgrounds, an event so alive with possibilities that it invited separate examination.

THE SIGNIFICANCE OF A TIME COVER APPEARANCE

For any person to appear on the cover of *Time* magazine is a significant event which carries with it extraordinary prestige. These effects result directly from the emphasis placed on the cover story by *Time*'s founder and longtime Editor-in-Chief, Henry R. Luce:

> He had a powerful sense of what people should read, what was good for them to read, and an essential belief worthy of the best journalist, that any subject of importance could be made interesting. Thus, the cover story, the personalizing of issues so that a lay reader could become more interested and more involved in serious reading matter. The cover story alone had a major impact on the journalism of our age.[4]

The practice of naming *Time*'s "Man of the Year' as the year's initial cover story is a continuing manifestation of this historical emphasis. The success of the weekly news magazine concept, originated with *Time,* further enhanced the effect of the cover story on public perception.[5] Raymond Horricks accurately referred to a *Time* cover appearance as representing "the ultimate in American acceptance."[6] The noted jazz author, Stanley Dance, in liner notes to the remastered *Ellington at Newport* recording, wrote that Ellington's cover appearance was "like a national seal of approval."[7] Joseph McLaren summarized the effect and meaning of the Ellington cover:

The most significant event of this rebirth was the appearance of the orchestra at the 1956 Newport Jazz Festival in Rhode Island. This performance was reviewed by *Time* in its August 20 issue that featured Ellington as the cover story, a sign of recognition that also reflected the importance of Ellington and his organization to American musical culture. Although Ellington had previously been the subject of cover stories by certain jazz periodicals of the day, the *Time* cover story was a most impressive accolade for an Afro-American musician who had maintained a big band orchestra for over twenty-nine years without disbanding, a feat which was unequaled by any other practitioner of popular American music and jazz.[8]

The *Time* cover story thus served both to acknowledge Ellington's stature and to confirm the renaissance of his orchestra. In coming years, the effect of Newport, as enhanced by this cover, will assume a significance of its own, as Ellington intended.

THE COVER STORY

The *Time* cover story was both a product and a reflection of the times and circumstances in which it arose. In the spring of 1956, Ellington turned fifty-seven. It was then an appropriate point for his stature, already of the highest magnitude, to be acknowledged in a national publication. Stanley Dance succinctly made this point: "When you consider . . . the stature Duke had acquired over the years, the *Time* cover doesn't seem so surprising now as it may have . . . then."[9]

There were more immediate factors at work. The first half of the decade of the 1950s had been a period of artistic highs and lows for the orchestra. Ellington's tone poem, "Harlem (A Tone Parallel to Harlem)," his last extended single work, premiered in January 1951.[10] He continued to produce any number of minor masterpieces, such as the little-known "Deep Night" (1951)[11] and "Ultra-Deluxe" (1953).[12] "Satin Doll" was another 1953 composition. A critical blow, however, was struck early in 1951 when Johnny Hodges,

Lawrence Brown, and Sonny Greer departed.[13] They were replaced, respectively, by Willie Smith, Juan Tizol, and Louis (Louie) Bellson. Despite a further infusion of talent in 1950 and 1951, which also saw Paul Gonsalves, Britt Woodman, Willie Cook, and Clark Terry join the band, there ensued a period of instability in personnel, particularly manifested in the drummer's chair.[14] The problems are generally considered to have reached their nadir with the Aquacades appearance in the summer of 1955, generally regarded as a debacle.[15] Even by then, however, the turnaround had begun. In January 1955, a new bassist, Jimmy Woode, joined the band. In the summer of 1955, Johnny Hodges returned, accompanied by a new drummer, Sam Woodyard.[16] Ellington's contract with Capitol Records expired at the end of 1955. Early in February 1956, an extended session for Bethlehem Records resulted in two recordings which demonstrated the band to be in outstanding form.[17] Ellington then signed a new contract with Columbia Records. Irving Townsend was assigned as his executive producer, and this association would prove exceptionally fruitful.[18]

The positive developments of this period did not go unnoticed by knowledgeable jazz critics. In the spring of 1956, the *Saturday Review* featured an extended appreciation of Ellington by Whitney Balliett, which could be viewed as a harbinger of the *Time* cover story. Although not biographical as the *Time* story would be (Ellington was not interviewed), the article summarized the history of the band, with emphasis on the recent past and the changing present. An excerpt from this warm and eloquent tribute is the following:

> Again, many listeners have been hypnotized by the trappings that often surround his music: the lushness, the use of the growl, the squatty brass and saxophone slurs, the striding humor, the seemingly insouciant, akimbo attitude of his musicians toward their music. This warm, overlaid picturesqueness is not ostentation, however; it is, rather, the result of a mind that moves through greener, more tangled musical meadows than those of the average journeyman jazzman. Ellington,

indeed, is perhaps the first, and as yet the only, complete jazz artist.[19]

In retrospect, for both long-term and short-term reasons, it was an appropriate point in Ellington's career for him to be accorded recognition other than by jazz critics or in jazz periodicals, as had previously been the case. It remained for two men in the midst of these developments, Joe Morgen and Carter Harman, to act effectively to get Ellington onto the cover of *Time.*

In the latter part of 1955, Ellington's publicist, Joe Morgen, conceived the idea of a *Time* cover story. He elected to approach *Time* both because of the exposure which would result from a cover appearance on the leading weekly news magazine and because his contact there, Carter Harman, shared his views about an Ellington cover story.

The personalities of Morgen and Harman were critical factors in the genesis of the *Time* cover story. Morgen was a Falstaffian character of little formal education or sophistication, with an unkempt appearance and an uncouth manner to match. His effectiveness as a publicist derived from the fact that he had the finesse and persistence of a bulldog. He died in 1981, but his forceful personality is vividly recalled by those who knew him. Stanley Dance has written:

> Joe Morgen was a very persistent publicity man. I wasn't in this country in 1956, but he himself always referred to the *Time* cover and story as one of his major coups. [He] was aggressive and hard to take at times, but he was absolutely loyal and devoted to Duke. He was also a hard worker. He knew all the press people and was always on their backs to give Duke publicity. Sometimes, I know, they did so to get rid of him, but they would not shake him for long.[20]

> It was part of Joe Morgen's job to make and maintain contacts with journalists who could give Duke . . . publicity of one kind or another. He was on good terms with Carter Harman, who wrote the story, and Carter had considerable understanding and affection for Duke's music.[21]

The DETS Newsletter of June/July, 1981, published shortly after Joe Morgen's death, contains this tribute:

> Those of us who knew Joe personally always admired his true sense of loyalty to Duke and his sincere love of the man. Joe was a bachelor, and in a sense, Duke was his mistress. I was proud to have known him these many years.[22]

Finally, we have Ellington's appreciation of Joe Morgen, in words which appear to have been written with the *Time* cover story in mind:

> Joe Morgen, who has been with me the longest—over twenty years—is the kind of p.r. who thinks only in terms of cover stories, full page pictures, and big, important articles in magazines. Maybe I exaggerate a little, for he will stand still for a good word in a column.[23]

Late in 1955, Morgen proposed the idea of an Ellington cover story to Carter Harman, music editor of *Time*. Harman now lives in Carmel, California. He is a 1940 graduate of Princeton University, having majored in music and studied under Roger Sessions. He became music editor of *Time* in 1952, after five years as a music reporter for *The New York Times*.[24] During his tenure as music editor, which extended until 1957, he wrote five cover stories, the subjects of which speak to his catholic taste: Rosemary Clooney,[25] George Balanchine,[26] Dave Brubeck,[27] Duke Ellington, and Maria Callas.[28] Harman first heard Ellington on radio in 1934 and first saw him in person in 1938 at the downtown Cotton Club on 48th Street in New York. He met Ellington briefly at a dance pavilion in New Brunswick, New Jersey, during his undergraduate years and retains to this day a deep love of and respect for Ellington and his music. Harman had known Joe Morgen casually for a number of years, but it was some time after they met before he became aware of Morgen's relationship with Ellington.

Morgen also did publicity work for the Hickory House, a steak restaurant on 52nd Street, which featured first-rate jazz

Carter Harman
Photograph by John Urban, Boston, Massachusetts

and was one of Ellington's favorite places to eat.[29] Much of what followed was planned and implemented there. It was through Morgen that Harman was again to meet Ellington and become involved in the cover story.

The first result of Morgen's efforts was an article which appeared in *Time* in January 1956.[30] In it, the band's resurgence is noted, and Sam Woodyard, whose picture appears, is the subject of high praise.[31] Carter Harman has said: "I wrote this article to keep Joe Morgen quiet. It didn't work and I knew it wouldn't."[32] This article was in fact far short of what Joe Morgen had in mind, and he continued into the spring of 1956 to promote Ellington as the subject of a *Time* cover story.

Morgen's dogged persistence and Harman's sympathetic ear would not have brought about the cover story had not responsible editors at *Time,* who never heard of or from Morgen, believed of their own accord that Ellington was a proper cover subject. Fortunately, a favorable editorial climate existed, both about jazz in general and Ellington in particular. For many years, the editorial thinking at *Time* had been that jazz was an American art form which deserved recognition as such. The Armstrong[33] and Brubeck[34] cover stories were manifestations of this editorial commitment to jazz.[35] Given the interval since the Brubeck story in November 1954, *Time* was seeking to reaffirm that commitment with a jazz cover. Given his stature, both in an absolute sense and in comparison to that of the jazz musicians who had previously graced *Time*'s cover, Ellington was clearly the logical subject. Robert Manning, senior editor, to whom Carter Harman reported, actively supported the idea of an Ellington cover. Otto Fuerbringer, assistant managing editor, who would make the definitive cover story recommendation, was also supportive, as was Roy Alexander, managing editor, who would ultimately approve that recommendation.[36]

In the spring of 1956, the efforts of Morgen and Harman, together with *Time*'s receptive editorial climate, began to produce results. From 10 May through 6 June 1956, Ellington had an extended engagement at the Flamingo Hotel in Las Vegas.[37] *Time*'s commitment to proceed with the Ellington cover was first manifested during this engagement. On 20

Otto Fuerbringer
Photograph by Bob Capazzo, Greenwich, Connecticut

May 1956, Otto Fuerbringer sent a telegram to Peter Hurd, inquiring whether Hurd would be interested in painting the cover portrait.[38] During the week of 27 May,[39] Harman flew from New York to Las Vegas, lived with Ellington in a rented house for three or four days, and gathered the background material for the cover story.[40] Morgen accompanied him, keeping å watchful eye on his favorite project. The day after the Flamingo appearance concluded, 7 June 1956, the band travelled to San Francisco to begin a ten-day engagement at the Macumba Club, during which the cover portrait was painted. Thus, by late June 1956, the cover story had been researched, although not yet written, and the cover portrait had been completed. At this point, publication of the Ellington cover story essentially became a reality. On infrequent occasions, cover stories for which portraits had been painted were not published, but Ellington's stature and his acceptance at all editorial levels of *Time* as the leading jazz figure of the period virtually assured that this story would be. A final editorial decision remained: when to publish. That decision would, for all practical purposes, be made by *Time*'s assistant managing editor, Otto Fuerbringer.

Fuerbringer now lives in retirement in Greenwich, Connecticut.[41] Early in 1960, he was named by Henry R. Luce to succeed Roy Alexander as managing editor. Hedley Donovan, who in 1964 would succeed Luce as editor-in chief of *Time*, wrote of this selection:

> Fuerbringer was an excellent choice, imaginative, energetic, as well organized as *Time* itself, as well informed about everything as *Time* sought to make its mythical cover-to-cover reader. His news antennae were beautifully tuned. He was alert to trends in show business, education, the arts, theology—all the "back of the book" departments that some readers who hated *Time*'s politics found indispensable. He had something of Luce's gift for latching onto a scrap of conversation or an obscure item in the paper and seeing a *Time* story in it.[42]

In 1956, one of Fuerbringer's principal responsibilities as assistant managing editor was to chair the weekly cover conference. Representatives of various departments of the magazine attended this conference, each prepared to advocate a cover story subject. Recommendations were developed concerning cover subjects for the ensuing several months. These recommendations were forwarded to Managing Editor Roy Alexander and, given the collegial journalism practiced within *Time,* were invariably followed.

These cover story recommendations necessarily took into consideration a number of editorial parameters intrinsic to *Time* as a weekly news magazine. The majority of its covers and stories dealt with events of the immediate past, or with anticipated future events, in national and world affairs. Periodically, *Time* also featured cover stories about topical matters, such as developments in the arts or sciences. These stories were referred to within the magazine as "back-of-the-book" stories, because their subject matter came from departments which appeared in the second part of the magazine, the first part being devoted to national and world affairs. Back-of-the-book stories were inherently of continuing interest, and were, in that sense, not date-sensitive. Nevertheless, these stories had to have a "news peg," some relationship to current events, even though that relationship need not be direct. The existence of this relationship was critical. The Ellington cover story, as it then stood, did not fit within these parameters because it had no relationship to any discrete current event. Although *Time* was firmly committed to publishing the Ellington cover story at some point, the story was in a posture to be postponed to await a news peg. Suddenly and unexpectedly, one appeared—Ellington's sensational appearance at the Newport Jazz Festival on 7 July.

Morgen recognized that Newport might provide the impetus to publish the *Time* cover story and saw an opportunity to make the point. Harman recalled the occasion vividly. On the evening of Saturday, 28 July 1956, Ellington appeared at the Connecticut Jazz Festival.[43] He returned to New York after the performance to attend an all-night party at the apartment of his longtime friend and onetime colleague, jazz writer Leonard Feather. Morgen invited Harman to the party and there advocated Newport as the current event needed to induce publication of the Ellington cover story. Harman thought Newport weak in this regard because of its increasing remoteness in time. Three weeks had passed since Newport: additional time would be required to write the story and edit it for publication. Nevertheless, he also recognized that Newport might be sufficient as a news peg. He presented the Newport concept to Senior Editor Robert Manning. A preliminary story conference for portions of the back-of-the-book part of the magazine, including music, was held in *Time*'s offices on the morning of Sunday, 29 July 1956. Manning, who chaired that conference, there agreed to active consideration of the Ellington story on the basis that the Newport success provided the necessary current event relationship. The final decision to proceed with the Ellington cover was made at the cover conference, chaired by Fuerbringer, held on the following Thursday, 2 August 1956.

The covers Fuerbringer had under consideration for the next several week all involved hard news. It was his judgement that reader interest would be enhanced by varying the fare of this succession of current events covers with a back-of-the-book cover.[44] An opening for the Ellington cover story was created.[45] Harman was then authorized to write the story, which he did during the remainder of the first week of August.

Fuerbringer and Harman described two particular aspects of the writing of the story. Speaking retrospectively to the current event requirement, Fuerbringer emphasized that by the date of his decision to go forward with the Ellington cover story, he considered Newport sufficient only for the purpose of providing a dramatic introduction to it. Had the story been further delayed, Newport's value as a lead-in would have diminished, and it would have been accorded a less prominent place in the cover story. Moreover, back-of-the-book stories were subject to preemption by events of appropriate magnitude in national or world affairs. Given the fortuitous and waning status of Newport, the Ellington cover story was somewhat vulnerable in this regard. Perhaps more than anyone realized at the time, the cover story on Ellington was nearly postponed, to await the occurrence of some other event which would bring him into the news.

The other aspect of the writing of the story related to a personal matter. Ellington, aware that the story was being written, expressed to Harman the concern that a literal portrayal of his relationships with his wife, Edna, and with his longtime companion, Beatrice (Evie) Ellis, would be embarrassing to all concerned. The details of these relationships would be published three years later in an article in *Ebony* magazine,[46] an event which infuriated Ellington. This section of the story was then rewritten to mention the matter only in passing:

> Before long he had a house, a car, a wife and a son, Mercer. But his musical friends then moved to New York, where the jazz was hot. Duke followed in 1922, though it meant a fresh start, many penniless months, and a separation from his wife that became permanent.[47]

The 20 August 1956 issue of *Time,* featuring Duke Ellington as the subject of its cover story, appeared on the newsstands on Monday, 13 August 1956.

THE HISTORY OF THE COVER STORY

Once printed, the *Time* cover story passed into the lore of Ellingtonia. A perception quickly developed concerning the relationship between the *Time* cover story and Newport. Harman described what occurred:

> Once we had decided to go ahead, everybody happily swallowed the idea that it was Newport that sparked the story and no evidence ever appeared to the contrary. It only would have weakened the story's credibility and nobody wanted that.[48]

Moreover, the Newport-*Time* linkage possessed a certain superficial but compelling logic. The sequence and timing of the events naturally followed one another, and the proposition was attractive in its simplicity. The fiction of the relationship, once advanced, thus acquired a rather vigorous

life of its own. When the Ellington literature began to
develop some fifteen years later, the treatment accorded the
relationship of Newport to the *Time* cover was consistent
with that which had gone before.[49]

In *Music Is My Mistress,* Ellington twice mentions the
Time cover. In the chronological narrative portion of the
book, the following appears:

> Nineteen fifty-six was an important year. The perfor-
> mance of *Diminuendo and Crescendo in Blue* (origi-
> nally written in 1937) at the Newport Jazz Festival, with
> an epic ride by Paul Gonsalves on tenor saxophone,
> brought us renewed attention and the cover of *Time*
> magazine. It was another of those major intersections in
> my career.[50]

Ellington concludes his appreciation of Joe Morgen,
quoted earlier, with these words:

> He was the one who engineered the *Time* cover story in
> 1956 after our success at the Newport Jazz Festival.[51]

Ellington's characterization of Newport as "another of
those major intersections" in his career is reinforced by
subsequent tributes in *Music Is My Mistress* to others who
had prominent roles in the Newport success—Jo Jones,[52]
Sam Woodyard[53] and Jimmy Woode.[54]

Stanley Dance refers to the *Time* cover in *The World of
Duke Ellington,* in a brief chronology of Ellington's career
which appears as an appendix:

> 1956–Triumph at Newport Jazz Festival, following
> performance of "Diminuendo and Crescendo in Blue,"
> which featured Paul Gonsalves extensively, resulted in
> Ellington's appearance on cover of *Time* magazine.[55]

Derek Jewell concludes his discussion of Newport in *Duke:
A Portrait of Duke Ellington,* which the following:

> The music, in a sense, wasn't the point. This was an
> event, a turning point, what Duke called "another of

Paul Gonsalves
Photograph: Rutgers Institute of Jazz Studies

those major intersections" in his career. *Time* magazine put him on its cover, and splashed his achievement over several pages. Ellington was back with a vengeance, and the world knew it.[56]

Mercer Ellington, in *Duke Ellington in Person: An Intimate Memoir,* relates the two events:

Paul [Gonsalves] played twenty-seven choruses [of "Diminuendo and Crescendo in Blue"], the band was really swinging behind him, and together they broke it up as nobody else ever had at Newport, before or since. There were scenes of the wildest enthusiasm, it was a big news item from coast to coast, and Pop's picture [*sic*] was on the cover of *Time* shortly afterward.[57]

Arnold Shaw makes reference in passing to the *Time* cover in *Black Popular Music in America:*

In 1956, Ellington made the cover of *Time* magazine after a "comeback" appearance at the Newport Jazz Festival.[58]

James Lincoln Collier cites two references to the *Time* cover in his biography of Ellington:

Rapidly, the word went out from Newport: Duke Ellington was back. And within weeks Ellington's picture was on the cover of *Time*. The record of the Newport concert sold in the hundreds of thousands and became Ellington's biggest seller.[59]

The wave of enthusiasm for Ellington that followed the Newport success did not immediately ebb. . . . Ellington was on the cover of the August 20 issue of *Time,* whose story said, in part, "The event last month marked not only the turning point of the concert, it confirmed a turning point in a career."[60]

The *Time* cover story is also mentioned in numerous secondary sources and in the liner notes to a number of Ellington recordings.[61] The common denominator of both primary and secondary sources is the explicitly stated or clearly implied proposition that *Time* began preparation of a cover story on Ellington only subsequent to and solely as a result of Newport. The facts now available simply do not support this proposition. How did it begin and why has it been perpetuated?

The most significant factor in the origination and perpetuation of the Newport-*Time* concept was Ellington's strongly held and frequently stated belief about the effect of Newport on his career.

> Whenever he was asked how old he was in the 1960s, Duke Ellington tended to give a mock scowl and say: "That's a dangerous question. I was born in 1956 at the Newport Festival."[62]

Patricia Willard echoed this characterization. She reiterated Ellington's feeling that he was "born at Newport" and that afterwards it was "Newport up." He expressed to her the feeling that his career prior to Newport was only of historical interest.[63] Ellington, of course, did not mean this in a literal sense. He consistently expressed the conviction that he preferred in all things to look to the future rather than to identify with the past.

In the two-part PBS series *A Duke Named Ellington,* Leonard Feather accurately summarized Ellington's view of Newport in a context which again emphasized and reinforced the connection with the *Time* cover. He concluded an extended interview about Newport with these words, spoken as the *Time* cover was strikingly displayed against a black background:

> And before you knew it Duke was on the cover of *Time* magazine. It represented a sort of renaissance for the orchestra and ever after that Duke would say "I was born at the Newport Jazz Festival on such-and-such a date in 1956."[64]

The text and physical arrangement of the cover story make it conspicuously amenable to the concept that it was prepared after and in response to Newport. The first three paragraphs are a graphic description of the festival appearance.[65] The second page features a page-width photograph captioned "Jazz Buffs Digging Ellington at Newport Festival."[66]

The critical importance Ellington attached to Newport leads to the conclusion that his recollection of all circumstances surrounding it would not have dimmed. To infer otherwise would be to ascribe to Ellington a forgetfulness and inattention to detail in lieu of the astute business practices he had acquired early in his career.[67] Ellington knew the sequence and timing of events, and knew that the *Time* cover story had been in preparation months prior to Newport. His treatment of the Newport-*Time* relationship in *Music Is My Mistress* was the written expression of a position he had taken since 1956—that Newport caused *Time* to prepare the cover story. Ellington's statements that Newport "brought us . . . the cover of *Time* magazine" and that the cover story had been "engineered . . . after our success at the Newport Jazz Festival" may therefore properly be viewed only in the larger context of his extraordinarily strong feelings about the effect of Newport. Through a subtle play on words, Newport and the *Time* cover were indelibly linked by a harmless but very effective fiction. It suited Ellington's purposes to characterize their relationship as one of cause and effect, and thereafter to promote it as such. From 1956 on he did so, and he knew exactly what he was doing.

THE COVER PAINTING

The letter written by the cover artist, Peter Hurd, confirms that *Time* began to prepare the Ellington cover story prior to Newport. On Tuesday, 5 June 1956, Peter Hurd wrote to his lifelong friend, the distinguished author Paul Horgan: "I will be off to San Francisco to paint a portrait of Duke Ellington on Thursday. . . ."[68] The Thursday referred to was 7 June 1956, exactly one month before Newport. San Francisco was agreed upon because of Ellington's engagement at the Macumba Club, which began on 8 June and extended through 17 June.[69]

Peter Hurd had come to paint cover portraits for *Time*

Peter Hurd
Photograph: *Houston Chronicle*

through the efforts of Otto Fuerbringer, who selected the cover artists. In 1953, when he assumed responsibility for covers, Fuerbringer embarked upon a project of his own creation to add a new dimension to cover art. *Time* covers in those years invariably featured portraits of persons painted from photographs by one of a number of artists on retainer.[70] Fuerbringer determined that henceforth, to the extent practical, cover portraits would be painted from life by recognized artists.[71] The resulting portraits, of which the Ellington portrait was one, would enhance an already outstanding body of cover art.[72] In the years to come, such notable artists as Henry Koerner, Marc Chagall, and Andrew Wyeth would paint cover portraits from life. Peter Hurd, a rancher and horseman from New Mexico, had come to the attention of Fuerbringer not only because of his stature as an artist and his ability to paint portraits, but also because he was Andrew Wyeth's brother-in-law.

Peter Hurd was born in Roswell, New Mexico, in 1904, and grew up in its frontier atmosphere. In 1921, he entered the United States Military Academy at West Point, New York, where he studied for two years and sold his first sketches. Recognizing his talent, he resigned from West Point in 1923 and studied art at Haverford College for one year. He then studied for two years in Chadd's Ford, Pennsylvania, under N.C. Wyeth. During this period, he met and courted the woman he would later marry, N.C. Wyeth's daughter, Henriette, and formed a lifelong personal and artistic relationship with Henriette's brother, Andrew.[73] Andrew Wyeth would later influence Peter Hurd's use of watercolors, and in turn would be introduced to the tempera-on-panel technique which Peter Hurd had perfected and which would be the medium for the Ellington cover.

In the 1930s Peter Hurd established his permanent residence in San Patricio, New Mexico, about 50 miles west of Roswell, at a home he called Sentinel Ranch. He spent the majority of his time there, except when on assignment. During World War II, he served two tours overseas as an artist-correspondent for *Life* magazine. He had a long, successful, and artistically productive career, and was the recipient of many honors, honorary degrees, and awards. He once wrote: "My credo is a simple one. It is to live just as intensely as possible, to keep my perceptions at a peak of sensitivity, and to try to realize to the fullest every moment of consciousness." He died in 1984 in Roswell, at the age of 80.[74]

Within these basic biographical facts lie a number of intriguing parallels between the lives of Peter Hurd and Duke Ellington. They were contemporaries in life: their lives overlapped by seven decades. Both evidenced talent as artists early in life. Both underwent a career change at about the same point in life: Peter Hurd from military service to artist; Ellington from commercial artist to professional musician.[75] Both enjoyed a mutually enhancing association with another artist in the same field: Peter Hurd's relationship with his brother-in-law, Andrew Wyeth, had many similarities to that of Ellington and Billy Strayhorn. Both had encounters at the White House in the 1960s.[76] Finally, they had an encounter with one other.

An account of the meeting between Peter Hurd and Ellington appears on the masthead page of the 20 August 1956 issue of *Time*. Appearing over the signature of Publisher James Linen, it is written in a delightfully tongue-in-cheek style, and accurately creates the impression that the artist was somewhat bemused by his encounter with the musician:

> The portrait of Duke Ellington is the first *Time* cover by one of the West's most distinguished artists, New Mexico's Peter Hurd. A *Life* correspondent during World War II, Hurd has painted on all five continents, but the people and scenes he likes best to portray are the ranch folk, the sun-blazed desert and the bare mountains near his New Mexican ranch. His precise tempera paintings of the U.S. Southwest are owned by such leading museums as New York City's Metropolitan, Kansas City's William Rockhill Nelson and the National Gallery in Edinburgh.
>
> For Hurd, a classical music fan, the Ellington assignment was his first brush with the world of jazz. He caught up with the Duke in San Francisco and spent the first two days trying to corner the elusive but affable

musician. "Hi, Hurd. You're the portrait man. Well,
fine. Excuse me, I have to see that cat over there,"
Ellington would say and fade away. But once the
portrait was started, Ellington liked to pose as he held
court for his innumerable friends in the artist's hotel
room.

Said Hurd: "It was an interesting assignment. As
they say here 'I wouldn't have taken for the experience!' "[77]

Another description of the meeting between Duke Ellington and Peter Hurd exists in a handwritten letter from Hurd
to Fuerbringer. The letter is reproduced below, with idiosyncrasies in style and punctuation intact:

SENTINEL RANCH SAN PATRICIO NEW
MEXICO

[COPY FROM TIME INC. ARCHIVES] [6/21/56]

Dear Otto.

The Ellington episode was most interesting and the
Duke, once he was badgered and harried enough by his
agent posed patiently each afternoon for four days. I
think he even enjoyed it for he stayed much longer the
final day than was necessary for the completion of the
portrait.

There was a more or less steady stream of phone calls
and visitors to the hotel room where we worked and
though I had known for years that California is over its
quota in strange individuals I was amazed at the
numbers and variety that turned up in my quarters to
pay homage (of a sort) to the Duke. I was delighted for
they serve to entertain him and keep his expression
animated during the sittings.

Nights I spent listening to the orchestra and making
pen sketches at the Macumba Club for at one time I
considered putting some of the musicians in the orchestra in the background along with the Duke; finally
abandoned this in favor of the simpler statement which
you will see.

I made friends with many of the musicians and with
Al Celley the manager who was invaluable to me. On

my last night in San Francisco I was invited by the Duke to a party he was giving after the concert at a place called Jimbo's Bop City. This was great fun—a party I'll never forget: we sat eating roast turkey followed by watermelon until 6:30 a.m. while a frenzied six piece colored orchestra seemed to pound my eardrums to ribbons—Say man, this Cat really has had it!

Hope you like the painting, Otto—it leaves air express today as I remember you are in somewhat of a hurry for it—

With warm regards to you I am

June 21st   Sincerely
1956
                   Peter

The portrait was received by *Time* on 23 June,[78] and Fuerbringer praised it highly:

The Ellington portrait is wonderful. I kept looking at it, seeing more and more nuances in his face, imagining more and more explosive expressions emanating from his mouth. The background is simple, direct and very convincing. I think it should reproduce very well.[79]

Many years later, in his unpublished autobiography,[80] Peter Hurd warmly recalled the occasion of his meeting with Duke Ellington. These reminiscences, written in his characteristic clear and precise prose, are reproduced below, again with idiosyncrasies in spelling and punctuation intact:

TIME COVER ADVENTURES

Duke Ellington 1956

Al Celli, Duke Ellington's manager, met me at my digs in San Francisco arranged for me by Time. Inc., in the Huntington Hotel. It would be best, he suggested, for me to hang around a few days getting the background material and watching Mr. Ellington and the band at the Mocambo, a night spot on Grant Street. This I agreed to do and immediately engaged a table there. I met Mr. Ellington the first evening; he was cordial but seemed a little remote—not really interested in posing for a Time cover by me. After three evenings of watching the show and making notes for the background I realized I was getting nowhere with Mr. Ellington who continued in our brief meetings elegantly courteous but definitely elusive. I was worried, for the deadline for delivery of the portrait was approaching. I decided to move to the hotel where Ellington and most of his band were staying. Much less elegant than the Huntington, it was on Grant Street and near the Mocambo. I went to Celli with my problem, saying that I could go home and complete a painting using photos but I felt this would not be nearly as successful in its outcome as it would be if my subject could give me some posing time.

"I will fix it", said Celli. "Leave it to me."

But nothing happened. I decided I'd better tackle my victim before he escaped.

"Mr. Ellington, do you know what an advertisement in color on the back cover of Time magazine costs?" I mentioned an astronomical figure, taken out of the blue. "Do you know what the front cover would cost?" I quoted another figure, larger. "Mr. Ellington, you are being offered the Front Cover—free. That's the number one slot and not for sale. You're getting it free. They can use a photograph of you, sure, but they've sent me out here to paint you. This is in a way a tribute to you."

I made my point; but it was born of desperation—and shameless on my part.

So it was arranged that my sittings would begin promptly at 2:00 next day. Paints all mixed (I decided on egg tempera), gesso panel cut to the proportion of Time's cover, I awaited my subject's arrival. Two o'clock came and passed, 2:05, 2:10, 2:15—while I impatiently waited. At 2:20 I called Al.

"What? Hasn't he come yet? I'll get him."

Five minutes later Al called.

"Pete, he wants you to go up to his room. He just woke up."

Not at all confident of the promptness of the elevator service in our hotel—the Beverly Plaza whose name

implied a tone of posh elegance, unfortunately nonex-
istent—I decided to try the back stairs. Upward I leapt,
two steps at a time, to reach Ellington's room as quickly
as possible. My first knock brought no answer although
I could hear someone moving around inside. A second
knock with more imperative authority brought a sleepy
answer, "All right, wait a minute." At the next sound of
the voice I walked in to see Mr. Ellington's long frame
stretched out in bed. He was wearing a silk kerchief of
olive green wound around his head which gave the
immediate impression of some royal personage out of
the Middle East.

Mr. Ellington after a brief apology, still very sleepy,
suggested that I step into the anteroom while he
dressed. I had just settled myself there when the
telephone rang. At the third ring I called through the
door to ask if I should answer it.

"Yes, would you please?"

I picked up the receiver and before I could say a word
an urgent female voice said,

"Duke, Oh Duke. It's me. It's Jennie. I'm down
stairs. I've got the baby."

"Just one minute" I said.

Speaking through the closed door I reported the
situation to Mr. Ellington. There was a long silence,
followed by a deep groan.

"O.K., tell her to come up."

The reader no doubt will guess what was running
through my mind at this point as to what sort of
dramatic meeting was about to take place. No such
thing. Jennie was one of his vast host of admiring fans
and it seems her marriage of two years had not been
blessed with a child. She and her husband had decided
to adopt a son. Mr. Ellington was the epitomy of
courtliness. "My dear, you are even more beautiful
than the last time I saw you", he said—a phrase I heard
many times repeated to other ladies during the next few
days.

This was the beginning of a procession of Ellington's
fans that trooped through my room as I worked on the
portrait. Again he reminded me of a story book king,
this time receiving his subjects in an informal levee.

Duke Ellington is a delightful person and proved to

be a patient and enduring model as he sat for me in my room. As I recall there were five afternoon sittings and on the fifth day at about 3:30 I announced to Duke and the dozen or so of the ardent admirers then present that the work was complete. I felt I could not improve it; anything more might result in harm. But the Duke looking like a benign maharajah continued the durbar until we all went out to dine at a Chinese restaurant farther down Grant Street.

Toward the end of the sittings I was invited to a wonderful party given by Duke. "Peter, bring along any friends you like and meet us at eight o'clock at. . . It will be a dinner dance." This was a great occasion— unforgettable in its *joie de vivre*. I had invited a doctor and his wife whom I had known during their tour of duty at Walker Air Force Base, and as it turned out, we were the only people of our race there. Most members of the orchestra were present—they and the entire group of guests were beautifully attired, handsome people.

All my travels as a "head hunter" for Time have yielded me rich dividends in the experiences I have had. But becoming well acquainted with Duke Ellington was one of the best and most rewarding of the entire twelve. We seldom meet these days and then always by chance—never with enough time.

I remember a call I had from Chicago on Christmas morning, 1956, the year I painted Ellington. At first I did not recognize the deep, rich voice that spoke to me, until I heard, "Peter, just wanted to say Merry Christmas and tell you how much I liked your cover portrait. Also a distinct rise in Capitol record sales I attribute to the Time cover story."

Since beginning this biography he has died. And I continue to mourn his passing.[81]

The original painting is today part of the collection of the National Portrait Gallery, Smithsonian Institution, Washington, D.C. It is there because *Time* has a longstanding agreement with the Smithsonian Institution to donate its cover art. It will come as no surprise that this agreement was initiated by Otto Fuerbringer.

THE COVER FILM—A STRANGE INTERLUDE

There is in circulation among collectors a five-minute film of Ellington which relates to the *Time* cover. The film begins with an announcer introducing Ellington as "an exciting person to read about in this week's issue of *Time* magazine." Ellington appears on screen, seated at a piano, and proceeds to tell fanciful allegories about how he came to compose and title "Mood Indigo," "Caravan," "Sophisticated Lady," and "Satin Doll," each of which he plays in abbreviated form. This is ostensibly done because these songs are to be mentioned in the *Time* story, although, of the four, only "Mood Indigo" and "Sophisticated Lady" are mentioned and then only in passing. A proof of the *Time* cover appears briefly on screen.[82] The film is obviously unfinished, has no titles or credits and is mentioned in only one source in jazz literature.[83] The purpose and medium for which it was intended remain uncertain. In all likelihood, the film was produced by *Time*'s promotions department for a use or purpose which was abandoned or did not come to fruition.[84]

CONCLUSIONS

Promotion of the *Time* cover as resulting from Newport, and the ensuing concomitant treatment of the cover in jazz literature, served Ellington's purposes admirably. To state that the *Time* cover resulted from Newport was to ascribe a tangible result—a cover appearance on the leading weekly news magazine—to the otherwise intangible effects of the festival appearance. "Success," "rebirth," "triumph" were now manifest in a vivid color portrait and a feature-length story. Newport and the *Time* cover, thus linked, were events which emphasized and enhanced one another. The effect of this linkage has been to consign the *Time* cover to a diminished and subordinate role, and thus to obscure the true nature of the actions taken by those responsible for it.

Months before Newport, Joe Morgen conceived the idea of an Ellington *Time* cover and set into motion the events which brought it about. His partner in this enterprise, Carter Harman, produced a story which, thirty-five years later, remains the definitive statement about an orchestra once again on the verge of greatness. Otto Fuerbringer, in furtherance of an editorial commitment to jazz which had been implemented during a period of turmoil and uncertainty, made the decisions to commence preparation of the cover story and to publish it.

The extraordinary prescience of the cover story, written only a month after Newport, is best exemplified in this striking paragraph:

> The event last month marked not only the turning point in one concert; it confirmed a turning point in a career. The big news was something that the whole jazz world had long hoped to hear: the Ellington band was once again the most exciting thing in the business, Ellington himself had emerged from a long period of quiescence and was once again bursting with ideas and inspiration.[85]

Newport was a "turning point" for Ellington, one of those "major intersections" as he confirmed seventeen years later in *Music Is My Mistress*. The favorable and widespread attention resulting from it brought him renewed commercial success and thrust him back into lasting prominence. In the years to follow, his "ideas and inspiration" would lead him to compose *Such Sweet Thunder, The Queen's Suite, Idiom '59, Suite Thursday, The Virgin Islands Suite, The Far East Suite, The New Orleans Suite, The UWIS Suite, the Goutelas Suite, The Latin American Suite, The Afro-Eurasian Eclipse,* and *The Togo Brava Suite.*[86] In 1957, Ellington's allegorical history of jazz, *A Drum Is a Woman,* was presented on national television.[87] He composed the background music for a television series, *The Asphalt Jungle,*[88] and the score for a ballet, *The River.*[89] He wrote the scores for the films *Anatomy of a Murder* (1959), *Paris Blues* (1961), *Assault on a Queen* (1966), and the obscure *Change of Mind* (1969). This period of unparalleled creativity culminated in the First,[90] Second[91] and Third[92] Concerts of Sacred Music.

Viewed in its proper perspective, the *Time* cover story can now be seen for what it is and always has been: at once a history of a pivotal time for the Ellington orchestra and a prologue to its future, conceived by an aggressive and effective publicist, crafted by a writer with knowledge of and sensitivity to Ellington's music, and published under the aegis of a visionary editor. Newport, when it inevitably occurred, merely confirmed their judgment.

NOTES

1. Leonard Feather described what occurred:

> Another unforgettable occasion was the chaotic scene at Newport, Rhode Island, during the three-day jazz festival in July 1956. Performing an extended and revitalized version of a fast blues entitled "Diminuendo and Crescendo in Blue," first recorded in 1938 [sic] and lengthened on this occasion to fourteen minutes and fifty-nine choruses, Ellington and his band (with particular help from the frenetic tenor sax of Paul Gonsalves) whipped the audience into such a furor that elder jazz statesmen could recall no comparable scene since the riots in the aisles of New York's Paramount Theater two decades earlier, during Benny Goodman's first wave of glory.

Leonard Feather, *From Satchmo to Miles* (New York: Da Capo, 1972), 54. The recording of the 1956 Newport concert remains in print: *Ellington at Newport,* Columbia Jazz Masterpieces CJ 40587 (LP); CK 40587 (CD).

The proposition that the artistic merit of a performance is inversely related to its popular success led to criticism of the Newport performance of "Diminuendo and Crescendo in Blue," particularly in comparison to the original version. Max Harrison, "Reflections on Some of Duke Ellington's Longer Works," in Max Harrison, *A Jazz Retrospect* (New York: Crescendo, 1977), 121–28.

2. Carter Harman, "Mood Indigo & Beyond," *Time*, 20 August 1956, 54.

3. Edward Kennedy "Duke" Ellington, *Music Is My Mistress* (New York: Doubleday, 1973) (hereinafter cited as "MIMM").
4. David Halberstram, *The Powers That Be* (New York: Knopf, 1979), 48. The influence of a *Time* cover appearance on the careers of Adlai Stevenson, Lyndon B. Johnson, Philip L. Graham, and Leon Jaworski, and on the perception of such events as Vietnam and the Watergate affair, is discussed throughout the book.
5. *Time* began publication on 3 March 1923. It was the first weekly magazine to present news of the previous week in an organized and departmentalized format. The development of this concept, and the rapid increase in circulation which followed, are chronicled in Edwin Emery and Henry Ladd Smith, *The Press in America* (New York: Prentice-Hall, 1954), 643–45; John Tebbel, *The American Magazine: A Compact History* (New York: Hawthorn, 1969), 227–30; and Sidney Kobre, *Development of American Journalism* (Dubuque: Brown, 1969), 722. There also exists a monumental history of Time, Inc. Robert T. Elson, *Time, Inc.—The Intimate History of a Publishing Enterprise, 1923–1941* (New York: Atheneum, 1968); Robert T. Elson, *The World of Time, Inc.—The Intimate History of a Publishing Enterprise,* Vol. 2, 1941–1960 (New York: Atheneum, 1973); Curtis Prendergast with Geoffrey Colvin, *The World of Time, Inc.—The Intimate History of a Changing Enterprise,* Vol. 3, 1960–1980 (New York: Atheneum, 1986).
6. Raymond Horricks, *The Jazzmen of Our Time* (London: Gollancz, 1959), 173. The reference is to the 8 November 1954 *Time* cover story on Dave Brubeck.
7. Stanley Dance, jacket notes, *Ellington at Newport,* Columbia Jazz Masterpieces CJ 40587 (LP).
8. Joseph McLaren, "Edward Kennedy (Duke) Ellington and Langston Hughes: Perspectives on their Contributions to American Culture, 1920–1966" (Ph.D. diss., Brown Univ., 1980), 195–96.
9. Stanley Dance, letter to author, 8 November 1989.
10. Luciano Massagli, Liborio Pusateri and Giovanni Volonte, comps., *Duke Ellington's Story on Records,* 16 vols. (Milan: Cartotecnica Bolzoni, 1966–1983), 265 (hereinafter cited as "DESOR"); W.E. Timner, *Ellingtonia: The Recorded Music of Duke Ellington and His Sidemen,* 3d ed. (Metuchen: Scarecrow, 1988), 117 (hereinafter cited as "Timner"). "Harlem" is discussed and analyzed in Jules Edmund Rowell, "An

Analysis of the Extended Orchestral Works of Duke Ellington Circa 1931 to 1972" (Master's thesis, San Francisco State Univ., 1983), 175–94.

11. Of "Deep Night" it has been written:

> What is certain is that Duke's mastery of the short composition remained; beautiful examples like "Deep Night," an exploration of trombone sonorities from 1951 when the band was apparently in some disarray, are clear evidence.

Andy Hamilton, "The Short and the Suite," *The Wire*, April, 1989, 33.

12. Ultra-Deluxe" is the subject of a vivid, if slightly flawed, description:

> In 1952, there slipped almost unnoticed from the barrage of commercial drivel Duke recorded for Capitol the mystical "Ultra-Deluxe," a remarkable creation slowly expanding from Gonslaves's opening tenor phrase. In the great surges of harmony and color rising from the orchestra we sense the thoughts of the most profound of jazz musicians; the original form of the blues is distorted, its rich spirit recreated in shades of orange and deep red.

Vic Bellerby, "Duke Ellington," in *The Art of Jazz: Essays in the Nature and Development of Jazz*, ed. Martin Williams (New York: Oxford Univ. Press, 1959), 157. "Ultra-Deluxe" was recorded in 1953, and the opening phrase is played by Harry Carney on baritone saxophone. DESOR, 329; Timner, 139.

13. Johnny Hodges had been with the band since 1928. He returned in August 1955 and remained until his death on 11 May 1970. Biographical portraits of him are found in Stanley Dance, *The World of Duke Ellington* (New York: Scribner's, 1970; New York: Da Capo, 1981), 91–102; Burnett James, *Essays on Jazz* (London: Sidgwick and Jackson, 1961; New York: Da Capo, 1990), 144–62; Whitney Balliett, *Dinosaurs in the Morning* (Philadelphia: Lippincott, 1962; Westport: Greenwood, 1978), 123–28; Humphrey Lyttleton, *The Best of Jazz II—Enter the Giants, 1931–1944* (New York: Taplinger,

1982), 132–56; and Max Jones, *Talking Jazz* (New York: Norton, 1988), 58–61.

Lawrence Brown had been with the band since 1932. He returned in 1960 and remained until he retired in 1970. His playing with the Ellington orchestra is analyzed in detail in Kurt Robert Dietrich, "Joe 'Tricky Sam' Nanton, Juan Tizol and Lawrence Brown: Duke Ellington's Great Trombonists, 1926–1951" (D.M.A. diss., Univ. of Wisconsin–Madison, 1989), 86–161. An interview of Lawrence Brown in retirement appears in Lowell D. Holmes and John W. Thompson, *Jazz Greats—Getting Better With Age* (New York: Holmes & Meier, 1986), 107–13.

William Alexander "Sonny" Greer had been Ellington's drummer since 1920. Frank Dutton, "Birth of a Band," *Storyville* 80 (December 1978–January 1979): 44–53. He returned for appearances with the band, or members of it, on single occasions in 1958, 1961, 1962, and 1972. His work with Ellington is discussed briefly in Theodore Dennis Brown, "A History and Analysis of Jazz Drumming to 1942" (Ph.D. diss., Univ. of Michigan, 1976), 421–24, and in Burt Korall, *Drummin' Men: The Heartbeat of Jazz—The Swing Era* (New York: Schirmer, 1990), 307–10.

14. This unsettled period is explored in depth in an aptly titled chapter, "1951–1959 Swing Low, Swing High," in Derek Jewell, *Duke: A Portrait of Duke Ellington* (New York: Norton, 1977), 110–37. Personnel changes within the band during this period are also summarized and discussed in Alun Morgan and Raymond Horricks, *Modern Jazz—A Survey of Developments Since 1939* (London: Gollancz, 1956), 183–90.

15. Ellington appeared in the "Aquacades" show at Flushing Meadow, Long Island, New York, from 22 June through 2 August 1955. Band regulars Paul Gonsalves, Willie Cook, Britt Woodman, Dave Black, and Rick Henderson did not appear because of union card problems. The band was augmented by an extra pianist, a string section, and two harpists. Alun Morgan, "Duke Ellington on Record—The Nineteen-Fifties," in *Duke Ellington: His Life and Music,* ed. Peter Gammond (London: Phoenix House, 1958; New York: Da Capo, 1977), 114.

16. Johnny Hodges and Sam Woodyard are said to have arrived on the same day. Mercer Ellington with Stanley Dance, *Duke*

Ellington in Person: An Intimate Memoir (Boston: Houghton, 1978), 109. Another source has spoken to the impact of their arrival:

> After four years as leader of his own small group, the nonpareil Johnny Hodges came back to him. And on the same day a great new drummer, Sam Woodyard, entered the band. It is not too much to say that the effect of these two men on the group's morale was comparable to that of Ben Webster and Jimmy Blanton fifteen years before. They were certainly an inspiration to Ellington himself and within a year, at the Newport Jazz Festival, he had scored the greatest single triumph of his career.

Stanley Dance, jacket notes, *The Private Collection, Volume One—Studio Sessions, Chicago, 1956,* LMR CD 83000 (CD).

A succession of drummers—Bill Clark, Charlie Smith, Louis (Louie) Bellson, Butch Ballard and Dave Black—had followed in the wake of Sonny Greer's departure. Sam Woodyard was Ellington's drummer from August 1955 through the spring of 1968, with minor breaks. He returned to the band for brief interludes in 1973.

17. *Historically Speaking—The Duke,* Bethlehem BCP-60 and *Duke Ellington Presents,* Bethlehem BCP-6005, recorded in Chicago, Illinois, 7 & 8 February 1956. DESOR, 363–67; Timner, 149. The title of the first album accurately reflects the historical nature of its contents."East St. Louis Toodle-o" (1926), "Creole Love Call" (1927), and "Stompy Jones" (1934) were featured, along with three songs from the extraordinary year of 1940—"Jack the Bear," "Ko-Ko," and "In a Mellotone." Other numbers became history: "Stomp, Look and Listen" would not again be recorded and the record contains the only commercially recorded performance of the intriguing "Lonesome Lullaby." The second album featured two additional songs from 1940, "Cotton Tail" and "Day Dream," together with non-Ellington numbers such as "Summertime," "Laura," "Deep Purple," and "Indian Summer."

18. Columbia released twenty-four long playing records by Ellington during the six-year period from 1956 through 1962. Much of the unissued material recorded during these years later appeared in a five-record, three-album compilation issued by

Columbia in Europe on the CBS France/Holland label. Duke Ellington, *"Duke 56/62"*, Vol. 1, CBS 88653; Vol. 2, CBS 88654; Vol. 3, CBS 23606.

19. Whitney Balliett, "Celebration for the Duke," *Saturday Review,* 12 May 1956, 30–31.
20. Stanley Dance, letter to author, 8 November 1989.
21. Stanley Dance, letter to author, 30 November 1989.
22. Jerry Valburn, ed., *D.E.T.S. Newsletter,* Vol. One, No. Three, June/July 1981, privately published by Marlor Productions, Hicksville, New York, in connection with issuance of the *Duke Ellington Treasury Series* of recordings.
23. MIMM, 435. These pointed recollections of Joe Morgen's aggressive character and pervasive presence invite speculation as to his role in the *Saturday Review* story. Carter Harman, for one, believes he was involved. "My guess is that Joe was there, lurking heavily among the shadows." Carter Harman, letter to author, 7 May 1990.
24. James A. Linen, "A Letter from the Publisher," *Time,* 19 October 1953, 18, contains a profile of Carter Harman.
25. Carter Harman, "Girl in the Groove," *Time,* 23 February 1953, 54.
26. Carter Harman, "Ballet's Fundamentalist," *Time,* 25 January 1954, 66.
27. Carter Harman, "The Man on Cloud No. 7" *Time,* 8 November 1954, 67.
28. Carter Harman, "The Prima Donna," *Time,* 29 October 1956, 60.
29. The Hickory House is mentioned twice in MIMM, 211, 400. Its atmosphere is affectionately recalled in Marian McPartland, *All in Good Time* (New York: Oxford Univ. Press, 1987), 19–28. Not coincidentally, the first manifestation of the collaboration between Morgen and Harman was an article on Marian McPartland, whose trio was a fixture at the Hickory House for many years. Carter Harman, "Post-Dixieland Piano," *Time,* 21 September 1953, 65.
30. Carter Harman, "The Duke Rides Again," *Time,* 23 January 1956, 53. Harman had previously written one other article on Ellington. "Duke's Anniversary," *Time,* 3 November 1952, 85.
31. The tribute to Sam Woodyard reads:

But the chief reason for all the internal excitement
is the Duke's new drummer, Sam Woodyard. He
sits, lean and still, behind his battery, neatly

punctuating every phrase, coming as close as any
man could to playing a tune on his four side drums
and three cymbals (he actually squeezes pitch
changes out of one drum by leaning on it with an
elbow), while keeping a rhythm as solid as
Gibraltar. When the band appeared bored with a
number, he seemed to get under and shove—and
the band came alive.

Time, 23 January 1956, 53.
32. Carter Harman, interview with author, Carmel, California, 20
January 1990 (hereinafter cited as "Harman Interview").
33. "Louis the First," *Time,* 21 February 1949, 52. *Time* articles
during these years carried no bylines. Articles by Carter
Harman are so cited because he is known to be the writer.
Time articles are today credited to the writer or writers.
34. Carter Harman, "The Man on Cloud No. 7," *Time,* 8
November 1954, 67. Oscar Peterson had been considered as an
alternative to Brubeck as a cover subject. Brubeck was
thought to play jazz more consistently, and Peterson's Cana-
dian citizenship was at odds with *Time*'s conception of jazz as
an American art form. Harman Interview; Carter Harman,
letter to author, 10 October 1990. The interest shown in
Peterson by *Time,* and the resulting story by Harman, are
detailed in Gene Lees, *Oscar Peterson: The Will to Swing*
(Rocklin: Prima, 1990), 83–99.
35. *Time*'s commitment to jazz continues. Wynton Marsalis is the
subject of a 1990 cover story. Thomas Sancton, "Horns of
Plenty," *Time,* 22 October 1990, 64.
36. Harman Interview.
37. Joe Igo, comp., "The Duke Ellington Chronicle," unpublished ms., Gordon R. Ewing, ed., a comprehensive itinerary
of Ellington's appearances begun by the late Joe Igo, presently
on deposit with the Duke Ellington Collection, National
Museum of American History, Smithsonian Institution, Washington, D.C. (hereinafter cited as "Igo Itinerary").
38. The telegram reads as follows:

Peter Hurd   1956 May 20 PM 5 07
Boswell, NMex [sic]

We are going to do a cover on Duke Ellington. He
is currently playing at Las Vegas and will be there

through June 7. Would you be interested in
painting him? Best regards =

Otto Fuerbringer Time Inc =

Otto Fuerbringer to Peter Hurd, telegram, 20 May 1956, *Peter
Hurd Papers,* Hurd-La Rinconada Gallery, San Patricio, New
Mexico (hereinafter cited as "Hurd Papers"). Documents
from the Hurd Papers were provided by Ms. Teresa Curry of
the Hurd-La Rinconada Gallery through the courtesy of Mr.
Michael Hurd, who kindly gave permission to use them.

39. This time period is established by a letter dated Friday, 1 June
1956, from Otto Fuerbringer to Peter Hurd, forwarding recent
photographs of Ellington to aid in painting the cover portrait.
The letter reads, in part:

> Carter Harman, our music writer, saw the Duke
> in Las Vegas early this week, found him fascinat-
> ing, and reports that he will cooperate fully.

Otto Fuerbringer to Peter Hurd, letter, 1 June 1956, Hurd
Papers.

40. Harman Interview. It was unusual for an editor to research a
story. This task was customarily performed by the editorial
researcher for the subject area, in this instance Dorothea
Bourne, assisted by *Time*'s network of correspondents and
stringers, as necessary. Harman's musical background, together with his friendship with Ellington and knowledge of
Ellington's music, made it appropriate for him to research the
story personally.

The relationship developed with Ellington in connection with
the cover story led, some years later, to Harman being
engaged as Ellington's biographer. Research began with
approximately twenty hours of tape-recorded interviews,
accomplished at various locations during 1964. The project
ended when it became obvious that author and subject were at
loggerheads over the tenor of what was to be written. Harman
planned a literal biography, one which would supplant the
novelistic one of Barry Ulanov, then almost twenty years old.
Barry Ulanov, *Duke Ellington* (New York: Creative Age,
1946). Ellington, ever protective of his private self, desired the
product to be a replication of his public persona. Ellington's

view prevailed, the eventual result being MIMM. Carter Harman, "The Duke Speaks Out," Ellington Study Group Conference, Los Angeles, California, 15 June 1991 (hereinafter cited as "Harman Presentation").

41. The summary of the cover story decisional process which follows was developed during numerous telephone interviews of Fuerbringer by the author during 1989–1992 (hereinafter cited as "Fuerbringer Interviews").

42. Hedley Donovan, *Right Places, Right Times—Forty Years in Journalism Not Counting My Paper Route* (New York: Holt, 1989), 193.

43. Igo Itinerary; DESOR, 383–84; Timner, 152. Ellington was still riding the wave of the Newport success when he appeared three weeks later at the Connecticut Jazz Festival at Fairfield University, Fairfield, Connecticut, on Saturday, 28 July 1956. On the program with him were pianists Willie "The Lion" Smith and Hank Jones, trumpeter Buck Clayton, bassist Walter Page, and drummer Art Trappier. "Diminuendo and Crescendo in Blue" was again featured, with an interlude of thirty-seven choruses by Paul Gonsalves. This performance appears on *Jazz Festival Jazz,* Queen Disc Q-044 (LP) and on *Diminuendo and Crescendo in Blue,* Koala AW 14165 (LP). Excerpts from the remainder of the festival appear on *Duke Ellington, His Orchestra and Friends at the First Annual Connecticut Jazz Festival,* IAJRC 45 (LP). A photograph of Ellington at Fairfield University appears in the cover story. *Time*, 20 August 1956, 55.

44. Fuerbringer Interviews. A number of newsworthy events occurred in the summer of 1956, all of which were reflected on *Time*'s cover. There was a major steel strike in the United States, repercussions from the Suez Canal crisis continued, the Democratic and Republican national conventions were held, and *My Fair Lady* opened on Broadway. The Ellington cover story appeared among cover stories relating to these events. The covers immediately preceding it depicted Prime Minister Jawaharlal Nehru of India (31 July), Greek shipping magnate Stavros Niarchos (6 August) and former President Harry S. Truman (13 August); those immediately following depicted President Gamal Abdel Nasser of Egypt (27 August) and Governor Arthur B. Langlie of Washington (3 September).

45. This would not be the last occasion on which Mr. Fuerbringer would demonstrate his ability to recognize artistic achievement in the midst of current chaos:

> And even his critics felt his sense of timing on cover stories was exquisite. Indeed, it was one of the ironies of his tour that though he was probably most remembered within the shop and within the profession for his dogmatic views on Vietnam, it was his idea to put the Beatles on the cover as 1965's Men of the Year.

Halberstram, *The Powers That Be,* 457. In this instance, however, current events prevailed. General William C. Westmoreland was named *Time's* Man of the Year for 1965.

46. Marc Crawford, "A Visit with Mrs. Duke Ellington," *Ebony,* March 1959, 132–36. Discussions of these relationships are found in Jewell, *Duke: A Portrait of Duke Ellington,* notably at 30–31 and 225–27. Ellington's private life with Evie Ellis is recalled in Leonard Feather, *The Jazz Years: Earwitness to an Era* (New York: Da Capo, 1987), 62–70.

47. *Time,* 20 August 1956, 56. A representative from *Time's* Washington, D.C., bureau had interviewed Edna Ellington in connection with the cover story. This led to the insertion into a draft of the story of an "unforgivably brusque" account of Ellington's marriage. Carter Harman, letter to author, 2 November 1990. The account was so at variance with Ellington's expressed desires that Harman took the extreme step of threatening to resign if it were not rewritten. Harman Interview; Harman Presentation.

48. Carter Harman, letter to author, 10 October 1990.

49. Two major works about Ellington contain discussions of Newport but make no mention of the *Time* cover. Peter Gammond, ed., *Duke Ellington: His Life and Music* (London: Phoenix House, 1958); G.E. Lambert, *Duke Ellington* (London: Cassell, 1959).

50. MIMM, 191.

51. MIMM, 435.

52. MIMM, 241.

53. MIMM, 227.

54. MIMM, 226.

55. Dance, *The World of Duke Ellington,* 297.

56. Jewell, *Duke: A Portrait of Duke Ellington,* 122.

57. M. Ellington with Dance, *Duke Ellington in Person,* 112. The Chico Hamilton Quintet, which preceded the Ellington orchestra on stage that night, had a similar experience with its rendition of "Blue Sands." Buddy Collette, reedman for the group, recalled the occasion:

> And we played for about ten minutes, giving it our best shot. And at the end, as we'd do, we just tapered off, and everything just stopped. And for eight or ten seconds nobody moved, and then they jumped up and screamed; they went wild, and it went on and on . . . Later, as we were moving off stage and Duke's band was setting up, we passed Duke on the stairs and he smiled and said, "Well, you sure made it hot for me."

Robert Gordon, *Jazz West Coast: The Los Angeles Jazz Scene of the 1950s* (London: Quartet, 1986), 139. The Chico Hamilton Quintet also appeared with Ellington at the Connecticut Jazz Festival three weeks later. See n. 43.

58. Arnold Shaw, *Black Popular Music in America—From the Spirituals, Minstrels, and Ragtime to Soul, Disco, and Hip-Hop* (New York: Schirmer, 1986), 151.

59. James Lincoln Collier, *Duke Ellington* (New York: Oxford Univ. Press, 1987), 264.

60. Ibid., 268. *See also* James Lincoln Collier, *The Making of Jazz: A Comprehensive History* (Boston: Houghton, 1978), 247:

> Then, at the 1956 Newport Jazz Festival, Paul Gonsalves, tenor soloist with the band, played a long, fervid solo on "Diminuendo and Crescendo in Blue" that left the audiences roaring. Suddenly the band was in the news again: Ellington even made the cover of *Time*.

61. Examples of jacket notes containing mention of the *Time* cover are those to *Duke Ellington—All Star Road Band*, Doctor Jazz W2X39137 (LP) and to *Ellington at Newport*, Columbia Jazz Masterpieces CJ 40587 (LP). *See also* Benny Aasland, ed., *DEMS Bulletin*, 1984/2:3, privately published by the Duke Ellington Music Society, Jarfalla, Sweden (hereinafter cited as "DEMS Bulletin").

62. Jewell, *Duke: A Portrait of Duke Ellington*, 110.

63. Patricia Willard, telephone interview, 7 August 1989. Ms. Willard was associated with Ellington for twenty-five years in research, editing, and public relations capacities. She is a former columnist for *Jazz Times* magazine and a former contributing editor of *Down Beat*. She recently completed two years as a member of the staff of the Duke Ellington

Collection, National Museum of American History, Smithsonian Institution, Washington, D.C.

64. "A Duke Named Ellington," narr., prod., and dir. Terry Carter, *American Masters Series.* Exec. prod. Susan Lacy, PBS, WNET, New York, 18 & 25 July 1988.
65. *Time,* 20 August 1956, 54.
66. Ibid., 55.
67. The sensation created at Newport by Paul Gonsalves's solo in "Diminuendo and Crescendo in Blue" was in itself another illustration of Ellington's acumen in the business of music. Gordon Ewing has explained how it came about:

> Bobby Boyd, who was a band boy and later road manager for Duke from 1951 to 1966, spent several days with me and provided some valuable information: One account, which you may already know, concerned the famous 1956 Newport Jazz Festival. Bobby said that before the concert, George Wein kept after Duke to let him know what he was going to play and offered a number of selections which Bobby said "went in one ear and out the other." Duke would tell him that he didn't know but would have something. Before that on 30 April 1956 the band was playing a dance in Durham, NC [North Carolina]. In the middle of the gig Duke suddenly called out 107–108 (Diminuendo and Crescendo in Blue) which the band hadn't played for years. The men shuffled through their music while Duke played a number of choruses and then the band fumbled around for several more before they got into the groove. Bobby said at that point they were really swinging and Paul Gonslaves, that night, didn't play 27 choruses, he played 36 and the crowd went wild. For the next two months the band played the number only once, at a concert, and Duke gave no indication to the men in the band that he was going to play it at Newport nor did any one else know ahead of time. This account is a little different from Mercer-Dance but so are a number of other stories in Mercer's book.

DEMS Bulletin, 1990/1:5–6 (Letter from Gordon Ewing). "Diminuendo and Crescendo in Blue," again featuring a Paul

Gonsalves solo, was also performed at a concert in Pasadena, California, on 30 March 1953. DEMS Bulletin, 1990/1:6 (Letter from Sjef Hoefsmit).

The account of Newport in Mercer Ellington's book incorrectly implies that "Diminuendo and Crescendo in Blue" was last performed during a Birdland engagement "[s]ome time previously." M. Ellington with Dance, *Duke Ellington in Person,* 112. The performance at Birdland was on 30 June 1951 and featured twenty-six choruses by Paul Gonsalves.

DESOR, 277–79; Timner, 122. The Durham and Pasadena concerts appear in the Igo Itinerary, but not in either DESOR or Timner, which cite no performances of "Diminuendo" between Birdland in 1951 and Newport in 1956. The remaining intervening performance, in May or June 1956, has not been documented.

These circumstances suggest that Ellington's decision to perform "Diminuendo and Crescendo in Blue" at Newport was made at the last moment, based upon his experience in Durham two months before, and possibly upon his recollection of similar experiences in Pasadena and at Birdland. The response of the audience to the Chico Hamilton Quintet which immediately preceded him certainly must have been a factor. See n. 57.

A summary of the interludes between "Diminuendo in Blue" and "Crescendo in Blue" for the period from 20 September 1937 through 28 July 1956 appears as an appendix.

68. Robert Metzger, ed., *My Land Is the Southwest–Peter Hurd Letters and Journals* (College Station: Texas A & M Univ. Press, 1983), 376.
69. Igo Itinerary.
70. The extensive use of these talented retainer artists is illustrated by the fact that one of them, Boris Artzybasheff, painted 219 covers for *Time* over the 24-year period from 1942 to 1966. Included among these were the cover portraits of Louis Armstrong (21 February 1949) and Dave Brubeck (8 November 1954). Other artists whose paintings frequently appeared on covers were Robert Vickery, Bernard Safran, James Chapin, and Boris Chaliapin. Their paintings represent the golden age of *Time* covers, and are a unique chronicle of the times. The reader is commended to a perusal of this

body of American art, particularly the covers of Boris Artzybasheff.

71. Although there were exceptional cases, it was generally true that the painting of a cover portrait from life was a time-consuming process which could only be accomplished infrequently. A cover assignment had to be completed on relatively short notice, but the artists were in demand and their schedules could not always be adjusted. Travel to the location of the subject was usually required. Finally, the subjects were frequently persons who had neither the time nor the inclination to sit for several days while a portrait was painted. Fuerbringer Interviews.

72. Improvement of the magazine in an artistic sense was a continuing theme of Fuerbringer's tenure as managing editor:

> Fuerbringer greatly invigorated the appearance of the magazine. *Time* moved away from the slightly fusty look of the 1950s and, without reducing its text content, began using photography with almost as much verve as *Life* and *Sports Illustrated*. More liberal use of color in takeouts on foreign countries and in stories on art, architecture, and the performing arts gave many pages of the magazine something its most ardent admirers had never before claimed for it: beauty.

Donovan, *Right Places, Right Times,* 193.

73. Andrew Wyeth painted a cover portrait of President Dwight D. Eisenhower for the 7 September 1959 issue of *Time*. He was, in turn, the subject of *Time*'s 27 December 1963 cover story, the portrait being painted by his sister, Henriette Wyeth Hurd. The extraordinary Wyeths are profiled in Richard Meryman, "American Visions—The Wyeth Family," *National Geographic,* July 1991, 78–109.

74. This summary was derived from Metzger, ed., *My Land Is the Southwest*. This book remains the definitive study of the life and work of Peter Hurd. The author is grateful to Professor Metzger for permission to use this material.

75. Ellington's brief but successful career as an artist is chronicled in Mark Thomas Tucker, "The Early Years of Edward Kennedy 'Duke' Ellington, 1899–1927" (Ph.D. diss., Univ. of Michigan, 1986), 135–37. This dissertation has been published in book form under the title *Ellington—The Early Years* (Urbana: Univ. of Illinois Press, 1990).

76. Ellington's 70th birthday was celebrated at the White House on 29 April 1969. He was a guest there on numerous other occasions, beginning during the Truman administration. MIMM, 424–33. In 1965, Peter Hurd was commissioned by the White House Historical Association to paint the official portrait of President Lyndon B. Johnson. The portrait was completed from photographs, since only one sitting was accorded, and was finished in 1966. President Johnson rejected it as "the ugliest thing I ever saw." Hurd returned his $6,000 fee and donated the painting to the National Portrait Gallery, where it remains. The resulting notoriety plagued him for the reminder of his life, much to his dismay. Metzger, ed., *My Land Is the Southwest,* 389–90.

77. James A. Linen, "Publisher's Letter," *Time,* 20 August 1956, 7.

78. Receipt was acknowledged by the following:

> Peter Hurd   1956 June 23 PM 3 24
> Roswell NMex
>
> Swell cover. Letter follows. All best = Otto
> Fuerbringer Time Inc New York =

   Otto Fuerbringer to Peter Hurd, telegram, 23 June 1956, Hurd Papers.

79. Otto Fuerbringer to Peter Hurd, letter, 24 June 1956, Hurd Papers.

80. Professor Metzger writes of Peter Hurd's autobiography:

> On his return to New Mexico in July, 1944, Hurd wrote several essays on his experiences overseas, and years later incorporated them into a draft of his autobiography, which many persons had asked for, and which he began writing in 1970. . . . He knew that the autobiography would take away from the time and concentration he needed for painting; nevertheless, he applied himself to it with wholehearted, though intermittent, effort. But failing health caused him to cease working entirely, and the manuscript was never completed.

   Metzger, ed., *My Land Is the Southwest,* xi–xii.

81. Peter Hurd, unpublished ms., c. 1970–1975, Hurd Papers.

The Beverly-Plaza Hotel was located on the southeast corner of the intersection of Bush Street and Grant Avenue. It is today called the Triton Hotel. The Macumba Club was located at 453 Grant Avenue, on the first block across Bush Street from the hotel. This site has been rebuilt in the intervening years, and the address 453 Grant Avenue no longer exists.

82. Fuerbringer confirmed that *Time*'s promotions department had access to cover portraits upon arrival for preparation of promotional materials. Fuerbringer Interviews. This would date the film no earlier than late June 1956, when the portrait arrived. Given the film's unfinished status and intended promotional use in connection with the cover story, a sufficient interval prior to the 13 August newsstand date would have been required for editing, thus making production in August unlikely. These facts suggest that the film was probably made in July. Possible dates are 9, 24 or 29 July, when Ellington is known to have been in New York State or New York City. Igo Itinerary.

83. Klaus Stratemann, *Duke Ellington Day By Day and Film By Film* (Copenhagen: JazzMedia ApS, 1992), 365–68.

84. Klaus Stratemann, letters to author, 25 June 1989, 15 January 1990, 1 March 1992. The author is indebted to Dr. Stratemann for his extensive and enlightening insights into the Ellington–*Time* film.

85. *Time*, 20 August 1956, 54.

86. The compositions listed represent a partial compilation of Ellington's post-1956 extended works. Many of these are discussed in Harrison, *A Jazz Retrospect,* supra, and in Rowell, "An Analysis of the Extended Orchestral Works," supra. A comprehensive listing of Ellington's compositions is found in Erik Wiedemann, "Duke Ellington: The Composer," *Annual Review of Jazz Studies* 5 (1991): 37–64, and reveals an extraordinary period of copyright activity by Ellington subsequent to 1956. Ellington's musical interpretations of literature, particularly as manifested in *Such Sweet Thunder* and *Suite Thursday,* and in his scores for the plays *Timon of Athens* and *Turcaret,* are explored in Theodore R. Hudson, "Duke Ellington's Literary Sources," *American Music* 9.1 (1991): 20. An excellent capsule history of the background of Ellington's extended works appears in Stanley Dance, jacket notes, *The Private Collection, Volume Ten—Studio Sessions New York & Chicago 1965, 1966, 1971,* SAJA 91234-2 (CD).

87. The work was presented on the United States Steel Hour, 8 May 1957. It was the first color production in the series, and the first

nationally broadcast one hour program featuring an all-black cast. Ellington always considered it one of his favorites. Jewell, *Duke: A Portrait of Duke Ellington,* 123. It received mixed reviews at the time, however, as reflected by the favorable and unfavorable reports published simultaneously in a leading jazz publication. Leonard Feather and Barry Ulanov, "Two Thumps on 'A Drum,' " *Down Beat,* 27 June 1957, 18.

88. Ellington's music was certainly the most memorable aspect of this short-lived series, which appeared weekly from 2 April through 24 September 1961. Tim Brooks and Earle Marsh, *The Complete Directory to Prime Time Network TV Shows, 1946–Present,* 5th ed. (New York: Ballantine, 1992), 56. "Asphalt Jungle Theme" remained in the band's book through early 1963.

89. *The River* was commissioned by the American Ballet Theater, choreographed by Alvin Ailey and premiered at the New York State Theater on 25 June 1970. Ellington's interpretation of its various sections appears in MIMM, 201–02.

90. This work premiered at Grace Cathedral, San Francisco, California, on 16 September 1965. DESOR, 726; Timner, 247.

91. This work premiered at the Cathedral of St. John the Divine, New York, New York, on 19 January 1968. DESOR, 852; Timner, 295.

92. The Third Concert of Sacred Music was performed only twice in its entirety. It premiered in Westminster Abbey, London, England, on 24 October 1973. DESOR, 1142–43; Timner, 389–90. Moving descriptions of the circumstances surrounding this performance appear in Jewell, *Duke: A Portrait of Duke Ellington,* 217–34, and in M. Ellington with Dance, *Duke Ellington in Person,* 192–97. Its second and final performance was in St. Augustine Presbyterian Church, Harlem, New York, New York, on 23 December 1973. Jewell, 226. Portions of the Westminster Abbey performance were issued by RCA Victor; the second performance appears not to have survived in recorded form. The Third Concert of Sacred Music was Ellington's last testament. The date of its first performance was seven months to the day prior to his death.

ACKNOWLEDGEMENTS

The interest and assistance of many people made this study possible. Edward L. Jamieson, Richard Woodbury, and

Elaine Felsher of *Time* provided access to otherwise inaccessible resources. Marian Powers and Reneé Mancini of *Time*'s Editorial Rights division facilitated reproduction of the cover and cover story. Carol Diehl, curator of *Time*'s cover art, located the Peter Hurd letter. The contributions of Stanley Dance, Gordon Ewing, Joseph McLaren, Robert Metzger, Klaus Stratemann, Jerry Valburn, and Patricia Willard are manifest throughout. Sjef Hoefsmit's encyclopedic knowledge of Ellingtonia is reflected in the text and in many footnotes. Willard H. Rosegay provided special insight into the geography of San Francisco. Staff members of the Houston Public Library and the libraries of Rice University and the University of Houston were most helpful. The Hurd Papers were made available by Teresa Curry of the Hurd-La Rinconada Gallery, with the kind permission of the artist's son, Michael Hurd.

Otto Fuerbringer and Carter Harman gave unselfishly of their valuable time to inform, comment, correct, and enhance. Helen Ruth Kuenstler, many years ago, established standards of excellence to which this writer's work can only be asymptotic. Theodore R. Hudson provided constant encouragement and valuable guidance. Melanie M. Theiss reviewed the manuscript and made many astute comments. Particular gratitude is extended to Rob L. Wiley, scholar, colleague, and friend, for his advice, knowledge, and inspiration. Finally, my wife, Saundra Carson Waters, endured the hours of work inherent in this project. She, too, made valuable suggestions to make this essay more readable. My deepest thanks go to her.

SUMMARY OF INTERLUDES BETWEEN "DIMINUENDO IN BLUE" AND "CRESCENDO IN BLUE" AS PLAYED BY THE DUKE ELLINGTON ORCHESTRA 20 SEPTEMBER 1937–28 JULY 1956

INTRODUCTION

The summary which follows lists all documented performances of "Diminuendo in Blue," "Crescendo in Blue," and the various interludes used to join them for the period from initial recording on 20 September 1937 through the first performance after Newport, that of 28 July 1956.

Performance of "Diminuendo" and "Crescendo," or either of them, together with an extended solo by Paul Gonsalves, inevitably became a staple of Ellington's post-Newport concert and club date repertoire. DESOR and Timner list some ninety performances of various combinations of these works from 28 July 1956 through 2 November 1973. As before Newport, presentation occurred in a variety of formats, all of which showcased Gonsalves's improvisational resourcefulness. Initial performances were simply a reprise of Newport: complete versions of "Diminuendo" and "Crescendo," joined by Gonsalves interludes of varying length. Later performances were sometimes shortened to consist only of "Diminuendo" followed by a Gonsalves solo which eventually acquired the almost onomotopaeic title "Wailing Interval." On other occasions, only "Crescendo" was played, but featuring an extended Gonsalves introduction. Ultimately, this latter variant became known as "Blow By Blow."

Although the documented performances of these works number over one hundred, the existence of numerous undocumented performances, both before and after Newport, is strongly suspected.

Reflected throughout this summary and the accompanying notes are the contributions of Dan Morgenstern, Sjef Hoefsmit, and Gordon Ewing, to each of whom the author expresses sincerest gratitude.

SUMMARY OF INTERLUDES BETWEEN "DIMINUENDO IN BLUE" AND "CRESCENDO IN BLUE"
AS PLAYED BY THE DUKE ELLINGTON ORCHESTRA
20 SEPTEMBER 1937 - 28 JULY 1956

DATE	INTERLUDE (VOCALIST)	DEBOR	TIMNER	RECORDING	LOCATION	REMARKS
20 SEP 37	NONE	158 d - g	26-27	CBS 88210	NEW YORK, NY	FIRST RECORDING; DESOR 1584 & f ISSUED ON BRUNSWICK 8004
29 MAY 38	NONE	NONE	NONE	NONE KNOWN	RANDALL'S ISLAND NEW YORK, NY	NOTE 1
9 JUN 45	"ROCKS IN MY BED" (ME)	337 l - a	71	DETS 9	PARAMOUNT THEATER TOLEDO, OHIO	TREASURY BROADCAST INTRODUCED AS "THE BLUES CLUSTER"
7 JUL 45	"CARNEGIE BLUES"	342 e - e	73	DETS 13	RADIO CITY STUDIO 6B NEW YORK, NY	TREASURY BROADCAST INTRODUCED AS "TRIO IN BLUE"
21 SEP 45	"ROCKS IN MY BED" (JH)	1946 p.LXV	79	JOYCE 1066	CLUB ZANZIBAR NEW YORK, NY	
13 OCT 45	"I GOT IT BAD" (AH)	364 k - m	82	DETS 26	RADIO CITY STUDIO 6B NEW YORK, NY	TREASURY BROADCAST INTRODUCED AS "THREE TUNES IN THE BLUE MOOD"
4 JAN 46	"TRANSBLUCENCY" (KD)	NONE	87	PRESTIGE 24074	CARNEGIE HALL NEW YORK, NY	PREMIERE OF "TRANSBLUCENCY"
20 JAN 46 (AFTERNOON)	"TRANSBLUCENCY" (KD)	NONE	NONE	UNISSUED	CIVIC OPERA HOUSE CHICAGO, IL	
20 JAN 46 (EVENING)	"TRANSBLUCENCY" (KD)	378 l - k	88	DETS 33	CIVIC OPERA HOUSE CHICAGO, IL	AFRS BROADCAST
4 MAY 46	"TRANSBLUCENCY" (KD)	383 f - h	90	DETS 36	DARTMOUTH COLLEGE HANOVER, NH	TREASURY BROADCAST

3 AUG 46	"TRANSLUCENCY" (KD)	393 e - g	93	DETS 42	GOLDEN STATE THEATER SAN FRANCISCO, CA	TREASURY BROADCAST
23 OCT 46	NONE	405 a	96	PRESTIGE 24029	NEW YORK, NY	NOTE 2
19 APR 47	ELLINGTON SOLO	416 d, e	99	STARDUST 204	BAILEY HALL CORNELL UNIV. ITHACA, NY	NOTE 3
31 AUG 47	"TRANSLUCENCY" (KD)	426	102 - 103	UNIQUE JAZZ UJ 001	HOLLYWOOD BOWL HOLLYWOOD, CA	NOTE 4
30 JUN 51	GONSALVES SOLO	492 m, n	122	JAZZ ANTHOLOGY 5209 STARDUST 202	BIRDLAND NEW YORK, NY	NOTE 5
30 MAR 53	GONSALVES SOLO	NONE	NONE	GNP CRESCENDO 9045	CIVIC AUDITORIUM PASADENA, CA	NOTE 6
30 APR 56	GONSALVES SOLO	NONE	NONE	NONE KNOWN	DURHAM, NC	SEE ENDNOTE 67
MAY OR JUN 56	GONSALVES SOLO	NONE	NONE	NONE KNOWN	UNKNOWN	SEE ENDNOTE 67
7 JUL 56	GONSALVES SOLO	618 j	150	COLUMBIA CL40387 (LP) CK40387 (CD)	NEWPORT, RI	NEWPORT JAZZ FESTIVAL SEE ENDNOTE 67
28 JUL 56	GONSALVES SOLO	624 g	152	QUEEN DISC Q-044 KOALA AW 14165	FAIRFIELD UNIV. FAIRFIELD, CT	CONNECTICUT JAZZ FESTIVAL SEE ENDNOTE 43

VOCALISTS: ME - MARIE ELLINGTON; JS - JOYA SHERILL; AH - AL HIBBLER; KD - KAY DAVIS

NOTES TO SUMMARY OF INTERLUDES

NOTE 1

Previously undocumented performances of "Diminuendo in Blue" and "Crescendo in Blue," discovered by Dan Morgenstern, confirm the power of these works from an early date to cause a crowd to respond. On Sunday, 29 May 1938, the Ellington orchestra appeared as part of a six-hour "Carnival of Swing" organized by broadcaster Martin Block and held at the outdoor auditorium on Randall's Island, New York, New York. Some 25,000 spectators were treated to a program featuring 25 separate orchestra units, including the bands of Woody Herman, Count Basie, Chick Webb, and Gene Krupa. The concert was the subject of a comprehensive review in the British weekly, *Melody Maker,* in which Ellington's appearance was reported in detail by New York correspondent Al Brackman:

> The first exciting moment of the occasion and the biggest thrill was the riotous reaction to Duke Ellington's Band.
> Martin Block announced Ellington's recent compositions, *Diminuendo and Crescendo in Blue.* During the first portion, which begins *fortissimo* and recedes to *pianissimo,* the crowd began to clap hands and stamp feet in rhythmic unison. In the second portion, which starts *pianissimo* and builds to *double fortissimo,* the riot started.
> ABOUT TEN PERSONS JUMPED FROM THE GRANDSTANDS ONTO THE FIELD, AND TAKING THIS CUE, THREE THOUSAND OTHER ENTHUSIASTS SWARMED THE FIELD FROM THE TIER SEATS IN AN EFFORT TO GET NEAR THE STAGE, CREATING TURBULENT HAVOC WITH THE FIELD ATTENDANTS.
> At the conclusion of the selection, with hundreds more pouring from the stands, Martin Block announced that unless order was restored and people returned to their seats the concert would be concluded immediately. A call was put in for extra policemen and the session was delayed about ten minutes.

When order was restored, Ellington and the band continued with inspired performances, so overwhelmed were the boys with the demonstration. Cootie Williams was featured in his familiar concerto, the band played *Rockin' in Rhythm, I Let A Song Go Out of My Heart,* and concluding with a new *St. Louis Blues* arrangement which gave Ivy Anderson an opportunity to sing her wares.

Following this rendition, W.C. Handy was brought forth and introduced to the assemblage.

Al Brackman, "25,000 American Swing Fans Go Crazy To Music Of Duke And Other Jazz Aces," *Melody Maker and British Metronome,* 11 June 1938, 9.

NOTE 2

The recordings of Musicraft Records, made during five sessions in the latter part of 1946, are available on *Happy-Go-Lucky Local,* Musicraft MVSCD-52 (CD). At the first session, on 23 October, four takes each of "Diminuendo in Blue" and "Magenta Haze" were recorded, take four of "Diminuendo" being issued. The prevailing practice, firmly established that year, was to join "Diminuendo" and "Crescendo" with the "Transblucency" interlude featuring Kay Davis, who is not present at this first session. She appears only in the third session, on 5 December, to sing the wordless vocal in "The Beautiful Indians—Part 2 (Minnehaha)." These circumstances may be viewed as either the cause of the anomalous recording of "Diminuendo" alone or the result of a decision to record only that work. As Jerry Valburn observes in the liner notes to the compact disc: "No one around today can recall why Duke recorded only the first part of this work."

DESOR, Prestige 24029, the compact disc and the Igo Itinerary correctly list the date of the first Musicraft session as 23 October 1946. Timner and DEMS Bulletin, 1984/5: 1 list the date of this session as 26 October 1946. No recordings were made on that date.

NOTE 3

Substantially all of the Cornell University concert was preserved on a numbered series of acetates privately issued by the Cornell Rhythm Club ("CRC"). The numbering of these acetates belies the fact that the sequence of performance of the entire concert has not been established, those set out in DESOR and Timner notwithstanding. Much of what was recorded was not of commercially acceptable quality. Accordingly, significant portions of this concert have not been generally available, the most extensive representation appearing on Stardust 204 (LP). "Diminuendo in Blue," the Ellington piano interlude and "Crescendo in Blue" appear on CRC 1204 and on Stardust 204. "Transblucency," also performed at this concert, appears on CRC 1001, but remains unissued on LP. "Transblucency" was performed in its full length, including Kay Davis's wordless vocal and Lawrence Brown's extended trombone solo. Applause heard after the performance confirms that it was played as a discrete number, and not as an interlude between parts of "The Beautiful Indians," as indicated in DESOR (from which the usual breakdown is curiously omitted) and in Timner.

DESOR incorrectly lists the location and date of this concert as being at Dartmouth College, Hanover, New Hampshire, on 30 April 1947. DEMS Bulletin, 1986/1: 3.

NOTE 4

The listing for this performance in DESOR is incomplete, and does not include "Diminuendo in Blue," "Transblucency" or "Crescendo in Blue."

NOTE 5

A description of the circumstances surrounding this performance is found in Mercer Ellington with Stanley Dance, *Duke Ellington in Person—An Intimate Memoir* (Boston: Houghton, 1978), 112.

NOTE 6

DEMS Bulletin, 1990/1:6 (Letter from Sjef Hoefsmit). The Pasadena concert also appears on *Duke Ellington–The 1953 Pasadena Concert,* Vogue 600105 (CD) and *Duke Ellington—Take the "A" Train,* Vogue 670208 (CD). On the LP and both CDs, Paul Gonsalves's solo appears to have been shortened. DEMS Bulletin, 1988/4: 3; 1988/5:1.

MUSIC

Mood Indigo & Beyond
(See Cover)

The chill of a moonless July midnight was in the air, and some of the 11,000 jazz buffs in Newport, R.I.'s Freebody Park drifted towards the gate. In the tented area behind the bandstand, musicians who had finished playing for the final night of Newport's third jazz festival were packing their instruments and saying goodbye. The festival was just about over. But onstage famed Bandleader Duke Ellington, a trace of coldness rimming his urbanity, refused to recognize the fact. He announced one of his 1938 compositions, *Diminuendo in Blue and Crescendo in Blue*. A strange, spasmodic air, that carried memories of wilderness and city, rose through the salt-scented night air like a fire on a beach. Minutes passed. People turned back from the exits; snoozers woke up. All at once the promise of new excitement revived the dying evening.

At that magic moment Ellington's Paul Gonsalves was ripping off a fast but insinuating solo on his tenor saxophone, his fancies dandled by a bounding beat on

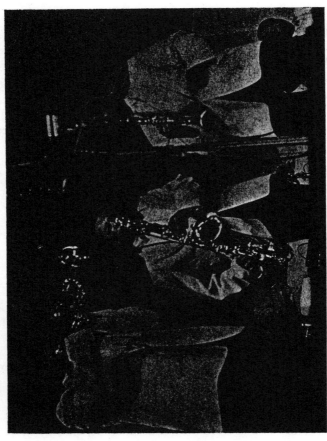

SIDEMEN TERRY, GONSALVES, HAMILTON

Robert Parent

bass and drums (Jimmy Woode and Sam Woodyard). The Duke himself tweaked an occasional fragment on the high piano. Gradually, the beat began to ricochet from the audience as more and more fans began to clap hands on the offbeats until the crowd was one vast, rhythmic chorus, yelling its approval. There were howls of "More! More!" and there was dancing in the aisles. One young woman broke loose from her escort and rioted solo around the field, while a young man encouraged her by shouting, "Go, go, go!" Festival officials began to fear that something like a rock 'n' roll riot was taking place. One of them was pleading with beaming Bandleader Ellington to stop. When the fellow's entreaties got too emphatic, Duke wagged a soothing finger at him and said mildly, "Don't be rude to the artists."

The event last month marked not only the turning point in one concert; it confirmed a turning point in a career. The big news was something that the whole jazz world had long hoped to hear: the Ellington band was once again the most exciting thing in the business, Ellington himself had emerged from a long period of quiescence and was once again bursting with ideas and inspiration.

At 57, Edward Kennedy Ellington, jazzman, composer, and beyond question one of America's topflight musicians, is a magic name to two generations of Americans. His *Mood Indigo, Sophisticated Lady, Solitude,* and countless other dreamy tunes have become as familiar as any other songs since Stephen Foster. As jazz composer he is beyond categorizing—there is hardly a musician in the field who has not been influenced by the Ellington style. His style contains the succinctness of concert music and the excitement of jazz. His revival comes at a time when most bandleaders who thrived in the golden '30s are partly or completely out of business,* and few have risen to replace them.

Last week Bandleader Ellington returned to New York from a four-night swing through New England and spent his first 24 hours in the company of his arranger, Billy Strayhorn, poring over a pad of hot score paper. Next night the band met to record the four new songs they had written, while wives and friends looked on. At midnight the whole crew got on the bus and left for Buffalo, where the next night they played for a Negro fraternity meeting. The affair lasted till 4 a.m. Back in New York Duke stayed up late (noon) and got up early (2 p.m.) in order to keep appointments with TV crews and the press. At week's end he was off for a handful of one-night stands before settling down for one of his periodic long runs: a fortnight's engagement in Chicago's Blue Note Café.

Hot Licks. Although Ellington's outfit is the only big band that has never been disbanded in its 29 years, its character has changed over the decades as death or a yen for adventure changed its roster. Yet the Ellington sound is as distinctive today as it ever was. Apart from the Duke himself, its dominant personality is provided by two men who have been with it longest: Harry Carney and the hoarse, jovial tone of his big baritone saxophone, Johnny Hodges and the refined, almost brutally sensual whine of his alto. The other characteristic sounds are the tantrum-tempered groans and howls

* Benny Goodman plays occasional weekend dates, Tommy and Jimmy Dorsey have combined their bands, Artie Shaw is out of the music business, Cab Calloway is appearing as a solo singing act. Such sweet-music bandleaders as Guy Lombardo and Sammy Kaye, however, are still going strong.

JAZZ BUFFS DIGGING ELLINGTON AT NEWPORT FESTIVAL

of the growl brasses with plunger mute,* an effect originally discovered by the late Trumpeter Bubber Miley, now played on trombone by Quentin ("Butter") Jackson and on trumpet by Ray Nance.

When the saxophones play together, their tone is tinted by one of Duke's innovations, the split harmony, which hauntingly inflects the whole quality of a chord. They seem to play with a fierce joy which is stimulated by the rude sting of the trumpets—or by their melting pleasure—and the short-tempered, but softhearted bleats of the trombones. The sound combinations are already fairly routine in almost any band of today. But in the Ellington band such background licks take on the coherence of speech and frequently turn into lively conversation. In *My Funny Valentine*, for instance, the blue mood of its start turns black in the second chorus; the dialogue becomes desperate and reaches a violent climax before tranquillity is restored.

Fickle Tricks. The man who is responsible for this remarkable musical idiom is a

* Actually, the business end of a "plumber's helper."

tall (6 ft. 1 in.), rangy (185 lbs.) fellow whose newfound trimness parallels his rediscovered energies. His habitual expression combines curiosity, mockery and humor. In his pleasant Harlem apartment or in his dressing room, he usually goes about in his shorts, possibly to preserve the creases in his 100-plus suits of clothes. His public personality resembles his public appearance, which is fastidious to the point of frivolity; few are the people who get a glimpse of the man beneath this polished exterior. "You gotta be older," he explains, "to realize that many of the people you meet are mediocrities. You have to let them run off you like water off a duck's back. Otherwise, they drag you down." Even his close friends say he never exposes himself to unpleasantness if he can help it. Says one: "He likes pretty pictures and pretty melodies."

Often, his efforts to avoid unpleasantness take the form of hypochondria—as he puts it, "I'm a doctor freak." Although his doctor says he is an unusually healthy specimen, Duke tends to mistrust his ability to stay well; if his pulse rate seems slow to him in Las Vegas, it means a call to New York for his doctor to take the next plane out. He will not tolerate air conditioning—"You know, I'm delicate. My hair gets wet, the air conditioning hits it, and I get a sharp pain right down the middle of my back." His personal vanity extends to his feet, which he exercises against the wall at odd moments during his busy days and nights.

Even the Duke himself has trouble fathoming the hidden truths of his personality, although he likes to try. "I may be a heel," he will say, "but I hate for people to think so." Or, "I always take the easy way." Perhaps his best estimate of his life and career is a self-deprecating one: "I'm so damned fickle," he says. "I never could stick with what I was doing—always wanted to try something new. I never accumulated any money, so I always had to keep working."

At Last, Clicks. When Edward Ellington was born in Washington, D.C. in 1899, the capital was jigging to the insolent rhythms of ragtime pianists. Farther west Buddy Bolden's fabulous cornet was shaking New Orleans' levees, and such young idolaters as Joe ("King") Oliver and Sidney Bechet were soon to hammer out the rudiments of instrumental jazz. Washington jazz tended to strings—pianos, banjos, violins—but it had the same ancestry: the sophisticated rhythms of African drums, which later took on a more succinct and sensuous character as they drifted through the Caribbean islands, gradually infiltrated the U.S. via New Orleans and the East Coast. The East Coast variety, with its own flavors added, eventually became the ragtime of Duke's childhood.

"Man, those were two-fisted piano players," he recalls. "Men like Sticky Mack and Doc Perry and James P. Johnson and Willie 'The Lion' Smith. With their left hand, they'd play big chords for the bass note, and just as big ones for the offbeat, and they really swang. The right hand played real pretty. They did things technically you wouldn't believe."

Ellington's father was first a butler, then a caterer, and eventually a blueprint technician, and he provided well for his family. Duke had art lessons, at which he did extremely well, and piano lessons, which he never mastered. He felt they cramped his style. He worked in a soda fountain after school, and spent his hours at home working out his own method of playing the piano. By the time he was 14, he had started a piece called *Soda Fountain Rag*, and he played it so many

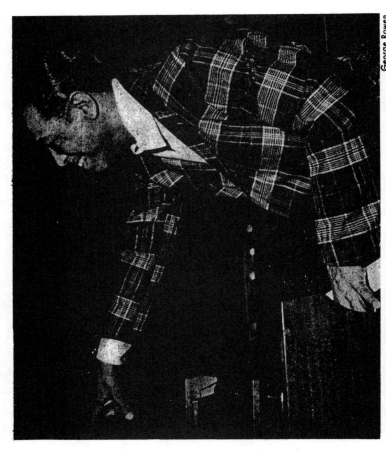

George Rowen

CONDUCTOR ELLINGTON (AT FAIRFIELD, CONN. CONCERT)

After that he never had to split his fees. Before long he had a house, a car, a wife and a son, Mercer. But his musical friends all moved to New York, where the jazz was hot. Duke followed in 1922, though it meant a fresh start, many penniless months, and a separation from his wife that became permanent.

Lucky Six. "A pal and I used to go see Willie The Lion at his club—the Capitol Palace—and Fats Waller at the Orient, and they'd let us sit in and cut in on the tips," Duke recalls. "Every day we'd go play pool until we made $2. With $2 we'd get a pair of 75¢ steaks, beer for a quarter, and have a quarter left for tomorrow." He did his own housework, including mending and pressing his tailor-made suits, always impeccably kept. Periodically, there was work for his five-man combo—Arthur Whetsel on trumpet, Otto Hardwick on bass and alto, Sonny Greer on drums and Elmer Snowden on banjo —but the real break came in 1927. "You know, I'm lucky," says Duke. "I'm lucky because I like pretty music—some people don't—and can write it down. And I was lucky when we auditioned for the Cotton Club job. Six other bands auditioned, and they were all on time. We were late, but the big boss was late too,

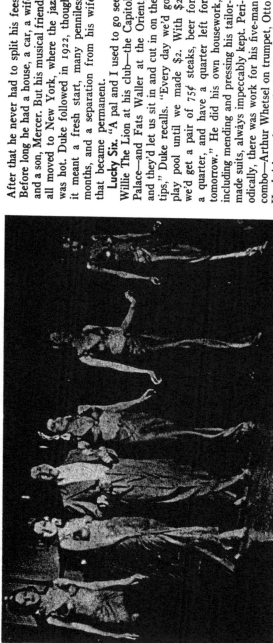

WITH COTTON CLUB DANCERS IN 1930
Willie The Lion let him sit in.

Max P. Haas—European

different ways that people thought it was several compositions.

Soon Duke and his friends were playing for private affairs and dances at Washington's True Reformers Hall. A musical contractor arranged bookings in return for half of the fees. Duke noticed that the contractor got his business from a small ad in the classified phone book, so the boy took an ad himself, and he clicked.

and he heard us and he never heard the others." Duke enlarged his band to eleven pieces and stayed at the Cotton Club on Harlem's Lenox Avenue for five years.

As soon as he got on his feet, Duke sent for his mother. "I was never out of her sight until I was eight," he says. "She and my father even used to take me to dances and set me on the bandstand while they danced." He bought her furs and a big diamond ring, and sought her advice constantly. When he toured, she would follow him around the country. When she died, Duke wept in his sister's arms. As for his father, Duke had long since made him road manager of his band.

Every man in the early Ellington band —as in today's—was a soloist, and the music they played was unlike anything anyone had ever heard. Recalls a friend: "One time at the Cotton Club the entire brass section arose and delivered such an intricate and unbelievably integrated chorus that Eddy Duchin, who was in the audience, literally rolled on the floor under his table—in ecstasy." Says Ellington: "We didn't think of it as jazz; we thought of it as Negro music."

It was, indeed, full of thudding tom-toms, sizzling cymbals and gongs. Much of it had an undulating, tropical beat that might have emerged from Africa, and its saxes wailed and its brasses growled in cheerful ill temper. The titles, themselves an important part of the magical atmosphere, were such things as *East St. Louis Toodle-oo*, *The Mooche*, *Creole Love Call* and *Black and Tan Fantasy*. By that time, Composer Ellington was already making some of his important innovations; *e.g.*, the use of a wordless soprano as if she were a musical instrument, and compositions of unusual length for a jazz band (his *Reminiscing in Tempo* was spread over four record sides).

Duke Ellington really started to get around. Recalls one of Duke's former managers: "I've traveled all over with him. I've seen Duke between a real duke and lady-so-and-so, and when he's dressed in those tails, he's as fine a gentleman as England could produce.

"Duke and his band played in England during the Economic Conference, in 1933. They were playing in Lord Beaverbrook's tremendous palace at a party. Jack Hylton's band played waltzes till midnight, and Duke took over at midnight. This mob, they'd never heard music like that. I was standing with Beaverbrook and Lady Mountbatten. We were watching all of these dignitaries, all diamonds and medals and what not. Beaverbrook was so taken with the music, and he said the mob was like a bunch of kids. He asked me questions about the band. I explained this was swing music. The Duke has the type of rhythm that more or less gets into your veins when you're dancing. Beaverbrook wrote an editorial about us."*

Quick Fix. In those days Negroes were still segregated on Broadway. Duke recalls going to work at a nightclub called the Hurricane, which he found a good spot until he began getting complaints from his Harlem friends; not one of them had been able to get in. Ellington spoke to the owner, and it was not long before the doors were opened. Duke is not a militant foe of segregation. He plays for segregated audiences on his annual swings through the South—"everybody does"—and feels lucky that there has never been an incident.

In 1926 Duke met an agent and lyric writer named Irving Mills, and Mills be-

* In the London *Daily Express*, advocating colored colonial Members of Parliament, Press Lord Beaverbrook took Ellington as a fine example of his race, described him as "a genius of Negro music. He sat by the side of his host, modest, dignified, delighting all the company with his gay mind and splendid bearing."

came manager of the band as well as Ellington's personal representative and partner. Out of this relationship came Duke's most successful years as a composer and bandleader, almost in spite of himself. "Oh yes," Mills would say, offhandedly, waving his fat cigar. "We've got a recording date tomorrow. Four new songs." Or, "Oh yes. We're going to introduce a new big work next week." *Creole Rhapsody*, Duke's first composition of greater than pop-tune dimensions (1932), came about after one of Manager Mills's press conferences. At that time *Creole Rhapsody* was just another little tune. A reporter wanted to know how come it was called "rhapsody," and Mills offhandedly said that it was "part of a larger work." And Duke Ellington, too proud to let his manager down, and unwilling to let such a whopper stand, produced the music on time—or almost on time.

Ellington, who seems to derive inspiration from being on the move, wrote many of the tunes in a taxi on the way to the studio, or even in the middle of bed in the night, grunt a tune that had just come to him and play it on the piano. It made little difference, since all new numbers had to be worked out anyhow. "You play

this," Duke would say to one musician at a time, while noodling out a tune on the piano. As soon as they heard a phrase, the musicians learned it, and then toyed with it until they made it sound as if they had invented it themselves.

Even accidents were turned to advantage. One day, when only half the band arrived for a recording session, a new distribution of voices was evolved on the spot to make the few sound richer. The tune was *Mood Indigo*, and the broad-spaced trio at the start became one of Duke's sound trademarks. Other tunes lay fallow in the band's books until somebody set words to them and they caught on, e.g., *Never No Lament (Don't Get Around Much Any More)*, *Concerto for Cootie (Do Nothin' 'Til You Hear from Me)*. Ellington is accustomed to hearing his ideas unexpectedly used by other songwriters, and is resigned to it.

Counting Chicks. Duke's fertile mind continued to turn out songs, even when there were no recording deadlines to meet. The band could now play a week's worth of dances and never repeat itself or play any composer except Ellington. During the early years, Ellington found that one hit tune a year was enough to keep the band popular. What kind of music did he think

he was writing? Mostly, he thinks it was folk music. In any case, he says, his songs are "all about women," and almost any

WITH MANAGER MILLS IN PARIS
International
The Beaver wrote an editorial.

one who listens receptively will agree. Duke is well qualified to discourse musically—or any other way—on the chicks, as he calls them. He has made a long and continuing study of the subject, and is himself the object of study by his subjects. As soon as he appears on a Harlem sidewalk, the street becomes crowded with chicks. The young ones merely ask for his autograph; older ones pass with glittering, sidelong g ances beneath lowered lashes.

In 1939 Musician Ellington and Manager Mills agreed to go separate ways (Mills has since become a successful music publisher). One of Duke's subsequent adventures was *Jump for Joy*, which he wrote and produced with a group of Hollywood artists. It was a revue designed to fight Uncle Tomism in the entertainment world, and the show folded after twelve weeks of backstage wrangling. As usual, Duke had written for his own band, and the band was in the pit. "We stayed out there for a while, just barely keeping our heads above water," he says. "But there were not enough people clamoring to buy at our price. So we put the price up. We gave a concert in Carnegie Hall."

Bop Kicks. It was about the same time that Duke got what he calls "the check." Things were very black. There was a recording ban on,* which meant no extra fees, and the band was taking a $500 loss a week just to play at a club with a "wire," *i.e.*, a radio hookup. "I was short of cash," he says, "so I went into the William Morris office to negotiate a small loan. While I was standing around, a boy came through with the mail, and handed me a letter from Victor records. I glanced at it. It was a check for $2,250. I slid it back into the envelope quick. Just what I needed, I thought. Two thousand, two-hundred-and-fifty dollars would do me nicely. But maybe I had misread it. Probably it was $22.50. I opened it again. It was $22,500 royalties for *Don't Get Around Much Any More*. I went out of there like a shot, and nobody saw me for two months."

During the '40s, Duke turned out several large jazz tone poems, notably *Black, Brown and Beige*, which has to do with states of mind rather than skin colors; *Harlem*, with its smooth changes of pace from nimble to noble; *Liberian Suite*, written on commission for the Liberian government centennial.

Despite the fame of these works, things continued strictly blue for the Ellington gang. Most of the original band members had either quit or died, and with their replacements, Composer Ellington seemed to have trouble writing new songs as distinctive as the old. The jazz world was getting its kicks from bop, but when Ellington tried to go along with the new style, he seemed to be regressing: he had been using their tricks for years. On the fringes of show business, men became reputable critics overnight simply by writing attacks on Ellington

The Clock Ticks. But the attraction of the Ellington band never faded among musicians. And today, joining him means both musical glory and financial security. "You hear the band, when you're not in it," says Butter Jackson, "and you like the way it sounds. You think you'd like to be playing that." Once in, every man is tempered by the fire of 14 other men's alert ears. There is no other discipline. Says Duke: "I told those guys in 1927 they were never going to drive me to the nuthouse. 'We may all go there,' I said, 'but I'm going to be driving the wagon.'"

* Instituted by Music Czar James C. Petrillo in a campaign to force radio stations, bars and restaurants to employ members of the American Federation of Musicians.

He can't remember ever firing anybody, but he has driven some to quit. One man regularly arrived tight and got drunker as the evening wore on. At the worst moment Duke would schedule the fellow's solo in racing tempo, so fast that he could not play the notes, and he eventually quit in humiliation.

Mercer Ellington (who is now in the recording business) well remembers the days when he was working his way up through the ranks of the band as baggage boy. "We got to Cleveland about 8 or 9 o'clock one morning," he says. "I complained that I was hungry. 'What!' said my father. 'Didn't you just eat yesterday?'" Today, things are different. The Ellington band, back on top, asks a tidy $2,500 a night for a dance, plus about half of the net gate receipts. The fee is $3,500 for a college concert-and-prom. Altogether, Duke Ellington, Inc. grosses between $500,000 and $700,000 a year. Part of the reason for the band's durability is the fact that, unlike most bands, it plays everything—concerts, proms, dances, theaters, nightclubs, hotel dining rooms, and even rock 'n' roll hops. Most of its time is devoted to living "on the other side of the clock" while playing one-night

George Rowen

THE DUKE (CENTER) & FAMILY*
Mostly on the other side of the clock.

* From left: Mercer Ellington and wife Evelyn, Duke, his sister Ruth, Arranger Strayhorn.

stands. The band packs up its instruments between 1 and 4 a.m., gets aboard the big bus with "Mr. Hi-Fi of 1956" on the fluted sides, and rides, argues and snores its way to the next town (favorite topics: chicks, music, food, geography). The arrival may be at dawn or dusk, depending on the distance. One musician described the rest of the process: "You go to the hotel, take a long look at the bed, go play the date, take another look at the bed and get on the bus." Such a life seems to agree with the Ellington bandsmen, who are cushioned against some of life's jolts by getting the highest pay in the business ($200-$500 a week).

Duke travels by car or train these days. He never flies, and has serious reservations about steamships. But when he hits New York between tours, his rounds of lawyers, music publishers, recording studios, photographers and tailors are fairly ducal. He likes to play the patriarch of his family which includes his sister, his son Mercer, 37, his three grandchildren and (by virtual adoption) his doctor and his arranger, Billy Strayhorn.

Ellington's second wind has been felt in the music business for months, and the major record companies have been bidding for his remarkable signature:

This week he plans to sign (with Columbia) a contract designed to give him the broadest possible scope. He will have time to write more big works, both instrumental and dramatic. Planned for the immediate future: a musical on the history of jazz, specifically composed for records. Ellington began work on this score 15 years ago in Hollywood, on a commission from Orson Welles, but he soon put it aside. "I wrote a piece of music . . just 28 bars," he wrote later. "It was a gasser —real great, I confess it. And I lost it. I always said, and I say to this day, that it was the greatest thing I ever wrote . . . I got the money, but they never got the 28 bars." Now, Duke is determined to go on with the project despite the missing 28 bars.

Says a friend: "Duke hasn't hit his stride yet. If he retired for a few years and just wrote, he would leave a wealth of music. The record companies should let Duke write tremendous symphonies that would represent America and a style of music. He should be allowed to write big works, to write and record with big symphony orchestras. He shouldn't be limited to 14 or 15 men."

To which Edward Kennedy Ellington replies: "We're not worried about writing for posterity. We just want it to sound good right now!"

THE JAZZ CANON AND ITS CONSEQUENCES

By Krin Gabbard

Jazz talk is becoming jazz discourse. Scholars at major universities are now granted the Ph.D. primarily on the basis of their contributions to jazz scholarship. The institutionalization of jazz in higher education would be consistent with current demystifications of the distinctions between high and low culture, with the growing trend toward multiculturalism in university curricula, and with the postmodernist cachet now enjoyed by marginal arts and artists. Signs of jazz's ascendancy can be found in such periacademic phenomena as the proliferation of jazz titles now being published by university presses, the birth of jazz repertory orchestras, and the new jazz division at New York's Lincoln Center. For several years Lincoln Center has also run a series of "Classical Jazz" concerts under the artistic directorship of Wynton Marsalis, himself an eminent symbol of jazz's new legitimacy.

Even television commercials testify to the music's rising cultural capital. In an advertisement a few years ago, a well-heeled white gentleman cited a Mozart concerto as the sound most appropriate for the total appreciation of his Mercedes-Benz; more recently, a cool, Milesian trumpet performed a similar function by providing elegant background music in a commercial for the Infiniti, a new luxury car. Concurrent with the Infiniti spot a faithful recreation of the Duke Ellington Orchestra's 1941 recording of "Chelsea Bridge" played behind a scene of casual affluence in a commercial for the American Express card; and at the time of this writing, Benny Goodman's 1952 recording of "How Am I to Know?" graces a series of spots for the Chase Manhattan Bank. Advertisers no longer use jazz to connote the night life and slumming that can be purchased along with their products—jazz can now signify refinement and upper class status, once the exclusive province of classical music.[1]

This new parity of jazz with classical music in the sign systems of popular media is an important breakthrough. Because jazz has historically been treated as a stepchild of "serious" music, the music's value is usually established with appeals to standards developed for classical music. The project is explicit, for example, in the title of Grover Sales's book, *Jazz: America's Classical Music.*[2] All jazz writers are richly aware of the various strains of prejudice that place classical music in a loftier position in the cultural hierarchy. A great deal of jazz writing implicitly or explicitly expresses the demand that jazz musicians be given the same legitimacy as practitioners of the canonical arts. When the arbiters of taste finally understand that the intrinsic value of jazz is unrelated to its exile from the Eurocentric canon, jazz will ascend to its rightful place in American culture as well as in the university, where jazz scholarship will flourish.

Or will it? The hypothetical ascension of jazz studies would take place at a peculiar moment in the history of academic institutions. Conditions that appear to bode well for jazz scholarship also conceal difficulties for the discipline. The canonization of jazz—or more precisely, the canonization of certain jazz artists and styles—would seem to be inescapable if the music is to claim its place within the academy, where an array of organizations such as grant-giving institutions support and further legitimize subjects of research and teaching. At the same time, however, humanistic disciplines are being re-canonized if not de-canonized while the entire process by which texts come under scrutiny is itself being scrutinized. And in spite of the occasional jazz group that called itself an "orchestra" or the jazz writer who composed a "fantasy," the music has almost from the beginning placed itself at odds with the canonizing language of high culture. The entry of jazz discourse into the dialogues of the university can only result in the transformation of that discourse. Scott DeVeaux has suggested that the term "jazz concert" once ran the risk of being an oxymoron.[3] Much the same can now be said for "the jazz canon."

My argument in this paper is arranged around two themes that complicate the attempt to establishment a jazz canon: (1) the resistance of jazz writing to the protocols of contemporary theory that follow canon-building wherever it takes place, and (2) the conviction on the part of many theorists that ideological forces masquerade as disinterested aesthetics in the discourse around *all* canonical works. I will make regular references to debates within other disciplines—film studies, most prominently—that offer instructive models for the imminent institutionalization of jazz. The creation of a jazz canon, I will argue, is as self-defeating as it is inevitable, especially as jazz studies move towards professionalization and autonomy.

CANONICAL STATUS

Although people inside and outside academia are now less inclined than ever to subscribe to the concept of the "masterpiece," canonical works of Western literature, classical music, and European painting still bear traces of the Benjaminian aura. Likewise, the term "canon" still carries the marks of its religious origins: the Oxford English Dictionary defines *canon* as "The collection or list of books of the bible as accepted by the Christian Church as genuine and inspired . . . . Any set of sacred books."[4] Although the sacral antecedents of canons are usually ignored in discussions of great art, music, and literature, those works that appear to have endured for centuries possess a mystifying sense of inevitability, as if they had been handed down by God. Like the books of the Bible, "great" works of art are "universal" and "timeless."

In stark contrast to the sacral haze that surrounds canonical texts, the actual path a work takes to "masterpiece" status has little to do with religion. In fact, canonization is usually determined by the likes and dislikes of the last few generations of university professors.[5] If nothing else, professors are more comfortable teaching the material once inflicted upon them in graduate school, if not in college and high school. Teachers can become self-conscious about the hidden politics of canon formation and cease referring to works as immortal masterpieces, even choosing to teach them anticanonically. Still, texts that are repeatedly inscribed in course syllabi possess a largely unquestioned claim upon the attention of scholars and students. This aura of inevitability masks the often tortuous paths such texts may have taken on their way to canonization. Lawrence Levine's account of Shakespeare's fortunes in mid-nineteenth century America provides a particularly revealing example of how texts can be wrested from a popular canon and sequestered within the academy for an educated elite.[6] But at least in part because English professors seldom teach history of reception, Shakespeare is widely regarded as an eternally stable fixture of the high art canon. We can also chart the ups and downs of novelists, painters, sculptors, and composers who now occupy equally unquestioned positions in our cultural hierarchies. In spite of the Infiniti and Chase Manhattan Bank commercials, few Americans today regard anything in jazz history as the auratic equal of Faulkner, Copland, or Wyeth. Consequently, the disciplines that attend to these works carry a legitimacy that jazz studies lack, if only because the music has not been around long enough to acquire real canonical status.

FILM STUDIES AS A MODEL

The progress of a youthful discipline such as film studies may offer a better model for contemplating the future of jazz studies. Cinema stood just outside the classroom door in the early 1960s, a position not unlike the one currently occupied by jazz. Colleges and universities had for many years provided meeting places for film societies and buffs, just as "hot record societies" and student jazz bands have long been fixtures at universities. Amidst the clutter of fanzines, a bare handful of journals published scholarly articles on movies; a few intellectuals had begun writing on the history and aesthetics of the cinema, in the case of the German-born psychiatrist Hugo Münsterberg as early as 1916.[7] Serious jazz criticism has historically lagged behind film criticism; although jazz was already a popular topic in newspapers and magazines by the second decade of the century, thoughtful jazz articles did not begin to appear in the United States and Europe until the 1930s.[8] In the academy, many universities developed professional schools for filmmakers; in the case of film history and criticism, some faculty members showed feature films in their classrooms to supplement more conventional pedagogical tools, and at a few schools, students could even take a course devoted entirely to cinema. Such courses, however, were usually ghettoized in departments of English or theatre. Much the same can be said for jazz today: while there are a number of schools that train young musicians to play the music (Berklee College, William Paterson College, North Texas State, etc.), these must be distinguished from schools where jazz is most often taught by musicologists more secure with Eurocentric forms or by a lone jazz musician retreating to the security of academia after several years of paying dues on the road. Institutes and archives such as those at Rutgers and Tulane are much more the exception than the rule.

Cinema, on the other hand, as been more successful in gaining acceptance at American colleges and universities. The first Ph.D. in film studies was granted by New York University in 1971. According to the latest survey by the American Film Institute, over 300 colleges and universities offered degrees in film study in 1980.[9] The number has surely grown since. By contrast, as late as 1990, only 100 colleges and universities in the United States offered degree programs in jazz, almost all of them undergraduate.[10] The success of cinema in becoming a recognized academic discipline might be attributed in part to the importation from France of *la politique des auteurs* in the 1960s. Andrew Sarris deserves substantial credit for Americanizing an auteur theory of cinema that identifies the director as the true author of a film.[11] The more romantic auteurists created an agonistic model of filmmaking, casting the director as a serious artist imprinting a unique vision on his films in spite of the arbitrary demands of studio bosses, star egos, and the Production Code. Anything that was aesthetically weak or unsavory in a film could be blamed on someone else so long as the auteur's signature was visible in the film's "privileged moments."

By authorizing the reading of a film around a single artist's work, auteurism gave a new aesthetic legitimacy to movies. In universities, films "by" Ford and Welles or Bergman and Antonioni could be collected and interpreted according to many of the same methods developed for, say, the novels of Henry James. Evidence of order and thematic unity, once the sole possession of high culture, was also found in works of cinematic auteurs, and canonized filmmakers were said to possess transcendent artistic visions that spoke to all humanity.[12] As the university was being transformed by the sea changes of the 1960s, auteurism helped clear room in the university for film study, bringing with it an aesthetics and a canonical list of director/authors. Sarris eventually became a professor of film studies at Columbia University in spite of his lack of conventional academic credentials.

Auteurism still has force today, even among the filmgoing public who now recognize a large variety of brand-name directors—Spike Lee and David Lynch as well as Steven Spielberg and Woody Allen. In academic film studies any number of theories from the 1970s and 1980s can be cited as refutations, revisions, or rethinkings of auteurism. In general, the mainstreams of the discipline have moved away from extolling the transcendent vision of a director and towards what Paul Ricoeur has called "a hermeneutics of suspicion."[13] Film theoreticians now rely on Marxist, psychoanalytic, semiotic, and poststructuralist methodologies to connect forces outside the text with meanings that lie beneath the film's smooth narrative surface. These meanings are usually uncovered through techniques of demystification developed by critics such as Roland Barthes who see bourgeois ideology passing itself off as nature. Canonical directors are still the subject of some research, but many scholars have found that the ideological workings of a film are more accessible to analysis when the director is relatively obscure and the film is more "typical" of the industry's production. As befits a discipline moving rapidly towards professionalization, film scholars have adopted a language that is notoriously remote. Most jazz scholars, for better or worse, still speak a language drawn from other disciplines and/or journalism.

As in the more established disciplines, the dominant canons of cinema study have been radically questioned by previously excluded groups, most prominently by women. Recently, however, feminist critics have become concerned that their critique of traditional male canons is equally applicable to the emerging feminist canons. Virginia Wright Wexman's essay on the various interpretations of Alfred Hitchcock's *Vertigo* (1958) is exemplary of a feminism that recognizes its own investment in an institutional dialectic of power that feminism itself has sought to expose.[14] *Vertigo* was singled out by Laura Mulvey in what is undoubtedly the single most influential essay in early feminist film theory.[15] Far from labeling the film a work of genius, Mulvey sees *Vertigo* as a convincing illustration of Hollywood's submission of female characters to the sadistic gaze of the male characters, who function as stand-ins for the men in the audience. Wexman suggests that many feminists—who promote a theory that may be illustrated most completely by the obsessive gaze directed at Kim Novak by James Stewart in *Vertigo*—have effectively secured their place in the discipline by helping to place Hitchcock's film on key lists that define the canons of film study.[16]

Wexman observes that canon formation is essential to the political prestige of groups and subgroups in the academy. Following Gramsci, Wexman distinguishes between "traditional intellectuals," who perpetuate and rationalize the values of a society, and "organic intellectuals," who advocate new value systems, in essence theorizing themselves into the society's structures of power.[17] Institutionally established critics have insisted that *Vertigo* is a work of "pure cinema," and, by extension, that as a work of art it transcends commerce. For Wexman, the interpretations of these traditional intellectuals promote bourgeois notions of the autonomy of art. She debunks these readings of the film by demonstrating that large portions of *Vertigo* are endorsements for the touristic delights of San Francisco as well as for the classical beauty of its star, Kim Novak. Wexman also finds alternatives to readings of *Vertigo* by certain feminist critics, "organic intellectuals" who have advanced their own cause by holding up the film as an important document for which they offer the most compelling interpretation. By laying claim to a film such as *Vertigo,* feminist scholars have hastened that film's rise to canonical status at the same time that they have rationalized their own ascent in American universities.[18] In much the same way, Sarris promoted himself by creating a pantheon of exclusively male auteur/directors in the 1960s.

The history of film studies suggests that a postcanonical study such as Wexman's is possible only after the discipline has built a foundation around key works. The current demystification and deconstruction of cinematic texts by film theorists might not have become so prominent without canonizing discourses to oppose. The concept of authorship, in both film and literary studies, has been under assault for some years now, most notably in the works of Barthes and Michel Foucault.[19] Coincidental with the collapse of the author has been the ascent of the critic. No longer required to pay tribute to infallible creators, critics gain autonomy and authority of their own. The privileged position of Jacques Derrida in today's critical canon is surely related to his liberation of the critic from subordination to literary texts. Critics establish autonomy most effectively by creating a metalanguage and a series of methodologies that close out the amateur. Anyone can engage in evaluation and express an opinion about a book, a play, or a film. Only a professional can speak a language and brandish a paradigm understood only by a small coterie of specialists with mastery over the same language and paradigm.[20]

AN EMERGING JAZZ CANON?

Turning at last to jazz studies, I would argue that the discipline has for a long time been in a phase comparable to the auteurist era of film studies in the 1960s and 1970s: ever since the first serious writings about jazz appeared, critics have sought to become organic intellectuals, who would theorize themselves and the music into positions of importance. Although a number of writers have ascended to stations with some power, they have not yet been able to carve their canon into the granite of American culture or to install their discipline in the structure of the university. If I am right that jazz may follow the path of film studies in becoming a stable fixture in constantly mutating university curricula, a number of its scholars will become more self-conscious about the problematic nature of canon formation even as they continue to write about the key artists of their discipline.[21] It is also likely that jazz scholars will develop a professional discourse that may at first draw upon the vocabularies of musicology, sociology, critical theory, and other disciplines but that ultimately will be unique to jazz studies.

In doing so, jazz scholars run the risk of losing touch with a group of critics who do not have conventional academic credentials but who nevertheless play a large role in the professional life of the discipline by reading grant proposals and evaluating manuscripts for university presses. In addition, the new metalanguage of the field may strike most jazz enthusiasts as impenetrable. This is the trade-off that professionals in other disciplines have accepted as they have gradually but inexorably separated themselves from the general public. For some time now, the vast majority of poetry lovers have *not* consulted *PMLA* and *Modern Philology* to supplement their enjoyment, just as few movie buffs today expend the effort necessary to read the articles in *Cinema Journal* and *Camera Obscura*. Most academics regret this situation; some of the most eminent among them even bemoan their isolation in speeches at plenary sessions during professional conferences.[22] Tenure, promotion, and job mobility, however, are based not on professors' fortunes with general readers but on their reputations among a handful of professional colleagues. Similarly, as the work of jazz studies expands, something more than the straightforward celebration of canonical artists is required if the field is to stand alongside established disciplines that have long since ceased making appeals to outsiders.

The actual development of a jazz canon—not to mention the critic's role in the process—is complex and multidetermined, caught in a complicated web of changing conditions. In the 1920s, for example, the entry of Louis Armstrong's recording of "West End Blues" into a jazz artist's canon can be documented at least in part by a King Oliver recording of the tune that appeared six months after Armstrong's version: on Oliver's record of "West End Blues," trumpeter Louis Metcalf attempted a note-for-note recreation of Armstrong's opening cadenza.[23] There are a number of reasons why Metcalf may have chosen to duplicate Armstrong's solo, just as Oliver—who in fact wrote "West End Blues" and considered Armstrong his protégé—may have had reasons of his own for directing Metcalf to recreate the difficult solo. We might also interrogate the processes that brought Armstrong and later Oliver into the recording studio as well as those forces that made their records available to large audiences. Basically, however, we have a case of canon formation through a somewhat uncomplicated process of communication by phonograph record. Today, this kind of homage to one artist by another is only one among numerous phenomena that contribute to the creation of a jazz canon: a partial list would include grant-giving agencies, recording contracts and sales, collections issued by mail order companies and the Book-of-the-Month Club, public appearances by artists, academic appointments, the political structures of universities, roles for jazz musicians in movies (Dexter Gordon in *Round Midnight,* for example), record reviews, "ten best lists" in the popular press, promotion by disc jockeys, Grammy awards, film scores, and faces on postage stamps.

In the academy, however, canonizers are more likely to adopt the strategy of romanticizing the artist. The improvising jazz artist is, after all, a composer as well as a performer, not unlike the mythologized composer/performers of the Romantic Era such as Liszt and Paganini who improvised on well-known works. Although this equation is seldom explicit in jazz writings, its traces can usually be found, hinting at why a music associated with prostitution and drug addiction is as valid as the music associated with landed gentry in premodern Europe. A disproportionate amount of jazz scholarship is and has been devoted to finding the most effective means for identifying and exalting favored artists.

DISCOGRAPHY AND CANON-BUILDING

Consider, for example, jazz discography. The practice has long been the almost sole province of an international network of devoted record collectors, largely uninterested in profits and often with careers outside of music.[24] From the beginning, discographers have been intimately and unavoidably involved with the work of canon-building. When Charles Delaunay published his first *Hot Discography* in 1938, he created a guidebook for those who agreed with him that the music had more than ephemeral value.[25] He was also committing an act of exclusion, declining to catalogue certain performers from "race records," blues, ragtime, and dance music whom he considered to be outside the charmed circle of jazz. Like the auteurists of cinema studies, he built the discography on a model that centered on great artists: Delaunay would combine, for example, all the recordings of Armstrong in one section of his book even when titles had not been recorded under Armstrong's name or when the trumpeter was only a sideperson at someone else's recording session. Delaunay did the same with Bix Beiderbecke, even less likely to be listed as leader during his recording history. Just as auteurist critics attributed an entire film to the director rather than to the producer, the screenwriter, the cinematographer, the stars, or some combination of coworkers, Delaunay in effect credited Armstrong or Beiderbecke with a recording even when the trumpeter was essentially an accompanist.[26] For Delaunay, the centrality of Armstrong and Beiderbecke was more consistent with an idealized jazz history than were the pedestrian blues singers and sweet dance bands with whom the two trumpeters had recorded. His view of jazz history was reflected in the very arrangement of his discography.

Delaunay's catalogue laid the groundwork for several generations of discographers who fall into two broad categories: (1) single artist discographers who fetishize the recordings of specific musicians, almost always to the point of detailing those sessions in which the artist is present but undetectable in a large ensemble; (2) Orin Blackstone, Dave Carey, Brian Rust, Jorgen Jepsen, Walter Bruyninckx, Erik Raben, and Tom Lord who have, like Delaunay, inventoried the music in large historical sweeps that inevitably repress artists who do not play in appropriate styles. While the discographers in the first category might be considered inclusionists, tracking down every recorded scrap of specific artists, those in the second are primarily exclusionists.[27] Walter Bruyninckx, surely the most catholic of all jazz cataloguers, provides a good illustration of the exclusionist at work. His regularly updated discography, currently known as *Seventy Years of Recorded Jazz,* is an international inventory of jazz as well as gospel, blues, and jazz-inflected pop that fills several feet of shelf space. Nevertheless, even Bruyninckx is likely to truncate the listings for an artist if he believes that at some moment the recordings cease to have jazz content. He also frequently writes statements such as the following: "Although negroid in origin this group recorded mainly for the white audiences and their recordings have very little of the sincerity and enthusiasm that is to be found in other negro recordings of religious oriented music."[28] Bruyninckx's candor becomes him well, but his didactic criterion for banishing one group instead of another is characteristic of any and all enterprises that seek to sort out the real from the ersatz. Discographers such as Bruyninckx unavoidably participate in the formation of a jazz canon, a project that is scarcely value free. Single artist discographies appear because a cataloguer has responded to a variety of forces that make an artist worthy of complete documentation. The methodologies operating in the larger, exclusionary discographies are invariably grounded in critically sanctioned judgments that discographers are seldom interested in interrogating. For example, Erik Raben, one of the more recent exclusionists, devotes two sentences to the issue:

> In many cases it has been difficult to decide where the boundaries to blues, R&B, dance-oriented big band

music, pop-vocal music, jazz/rock fusion music and Latin music should be drawn. In some cases non-jazz recordings are included to "complete" the discography of a musician or a group/band.[29]

Like his predecessors, Raben does not reveal how he drew the boundaries between jazz and nonjazz.

The canonization of jazz artists has almost always been the major thrust of jazz scholarship, regardless of whether the writers take their methodology from traditional musicology or from social science. Two articles from the Austrian journal *Jazzforschung/Jazz Research* provide extreme examples of both approaches. An essay on Clifford Brown begins with the following paragraph:

> It is now twenty-two years since the passing of Clifford Brown, yet his loss is felt today almost as much as it was in the late summer of 1956. Musicians and fans alike, some of them too young to have heard him in person, pay tribute to this creative person. For many people, there is something amazing about the way that beautifully developed musical structures flowed from his horn with ease and joy. There is something phenomenal about the way that his improvisations are understood and appreciated even by those who ordinarily are not jazz lovers. Clifford Brown was possibly the rare musician who comes along only once in a generation.[30]

The body of the essay, however, is devoted to a highly technical, Schenkerian analysis of Brown's improvisations, devoid of the adulatory tone that opens the essay. Here is a representative sample: "The middleground structure of the original piece includes the neighbornate, b^1, which serves to prolong a^1, and the movement d^1 in measure 8 which serves to provide acoustical support for a^1 by virtue of the fifth relationship" (136). At this point, the rhetoric of jazz studies is indistinguishable from that of academic music theory.

An article on Lester Young, also published in *Jazz-forschung*, grafts the history of racist violence against African-American people onto a biographical sketch of Young. Here is the conclusion of the article:

The sensibilities of Lester Young and other Black
artists assume even more impressive significance when
compared to the callow, materialistic, and often violent
nature of the world they inhabited. Young's humanistic, benevolent, and non-materialistic values set him
apart from both businessmen and conformist consum-
ers. He represents an ideal example of the qualities
allegedly treasured by the people whose actions suggested the very opposite.[31]

Without in any way rejecting the judgments of these two
writers, I would point out that both insist on the value of their
subjects even when it means speaking with two voices: each
scholar writes almost entirely in the professional language of
a canonical discipline, but at the beginning or end of his
piece, he switches to the vocabulary of the fan and the record
collector. Their praise for jazz artists is not and cannot be
documented with traditional scholarly apparatus. Footnotes
and musical examples disappear when the scholar becomes
essentially indistinguishable from the fan. The collapsing of
these two categories has run through a great deal of jazz
writing ever since the appearance of the first books that dealt
with the music.

By contrast, scholarly writing today in literature, music,
and art is increasingly less likely to be built around the
unequivocal glorification of the artist or the bald valorizing of
one artist over another. In literary studies, Northrop Frye
was calling such evaluative criticism "debaucheries of judi-
ciousness" in the 1950s.[32] Hyperbolic praise for the auteur
has been largely abandoned by film scholars during the past
two decades—it is now left almost entirely to critics in the
popular press. If a discipline can be considered "profession-
alized" when it develops its own metalanguage and a
self-consciousness about its canon, then jazz study is still in
its infancy. The discipline's lingering preprofessionalism is
especially evident in Gunther Schuller's *The Swing Era,*
doubtlessly one of the most important jazz texts in recent
years.[33] Schuller brings impressive credentials to this and his
already canonical study of early jazz.[34] In both books,
however, he rejects scholarly prose in favor of journalistic

terms such as "truly magnificent," "totally unredeemable," and "heartrendingly moving." Because Schuller is also devoted to the myth of jazz's autonomy, he seldom considers the music's contextual and historical relationships.[35] His consistent reluctance in *The Swing Era* to press his analyses beyond his own impressions is most explicit when he states, for example, that Billie Holiday's talent is "in the deepest sense inexplicable" (528), or when he writes of Ben Webster, "as with most truly great art, Webster's cannot be fully explained" (590), or when, after a few words on Lester Young's mastery of understatement, he calls Young "The Gandhi of American jazz" (562). These passages are likely to become increasingly uncharacteristic of jazz writing as the subject advances into the academy. No assistant professor in any discipline is tenured today for declaring a phenomenon to be "in the deepest sense inexplicable" (unless that professor is a deconstructionist, and Schuller is no deconstructionist).

AN AESTHETIC OF UNITY AND COHERENCE

Even when jazz writers perform close analysis on the music, they engage in a kind of canon-building based in paradigms that have been radically questioned in other disciplines. One historically prominent strategy for canonizing the jazz artist is based in an aesthetic of unity and coherence. Few writers employed this strategy as persuasively as Martin Williams, who studied the New Criticism in the 1950s while working on a graduate degree in English at Columbia University. A striking but not atypical example of William's application of formalist literary principles to jazz is his discussion of Charlie Parker's 1946 improvisation on the first take of "Embraceable You":

> In his one-chorus improvisation on "Embraceable You," Parker barely glances at Gershwin's melody. He begins with an interesting six-note phrase which he then uses five times in a row, pronouncing it variously and moving it around to fit the harmonic contours of

> Gershwin's piece. On its fifth appearance the six-note
> motive forms the beginning of a delicate thrust of
> melody which dances along, pauses momentarily, re-
> sumes, and finally comes to rest balanced at the end
> with a variant of that same six-note phrase . . . [I]t is the
> core of his improvisation, and, speaking personally, I
> have seldom listened to this chorus without realizing
> how ingeniously that phrase is echoed in Parker's
> remarkable melody.[36]

As many theorists have pointed out, a work's value is not
simply a function of how well its artist understands internalist
principles of unity and coherence. Jonathan Culler has
written, "The notion that the task of criticism is to reveal
thematic unity is a post-Romantic concept, whose roots in
the theory of organic form are, at the very least, ambigu-
ous."[37] Parker's work might just as easily be discussed in
terms of how he *destroys* the illusion of organic unity in his
solos by inserting easily recognizable fragments from other
musical traditions such as the Habenera from Bizet's *Carmen,* "The Campbells Are Coming," and Alphonse Picou's
clarinet solo from "High Society."[38] Williams overlooked the
ways in which Parker resisted recuperation into a Eurocentric aesthetic by in fact "Signifyin(g)" upon it, as Henry
Louis Gates, Jr., might suggest.[39]

    Because of the music's youth, jazz writers have gone about
the business of canon-building without having to look over
their shoulders at those who would demand alternative
canons. The infamous battle between "the ancients and the
moderns" in the 1940s was easily resolved by making room in
the canon for bebop alongside older forms associated with
New Orleans and Chicago. No legitimate history of jazz
today can afford to omit either one.[40] In other disciplines,
however, canons have faced powerful challenges from
women, minorities, and those working with various
poststructuralisms (and more recently from resurgent white
males such as Allan Bloom, William Bennett, and Roger
Kimball). The progress of various teaching anthologies is a
good index to canon struggles in literature departments. In
the 1970s, newly acquired female and minority editors began
to effect the contents of W.W. Norton Company's well

established anthologies of English and world literature. For some time Norton had invested in the belief that single, two-volume anthologies could present coherent canons for an entire discipline. Other presses subscribed to the same proposition and published their own one- and two-volume selections from the canon. Today, however, in addition to more pluralistic anthologies of English and world literatures, Norton has published an anthology of women writers, and Henry Louis Gates, Jr., perhaps the single most articulate critic of the old canon, is currently editing a Norton anthology of African-American literature.[41] Although Gates is clearly ambivalent about his new role as canonizer,[42] he has taken the original step of including in the anthology a sound recording of African-American writers reading from their work. Not only has Gates emphasized the performative dimensions of a great deal of black literature; he has also changed the rules for canon formation. By contrast, *The Smithsonian Collection of Classic Jazz,* now in its second edition and available on compact discs, stills stands as the only major listening text for an introductory course in jazz history. Many critics have second-guessed Martin Williams's choices for what ought to be included in the box, but as of this writing, no one has undertaken to replace it with a comparable anthology of favored recordings.[43]

PITFALLS OF CANON FORMATION

Although jazz scholars may need a canon to establish their legitimacy, there are other consequences of acquiring one. Like feminists who have found themselves in the uncomfortable position of deploying an institutional politics not unlike the one which had once been used to exclude women, jazz canonizers may find it difficult to be true to the full range of jazz culture at the same time that they rely upon Eurocentric traditions. Bernard Gendron has broached the subject of what is at stake as the discipline solidifies around a canon.[44] In discussing André Hodeir's preference of Igor Stravinsky's appropriation of jazz over that of Darius Milhaud, Gendron refers to Hodeir's "inadmissibly essentialist construction of 'authentic' jazz'' (13). Milhaud most likely understood jazz as anything influenced by the rhythms of African-American music. Gendron argues that Hodeir and other historians have defined jazz more narrowly as an art music with specific qualities that they have then "read back" into earlier, amorphous forms of the music.

> We can understand this exclusionary re-reading of history as part of a decades-old struggle to establish jazz as a genuine art music, indeed as "America's classical music." Recent histories of jazz have bypassed those early types of nominal jazz which do not fit into the trajectory leading to modern jazz or give sense to its aesthetics; it is not that they have succeeded in separating the genuine from the counterfeit. . . . Much of what [Milhaud] called "jazz" is no longer part of the canon of jazz history. (14)

The tendency of jazz historians to search for predecessors of the more ambitious modernists may in part explain the inordinate amount of attention afforded Jelly Roll Morton, whose 1920s recordings are said to anticipate the "orchestral" aspects of swing and modern jazz. Schuller has called him "The First Great Composer."[45] The centrality of Morton in many jazz histories is consistent with a "masterpieces only" approach that tends to create a series of museum pieces alleged to possess universal meanings that travel with the work beyond its time and place.

The exclusion of anything not consistent with the "art" of jazz is complemented by the somewhat opposite phenomenon of celebrating the down-and-out, subcultural appeal of a repressed artform. This tradition in jazz criticism dates back at least to the various critical uproars in the 1930s and 1940s that accompanied each stage in Duke Ellington's progress towards concert music and away from his titillating "jungle music." Ellington perfected his jungle style in the late 1920s while his band was in residence at the Cotton Club playing behind gyrating, light-skinned, African-American female dancers.[46] A comparable fascination with the sordid aspects of substance abuse and mental illness has surely enhanced the charisma of artists such as Beiderbecke, Holiday, Young,

Parker, Chet Baker, and Bud Powell (and perhaps detracted from the amount of attention devoted to the clean-living Clifford Brown). The trend has culminated most recently in documentary and fiction films, such as *Round Midnight* (1988), *Bird* (1989), and *Let's Get Lost* (1989), that center on the broken lives of jazz artists.[47] In the academy, however, the ideology of jazz criticism has tended away from pathobiography and towards explicit or implicit connections between jazz and canonical aesthetics. Although a jazz musicologist influenced by André Hodeir may not overtly argue that Duke Ellington is the equal of Brahms, his use of analytical methods designed for Brahms makes the argument all the same.

In this context, few jazz scholars have yet to grapple with the critique of canons that has become central in many humanistic disciplines.[48] A consensus is now emerging that canon formation is a discourse of power, reinforcing the values of the canonizers. Groups that have been marginalized by generations of Eurocentric, mostly male academics can legitimately question the claim that certain works speak to us across the ages and possess universal truths. Barbara Herrnstein Smith has argued that any value attributed to a work of art

> is radically contingent, being neither a fixed attribute, an inherent quality, or an objective property of things but, rather, an effect of multiple, continuously changing, and continuously interacting variables or, to put this another way, the product of the dynamics of a system, specifically an *economic* system.[49]

Smith does not adopt a vulgar Marxist concept of an economic system driven by monopolistic forces, urging instead that we understand how certain works perform desired or desirable functions for certain groups at certain moments in history. A work that continues to provide these functions through extended periods of time becomes amenable to new generations with new economies largely because it has been carefully transmitted and preserved and is thus most easily discovered by a new generation searching for its central texts. Once canonized, a work need not answer to all the demands of a newer culture because its guardians will find reasons why objectionable features—Smith lists "incidents or sentiments of brutality, bigotry, and racial, sexual, or national chauvinism" (49)—ought to be overlooked in favor of other features, usually those that accommodate themselves comfortably to humanist ideologies. Those people in whose economy the canonical authors of the West have little or no value are frequently characterized as primitive or culturally deprived by canonizers who are reluctant to acknowledge that other cultures find value in activities bearing little resemblance to Western conceptions of art.

Smith goes to special lengths to rebut the "axiological logic" of writers such as Hume and Kant who have explicitly argued that aesthetic judgments can have objective value.[50] In deconstructing the prose of Hume, Smith finds a pattern of qualifications and hedges that ultimately undermines his claim for universal standards of judgment:

> Hume's claim is that there is empirical, factual evidence for a natural norm of taste. When restated with the conceded qualifications, however, the foundation of that norm, the alleged fact that some objects, by the very structure of the mind, are naturally calculated to please and others to displease, becomes the limp truism, *some objects tend to please or displease some people under some conditions. . . . (63)*

Kant's argument for the objective validity of some judgments is rooted in the premise that we are capable of putting aside all stimuli that distract from a direct appreciation of "the beautiful." Once subjects achieve this uncontaminated state, they will, according to Kant, invariably arrive at the same judgments. Smith points out that Kant's list of what one must put aside in order to become uncontaminated amounts to the sum total of one's humanness.

> Contrary to the key requirements of Kant's analysis, then, our interactions with our environments are always and inevitably multiply contingent and highly individuated for every subject: our "sensations" and "percep-

tions" of "forms" or of anything else are inseparable from—or, as it might be said, thoroughly contaminated by—exactly who we are, where we are, and all that has already happened to us, and there is therefore nothing in any aspect of our experience of anything that could ever be, in the required sense, pure. (69)

I have quoted Smith at length because her work is especially persuasive and systematic in refuting the notion that one work of art can be declared intrinsically superior to another. By appropriating her work, jazz scholars need no longer argue with those who find classical music more valuable, more beautiful, or—as a colleague of mine once phrased it—"more interesting" than jazz. Although Smith bases her work in rigorously philosophical procedures, she is nevertheless working within the hermeneutics of suspicion that has yet to cast a significant shadow over jazz studies. Once jazz scholars have followed out her arguments in order to dispose of the assertion that Brahms is intrinsically superior to Ellington, they must then face up to equally valid proposition that Ellington is not necessarily superior to Brahms, nor for that matter that Ellington is necessarily superior to Jimi Hendrix or even to Kenny G. They must also confront the possibility that a solo by a canonical jazz artist in no way communicates universal emotions but rather communicates to both the initiated and uninitiated listener through highly mediated complexes of cultural forces. Jazz studies will come of age only when these cultural forces have been thoroughly investigated.

Of course, jazz scholars may choose to resist Smith's gambit and continue to build their canon with preprofessional professions of faith in the transcendent value of favored artists. Ironically, the impulses that have driven jazz writers to avoid a rhetoric based in suspicion share many of the same radical aspects that have led to the recent transformation of other disciplines. Literary critics today who *attack* the old white canon for marginalizing minority authors have a good deal in common with jazz critics who *defend* what could soon become the old canon in their discipline. Since the vocation of the jazz scholar is intimately bound up with highly charged issues of race, a large group of scholars has almost always shied away from positions that might in some way suggest white-against-black racism. A white critic, for example, may feel more secure in simply praising the achievements of an African-American artist than in coming to terms with the forces that may have affected what the artist played and how that playing was received. Any number of jazz writers have continued to write laudatory interpretive criticism even after musicians such as Archie Shepp and critics such as Frank Kofsky have accused the critics of paternalism and of pretending to speak for black artists.[51]

The need to find tortuous paths around and/or through the currents of racism is only one factor that inhibits a thorough interrogation of canonizing traditions in the study of jazz.[52] A hermeneutics of suspicion has much less raw material when the subject is music. Catherine Clément and Carolyn Abbate have both written feminist critiques of opera,[53] but the uncovering of sexism and racism or the deconstruction of false binarisms is substantially more difficult when the music is attached to no program or literary text. Perhaps as a result, traditional musicology has only recently begun to develop feminist, ideological, and metacritical practices.[54]

ELEMENTS OF RESISTANCE
TO CRITICAL THEORY

There may also be a psychological dimension to musicology's resistance to contemporary critical theory. In an argument that can be applied to the work of musicologists, Donald Kuspit has offered reasons why many art historians react negatively to the introduction of structuralist and poststructuralist theories into their discipline.[55] He lists four assumptions that account for what he calls "the peculiarly hermetic, cult-like character of so-called traditional art history" (346): (1) the artwork possesses a sacral quality that distinguishes it from ordinary objects and that induces the critic to explain why it is special; (2) the visual is closer to the "madness of inner life" than the verbal—to reduce the visual artwork to a series of linguistic gestures is to repress its sensual, libidinous, and/or transgressive character; (3) correlatively, the visual has more to do with "bodiliness," the gut feelings that effect the spectator more profoundly than can anything expressed in words; (4) and finally, the activity of the critic is secondary to the activity of the artist—to suggest otherwise is to embrace the profane over the sacred.

Most of what Kuspit says about "traditional art history" can be adapted to jazz studies in particular and to musicology in general. Like almost everyone else, disciples of jazz respond to the sensual, libidinous dimensions of their music. If jazz has few conventionally sacral dimensions, it may have an even greater agonistic appeal as its advocates resist the class and racial prejudices that regularly stigmatize their work. With jazz in particular, strong emotional attachments of youth can persist throughout the devotee's life, especially when that attachment signifies a crucial developmental moment such as the willful rejection of bourgeois values. In addition, what Kuspit calls the "bodiliness" of the visual may have its equivalent in the gut feelings of jazz that seem to render words impotent: "If you have to ask, you'll never know." The jazz writer's corresponding discomfort with words takes many forms. One is the critical trope of privileging the experience of musicians—even when unarticulated—over any written statement by outsiders, i.e., other writers and critics.[56]

Popular music, meanwhile, has quickly followed cinema in acquiring a theoretically sophisticated body of scholarship. Like cinema, rock 'n' roll involves a huge industry and a highly conventionalized sign system and thus becomes especially accessible to critics skilled in the theories of Barthes, Foucault, Louis Althusser, Raymond Williams, and the Frankfurt School.[57] And because rock critics, unlike their jazz counterparts, have seldom laid claim to the formalist aesthetics developed for classical music, they have been more attentive to the contexts of the music. Lawrence Grossberg has suggested a useful model for writing about rock and roll, conceptualizing it as what Foucault calls "an apparatus."[58]

The rock and roll apparatus includes not only musical
texts and practices but also economic determinations,
technological possibilities, images (of performers and
fans), social relations, aesthetic conventions, styles of
language, movement, appearance and dance, media
practices, ideological commitments and media representations of the apparatus itself. The apparatus describes 'cartographies of taste' which are both syn-
chronic and diachronic and which encompass both
musical and non-musical registers of everyday life.
(236)

As I have pointed out, many jazz writers tend to ignore the
extramusical aspects of the music by conceptualizing it as a
safely autonomous domain. In doing so, however, they close
themselves off from the kind of work undertaken by
Grossberg and the more sophisticated commentators on pop
music.[59] Although theoretically informed studies of canonical artists have already been written and should continue to
be written, there still seems to be a vacuum in the academic
literature of jazz relating to fusion and the more commercial-
ized forms of jazz. Gary Tomlinson's evocative and erudite
defense of Miles Davis's post-1969 recordings is one of the
more promising signs of a new turn in jazz writing.[60]

CONCLUSION

I must make it clear that I am not unequivocally valorizing
terms such as "theory" and "professionalism" in this essay. I
have no illusions about the jargon-mongering that passes
itself off as theory in many quarters of academia today. I am
also ambivalent about the trade-offs that seem to be
necessary as disciplines move away from public concerns and
into a sequestered world of professionalism. As DeVeaux
has suggested, it may be a little unfair to deconstruct a
canonical view of jazz history so soon after it has been
constructed.[61] My goal has been to take a long view of jazz
studies as it makes its way along the arduous path to
institutionalization. I would hope to see more analyses
consistent with Grossberg's "apparatus" model that address

the actual function of jazz within culture rather than a disciplinary teleology of jazz's equality with classical music. Whether or not such projects prove to be compatible with the current and future place of jazz within academic political structures remains to be seen.

I conclude by returning once again to the paradigm of film studies to conceptualize the course of jazz studies. The late Charles Eckert, a film theorist of some prescience, wrote in 1974 of the new methods entering his discipline: "there is a stiff, cold wind blowing against partial, outmoded, or theoretically unsound forms of film criticism—and it just might blow many of them away."[62] Having boarded up the windows against the winds for some time now, jazz scholarship now faces two significant choices: it may continue developing and protecting its canon, or it may take the consequences of letting in some fresh, if chilling, air.

NOTES

I am extremely grateful to the following colleagues who commented on earlier drafts of this paper: Burton W. Peretti, Ronald M. Radano, Lewis Porter, Vera Micznik, Steven Elworth, Michele Bogart, William Howland Kenney III, John L. Fell, John Hasse, and Dan Morgenstern.

1. Since I will be attributing a number of qualities to "jazz" throughout this essay, I feel obliged to offer a definition of the term that distinguishes it from "classical music." Realizing that numerous artists complicate any such distinction (James Reese Europe, Duke Ellington, Benny Goodman, John Lewis, Anthony Davis, John Zorn, Anthony Braxton, Willem Breuker, and many others), I would define jazz as a music that is rooted primarily in the confrontation between African-American traditions and European music, involving some improvisation and syncopation, and performed more often in night clubs and dance halls than in concert halls. The music has changed too quickly throughout its history to accommodate a more precise definition. I am convinced that any attempt to arrive at such a definition must be based in a socio-cultural analysis of jazz rather than in its internal aesthetics. In this

sense, I am in almost total disagreement with assumptions underlying the otherwise convincing essay by Lee B. Brown, "The Theory of Jazz Music: 'It Don't Mean a Thing . . .'," *Journal of Aesthetics and Art Criticism* 49 (1991): 115–27. In his rigorous analysis of André Hodeir's writings, Brown never questions the purely formalist criteria that Hodeir and others employ in their attempts to define jazz. Nowhere does he ask crucial questions about who is listening, what the listener expects, or under what conditions the listening is taking place. Nor does Brown ask what cultural and ideological forces lay behind Hodeir's decision to write a definition of jazz in France in the 1950s.

2. Grover Sales, *Jazz: America's Classical Music* (Englewood Cliffs, N.J., 1984); also see Billy Taylor, "Jazz—America's Classical Music," *Black Perspective in Music* 14, no. 1 (1986): 21–25. On the other hand, a number of critics have made claims for jazz as the *antithesis* of classical music, most notably Hugues Panassié. In *The Real Jazz,* trans. Anne Sorelle Williams (New York, 1942), Panassié effectively redefines music in order to privilege jazz and to reverse the familiar musical hierarchies: "For music is, above all, the cry of the heart, the natural spontaneous song expressing what man feels within himself" (6). He is thus in a strong position to denigrate the environment in which classical music is consumed: "Likewise many feel that it is ridiculous for Negroes to clap their hands, dance in their seats, sing and cry when listening to an orchestra . . . But to me the most ridiculous spectacle is the sight of a concert hall filled with hundreds of spectators who sit statue-like in their seats listening with a lugubrious expression to solemn music which is served up to them in massive doses" (29).

3. Scott DeVeaux, "The Emergence of the Jazz Concert, 1935–1945," *American Music* 7 (1989): 7.

4. *Oxford English Dictionary,* s.v. "canon, 4." In addition, canon is a rule, law or decree from the church or from the Pope, as in canonical law. The portion of the Catholic Mass between the Preface and the *Pater,* containing the words of the consecration, is also known as the canon. Finally, a canon is a clergyman or anyone living a canonical life, that is, one devoted to the canons of the church.

5. "The problem of the canon is a problem of syllabus and curriculum, the institutional forms by which works are preserved as *great* works. One might contrast this institutional

function of the school with the function of the library, where ideally *everything* is preserved and where the system of preservation makes no distinction at all between good books and bad." From John Guillory, "Canon," in Frank Lentricchia and Thomas McLaughlin, eds., *Critical Terms for Literary Study* (Chicago, 1990), 240.

6. Lawrence W. Levine, *Highbrow/Lowbrow: The Emergence of Cultural Hierarchy in America* (Cambridge, Mass., 1988).

7. Hugo Münsterberg, *The Film: A Psychological Study* (1916; rpt. New York, 1970).

8. For a good deal of original research on the earliest jazz criticism, see James Lincoln Collier, *The Reception of Jazz in America: A New View*, I.S.A.M. Monographs, no. 27 (Brooklyn, 1988). Also see Ron Welburn, "The American Jazz Writer/Critic of the 1930s: A Profile," *Jazzforschung/Jazz Research* 21 (1989): 83–94.

9. Charles Granada, Jr., ed., *American Film Institute Guide to College Courses in Film and Television*, 7th ed. (Princeton, 1980).

10. Susanna L. Miller, "Classroom Gigs—Funding for Musician/Clinicians," *Down Beat* 57, no. 6 (June 1990): 56.

11. Sarris's seminal essay, "Notes on the Auteur Theory in 1962," first appeared in *Film Culture* (Winter 1962–63). It is collected along with responses by Peter Wollen and Pauline Kael in Gerald Mast and Marshall Cohen, eds., *Film Theory and Criticism*, 3rd ed. (New York, 1985), 527–62. The bible of American auteurism is still Sarris's *The American Cinema: Directors and Directions, 1929–1968* (New York, 1968).

12. Janet Staiger, "The Politics of Film Canons," *Cinema Journal* 24, no. (Spring 1985):4–23.

13. Paul Ricoeur, *Freud and Philosophy* (New Haven, 1970), 29–33.

14. Virginia Wright Wexman, "The Critic as Consumer," *Film Quarterly* 39, no. 3 (1986): 32–41.

15. Laura Mulvey, "Visual Pleasure and Narrative Cinema," *Screen* 16, no. 3 (Autumn 1975): 6–18, rpt. with afterthoughts in Mulvey's *Visual and Other Pleasures* (Bloomington, Ind., 1989).

16. Perhaps the best place to look for a scholar's film canon is the ten-best list published every decade—to considerable media attention—in the British journal *Sight and Sound*. Although *Vertigo* did not appear on previous editions of the list, it appeared in 1982, the prime time of a Mulveyian method of

feminist analysis. For the 1982 list, published alongside the previous three lists, see *Sight and Sound* 51, no. 4 (Autumn 1982): 243. Significantly, *Vertigo* is also on the first list of 25 protected American films established by the Librarian of Congress in 1989.

17. Wexman references Antonio Gramsci, *Selections from the Prison Notebooks,* ed. and trans. Quintin Hore and Geoffrey Nowell-Smith (New York, 1971).

18. Wexman has not had the last word on the feminist canonization of *Vertigo.* Susan White, an eminent feminist film theorist in her own right, has responded to Wexman's assertion that feminists have been "blind" to the vested interests of their critical positions on key films. In "Allegory and Referentiality: *Vertigo* and Feminist Criticism," *MLN* 106, no. 5 (1991): 910–32, White asks first "how it is that Wexman, a white, feminist, academic critic, is *not* blinded by her own position" (923). Employing a strategy developed by Paul de Man, White then deconstructs the opposition "blindness/insight," suggesting that blindness is in fact what makes insight possible. She concludes by arguing against the claim that *Vertigo* or any other text can be read "from a single, dominating reality that knows itself, knows its priority, comes from a position that knows no blindness and seems to have no vested interest . . . " (931).

19. Roland Barthes's "The Death of the Author" and Michel Foucault's "What Is an Author?" are collected with other relevant material in *Theories of Authorship: A Reader,* ed. and trans. John Caughie (London, 1981).

20. Brian McCrea has written an extended critique of "the professional" in English studies, *Addison and Steele Are Dead: The English Department, Its Canon, and the Professionalization of Literary Criticism* (Newark, N.J., 1990), esp. chapters 7 and 8. For a more polemical but compatible argument, see Leslie A. Fiedler, "Literature as an Institution: The View From 1980," in Leslie A. Fiedler and Houston A. Baker, Jr., eds. *English Literature: Opening Up the Canon,* Selected Papers from the English Institute, 1979 (Baltimore, 1981), 73–91.

21. Scott DeVeaux has recently published an extensive and well-argued article that confronts many of these issues. In "Constructing the Jazz Tradition: Jazz Historiography," *Black American Literature Forum* 25, no. 3 (Fall 1991): 525–60, DeVeaux addresses problems in jazz writing such as a chronic insistence upon the music's autonomy from social praxis, the

"romance" paradigms promoted by its historians, and the need for canonical figures. Ultimately he calls for "an approach that is less invested in the ideology of jazz as aesthetic object and more responsive to issues of historical particularity" (553).

22. In *Addision and Steele Are Dead*, McCrea describes the typical presidential address at the annual meeting of the Modern Language Association as

> the address in which a man or a woman who has achieved eminence on the basis of publications and holds an endowed chair at a major research university laments our failure to pay enough attention to introductory classes and the task of bringing undergraduates to know the joys of studying literature. (147)

McCrea, however, observes that "all such talk is nostalgic and largely empty" (147). The demands of professionalism take precedence over goals expressed in the official rhetoric.

23. Louis Armstrong, "West End Blues," rec. 28 June 1928, *Louis Armstrong, Vol. IV: Armstrong and Earl Hines* (Columbia CK 45142); King Oliver, "West End Blues," rec. 16 Jan. 1929, *King Oliver and His orchestra 1928–1930* (Classics 607). There is also a 1929 recording by a territory band, Zach Whyte's Chocolate Beau Brummels, that includes a passage for two unison trumpets and rhythm based on Armstrong's cadenza in "West End Blues."

24. Recently, however, discography has begun to move into the academy. The Institute of Jazz Studies in Newark has begun publishing exhaustive discographies of artists such as Benny Carter, Duke Ellington, Art Tatum, Erroll Garner, James P. Johnson, and Benny Goodman. As a participant in this project, Ed Berger has written on the problems of compiling a complete listing for Benny Carter, who has recorded as a multi-instrumentalist and an arranger in conventional jazz formats but also as the composer and arranger of movie scores and television soundtracks: "Benny Carter: A Discographical Approach," *Journal of Jazz Studies* 4, no. 1 (1976): 47–64. In fact, the *Journal of Jazz Studies* itself was effectively inaugurated by the single issue of *Studies in Jazz Discography* (1971), also published by the Institute of Jazz Studies and with the same cover design as *JJS*.

25. Charles Delaunay, *Hot Discography* (Paris, 1938).

26. The work of Gary Giddins, who regularly reviews movies as well as jazz, provides an equally revealing parallel between cinema auteurism and jazz criticism. Auteurist critics transformed previously neglected films into significant texts if they happened to appear in the filmography of a "pantheon" director such as John Ford or Orson Welles. In particular, the late works of the auteur were extolled in spite of previously received notions of his decline. Similarly, Giddins has responded to negative judgments of aging jazz artists (in the writings of André Hodeir, most prominently) by celebrating the later phases of their work. In his book on Louis Armstrong, for example, Giddins confronts critical commonplaces about the trumpeter's decline by bestowing praise on Armstrong's recording of "Hello Dolly" (1963) as well as on his 1968 album of Disney Songs. See Giddins, *Satchmo* (New York, 1988), 191, 203.

27. The label discographies of Michel Ruppli ought to be considered inclusionist rather than exclusionist. Ruppli's inventories of canonical jazz labels such as Blue Note, Prestige, Savoy, Chess, and Clef/Verve are meant to be complete, even when this necessitates the inclusion of whatever blues, folk, pop, or comedy acts the labels recorded along with the jazz material.

28. Walter Bruyninckx, *Seventy Years of Recorded Jazz, 1917–1987* (Mechelen, Belgium, 1978–1990), F110a. The group is "Fiske [sic] Jubilee Singers."

29. Erik Raben, *Jazz Records 1942–80: A Discography,* Vol. 1: A–Ba (Copenhagen, n.d., issued in 1989), iii.

30. Milton L. Stewart, "Some Characteristics of Clifford Brown's Improvisational Style," *Jazzforschung/Jazz Research* 11 (1979): 135–164.

31. Douglas Henry Daniels, "History, Racism, and Jazz: The Case of Lester Young," *Jazzforschung/Jazz Research* 16 (1984): 87–103.

32. Northrop Frye, "Polemical Introduction," *Anatomy of Criticism* (Princeton, 1957), 18.

33. Gunther Schuller, *The Swing Era: The Development of Jazz, 1930–1945* (New York, 1989). Further references to this book will be included in the text.

34. Schuller, *Early Jazz: Its Roots and Musical Development* (New York, 1968).

35. In "Constructing the Jazz Tradition," DeVeaux calls Schuller's work "a monument to the ideal of jazz as an

autonomous art" (542). For a thorough analysis of *The Swing Era* and the problems it raises, see Lewis Porter's review in *Annual Review of Jazz Studies* 5 (1991): 183–200.

36. Martin Williams, *The Jazz Tradition*, rev. ed. (New York, 1983), 137. The passage appeared with the exact same wording in the first edition of *The Jazz Tradition* (1970).

37. Jonathan Culler, *Structuralist Poetics: Structuralism, Linguistics, and the Study of Literature* (Ithaca, N.Y., 1975), 119.

38. See my essay, "The Quoter and His Culture," in Reginald T. Buckner and Steven Weiland, eds. *Jazz in Mind: Essays on the History and Meanings of Jazz* (Detroit, 1991), 92–111.

39. Gates, *The Signifying Monkey: A Theory of Afro-American Literary Criticism* (New York, 1988).

40. DeVeaux has identified the notion that jazz has undergone an *organic* growth process as the legitimating force behind the eventual reconciliation between bebop and older forms: "In the long run, it proved as much in the interests of the modernists to have their music legitimated as the latest phase of a (now) long and distinguished tradition, as it was in the interests of the proponents of earlier jazz styles (whether New Orleans jazz or swing) not to be swept aside as merely antiquarian" (DeVeaux, "Constructing the Jazz Tradition," 539).

41. Gates, "Canon-Formation, Literary History, and the Afro-American Tradition: From the Seen to the Told," in Houston A. Baker, Jr., and Patricia Redmond, eds., *Afro-American Literary Study in the 1990s* (Chicago, 1989), 14–39. Gates's most important transformation of the literary canon is surely his multi-volume edition of African-American woman writers.

42. See Gates's *Loose Canons: Notes on the Culture Wars* (New York, 1992).

43. For a survey of anthologies of jazz recordings that *preceded* the *Smithsonian Collection,* see John Hasse, "The Smithsonian Collection of Classic Jazz: A Review-Essay," *Journal of Jazz Studies* 3, no. 1 (Fall 1975): 66–71. Creating real competition for the *Smithsonian Collection* has always been complicated by legal issues related to acquiring permissions from a wide variety of record companies. Now that the major jazz catalogues are owned by Japanese (Columbia, Decca) and European (RCA, Verve) corporations, the opportunities for a competing anthology may be even more diminished.

44. Bernard Gendron, "Jamming at Le Boeuf: Jazz and the Paris Avant-Garde," *Discourse* 12, no. 1 (Fall-Winter 1989–90):

3–27. Further references to this work will be included in the text.

45. Schuller, *Early Jazz,* 134.

46. James Lincoln Collier is especially sensitive to the tension between Ellington and his critics in *Duke Ellington* (New York, 1987).

47. Self-destructive artists are not, of course, the sole province of jazz history. Americans are especially fond of crash-and-burn legends among their poets (Lowell, Berryman, Plath), painters (Rothko, Pollock) and rock stars (Joplin, Hendrix, Morrison). Spike Lee has claimed that his film *Mo' Better Blues* (1990) corrected the myth of the doomed jazz artist promoted in *Bird* and *Round Midnight.* I have argued to the contrary that, although the trumpeter-hero of Lee's film is not a drug addict or an alcoholic, he can only be "saved" when at the end he gives up the jazz life with its attendant dangers. See my article, "Signifyin(g) the Phallus: *Mo' Better Blues* and Representations of the Jazz Trumpet," *Cinema Journal* 32, no. 1 (1992): 43–62.

48. See, for example, the papers published in various issues of *Critical Inquiry* and collected as Robert von Hallberg, ed., *Canons* (Chicago, 1984).

49. Barbara Herrnstein Smith, *Contingencies of Value* (Cambridge, Mass., 1988), 30. Further reference to this book will be included in the text.

50. The crucial texts here are Hume's "Of the Standard of Taste" and Kant's *Critique of Judgment.*

51. Ronald M. Radano's forthcoming book on Anthony Braxton (Chicago, 1993) has much to say about the artist's struggle to make himself heard above the voices of critics, many of them well intentioned and supportive if ultimately unhelpful.

52. The many African Americans writing about jazz and related subjects (Stanley Crouch, Albert Murray, Amiri Baraka, Gates, Houston Baker, etc.) will undoubtedly continue to have much to say about jazz canons in years to come. In a personal communication, Burton W. Peretti has suggested that jazz is most likely to be grouped with other black musics and with the study of African-American oral traditions as it moves into the academy: Gates and Baker in particular have regularly made implicit and explicit arguments for the inseparability of jazz from African-American traditions that long preceded its emergence.

53. Catherine Clément, *Opera, or the Undoing of Women,* trans. Betsy Wing (Minneapolis, 1988); Carolyn Abbate, *Unsung Voices: Opera and Musical Narrative in the Nineteenth Century* (Princeton, 1991).

54. The most widely heard call for a new hermeneutics in musicology is probably that of Joseph Kerman, *Contemplating Music: Challenges to Musicology* (Cambridge, Mass., 1985). The several books that have responded at least in part to that call include Leo Treitler, *Music and the Historical Imagination* (Cambridge, Mass., 1989); Susan McClary, *Feminine Endings: Music, Gender, and Sexuality* (Minneapolis, 1990); Katherine Bergeron and Philip V. Bohlman, eds., *Disciplining Music: Musicology and Its Canons,* (Chicago, 1992); and Steven Paul Sher, ed., *Music and Text: Critical Inquiries* (Cambridge, 1992).

55. Donald Kuspit, "Traditional Art History's Complaint Against the Linguistic Analysis of Visual Art," *Journal of Aesthetics and Art Criticism* 45, no. 4 (1987): 345–49. Further references to this article will be included in the text.

56. See, for example, Stephan Palmié, "Jazz Culture in the Thirties: 'Kansas City, Here I Come!' " *Jazzforschung/Jazz Research* 16 (1984): 43–85, in which Palmié scorns those writers who claim to be "more knowledgeable than the musicians themselves" (43). Ira Gitler and Stanley Dance are two of the most prominent critics who have for decades uncritically reported the utterances of jazz artists.

57. A full account of how these various authors and schools have come together in the study of mass culture appears in the editors' introduction to James Naremore and Patrick Brantlinger, eds., *Modernity and Mass Culture,* (Bloomington, Ind., 1991), 1–23.

58. Lawrence Grossberg, "Another Boring Day in Paradise: Rock and Roll and the Empowerment of Everyday Life," Richard Middleton and David Horn, eds., *Popular Music,* Vol. 4 (London, 1984): 225–58.

59. Also see Simon Frith and Howard Horne, *Art Into Pop* (London and New York, 1987); Greil Marcus, *Lipstick Traces: A Secret History of the Twentieth Century* (Cambridge, Mass., 1989); and the several essays in the "Rock & Roll Culture" issue of *South Atlantic Quarterly* (90, no. 4 [1991]).

60. Gary Tomlinson, "Cultural Dialogics and Jazz: A White Historian Signifies" in Bergeron and Bohlman, *Disciplining*

Music. Also see Robert Walser, " 'Out of Notes': Significa-
tion, Interpretation, and the Problem of Miles Davis"
(forthcoming).
61. DeVeaux, "Constructing the Jazz Tradition," 553.
62. Charles Eckert, "Shall We Deport Lévi-Strauss?" *Film Quarterly* 27 (1974): 63–65, rpt. in Bill Nichols, ed., *Movies and Methods, Vol. II,* (Berkeley, Cal., 1985), 426–29.

BILLIE HOLIDAY AND BETTY CARTER: EMOTION AND STYLE IN THE JAZZ VOCAL LINE[1]

By William R. Bauer

I

One of the many pleasures of listening to jazz may be found in the way a performer plays around with what we know to be "the song." In the process of weaving variations from a standard tune, the player dances fluently between literal quotation and liberal elaboration. No mere game, however, this process serves as a means of exegesis through which a performer subjectively colors her rendition with personal responses to the tune. Regardless of the degree to which she improvises, a jazz performer contributes her own perspective to the materials.[2]

At the risk of oversimplification, we may contrast this approach with that of the classical musician, for whom adherence to the written score usually precedes and informs the making of an interpretation. While the classical musician holds up the making of a personal statement as the ultimate achievement, even a mediocre jazz performer must produce some form of personal statement. The difference in the two approaches may hinge upon whether the listener hears the emotion expressed in the performance as the composer's or the performer's. In the classical world, the work embodies the composer's feelings, and we perceive the performer as someone who recreates and communicates these feelings. In the jazz world, however, no clear boundary separates composer, arranger, and performer, and thus the song can function as a vehicle for the performer's own personal expression. While such expression may take root in the emotions suggested by the performer's material, the performance must ultimately grow into a full blown revelation of the performer's feelings in order for it to exist *as jazz*.

Manipulating given materials has its risks and its limits, however, especially when these materials consist of well-known favorites. Thus a musician's alterations of a standard tune can easily slip from playful modifications into full-scale distortions that threaten the listener's ability to recognize the tune.[3] The degree to which a listener will accept the manipulation of familiar material depends upon many factors, including the style of the performer. When paraphrasing a standard, some jazz musicians make an expressive point via barely noticeable digressions from the original, while others will use crossing the threshold of recognizability itself as an expressive tool.

The relationship between emotional expression and personal style in music tends to resist analysis. One obstacle to such analysis lies in the abstract nature of sound. We can identify elements in an instrumental performance that act as general stylistic features, but we cannot consistently or precisely articulate what elements of a performance result from and indicate the performer's emotional contribution to it. However, by using words, vocalists communicate concrete meanings in sound. Thus by examining the work of singers we can gain a better understanding of how the specific meanings of words interact with musical expression to shape individual style. For this reason the work of singers provides the basis for this study.

In a jazz vocal performance, lyrics provide concrete images for the nonverbal meanings suggested by the music, and therefore play a significant role in the singer's response to the song. Furthermore, by providing grammatical structure (words functioning in different roles as parts of speech, their inflection, and their syntax), lexical meaning (or, semantics) and phonetic content (vowel length, accent, and rhyme), the lyrics also affect how a singer approaches her musical decisions, especially if she wants the listener to understand the words.[4] In responding to the emotional and linguistic contents of the lyrics, and in making her musical choices grow out of her response, the singer brands the reading of a song with her personality. An examination of a singer's rendering of a song's lyrics, and specifically how she alters the song's melody in order to accommodate linguistic features, will therefore help us to identify how stylization occurs.

The works of Billie Holiday and Betty Carter, two of music's greatest stylists, offer ample opportunity to study the process of stylization. Distinguished from one another by important temperamental differences, both singers nonetheless share two traits which intensify this process: a strong commitment to improvisation and an equally strong commitment to communicating the lyrics. In sharing these traits, both singers stand apart from many other jazz vocalists.[5] A fluid approach to what constitutes the tune may at first seem incompatible with an emphasis upon intelligibility. Yet both singers' improvisational decisions actually enhance our understanding of the words, by revealing personal meanings that the words hold for each singer. Thus we may most readily observe the process of stylization when singers have the freedom and the inclination to allow verbal meanings in the lyrics to interact with nonverbal meanings in the music.

In order to identify how the interaction of verbal and nonverbal meanings enables each of these singers to make a song distinctively hers, we will analyze Billie Holiday's and Betty Carter's performances of the Rodgers and Hart song "I Didn't Know What Time It Was." A musical transcription will serve as a means of referring to specific moments in each singer's performance. We will also need to differentiate among the registers of language each singer uses: phonetic, semantic, and syntactic, and to understand how these distinct registers interact with musical elements of the performances. Thus, in addition to describing the musical features of each performance, these transcriptions also must describe phonetic features. I use the modified Trager-Smith phonetic notation found in the American Heritage Dictionary[6] to identify specific speech sounds produced by each singer and to relate them to corresponding moments in the vocal line. Phonetic relationships within the lyrics, such as rhyme, also emerge more clearly without the incongruities of traditional spelling. Table 1 presents the song's lyrics respelled phonetically, based upon standard American pronunciation.

Table 1:   American Pronunciation of the Lyrics to "I Didn't Know What
Time It Was," Spelled Phonetically Using the Trager-Smith System
(Underlined Syllables Receive Accents)

I didn't know what time it was,
/ay/<u>didn</u>/now/wə t/taym/it/wə z/

Then I met you.
/ðen/ay/met/yuw/

Oh, what a lovely time it was,
/ow/wə d/ə /<u>lə v</u>liy/taym/it/wə z/

How sublime it was too!
/hæw/sə <u>blaym</u>/it/wə z/tuw/

I didn't know what day it was.
/ay/<u>didn</u>/now/wə t/dey/it/wə z/

You held my hand,
/yuw/held/may/hænd/

Warm like the month of May it was
/wohrm/layk/ðə /mə nθ/ə v/mey/it/wə z/

And I'll say it was grand.
/ænd/ayl/sey/it/wə z/grænd/

Grand to be alive,   to be young,   to be mad,   to be yours alone!
/grænd/tuw/biy/ə layv/tuw/biy/yəŋ /tuw/biy/mæd/tuw/biy/yohrz/ə lown/

Grand to see your face, feel your touch, hear your voice say I'm all your
/grænd/tuw/siy/yohr/feys/fiyl/yohr/təč /hihr/yohr/voys/sey/aym/ohl/yohr/

own!
own/

I didn't know what year it was.
/ay/didn/now/wə t/yihr/it/wə z/

Life was no prize.
/layf/wə z/now/prayz/

I wanted love and here it was
/ay/want id/ləv/ænd/hihr/it/wə z/

Shining out of your eyes,
/šayniŋ /æwt/ə v/yohr/ayz/

I'm wise and I know what time it is now!
aym/wayz/ænd/ay/now/wət/taym/it/iz/næw/

We see that traditional spelling does not adequately represent the generally connected quality of speech sounds. However, singers exploit this connected quality in order to produce a flowing vocal line. The table does not show how certain words receive more emphasis within sentence, because each performance may emphasize different words.

An initial examination of each singer's performance reveals that while certain linguistic features of the song remain relatively constant between the two versions, the dramatic implications of the lyrics as they unfold in each singer's treatment vary considerably, due to different musical choices made by each singer. (Transcriptions of their performances appear as Examples 1 and 2, published as inserts to this volume to facilitate comparison and reference in reading the analysis which follows.)

Comparison of the performances also reveals slight differences in pronunciation, but as these differences do not strongly affect the analysis they will receive little attention. One obvious way that the transcriptions reflect the interaction between musical and textual elements of each performance becomes apparent when we look at and listen to the ends of phrases. The "x" in the melodic line which indicates the rhythmic placement of final consonants reveals that both singers end words and phrases with careful regard to the beat.

Before we make any further comparisons between the two singers, we must first hear how the text influences each individual singer's approach to the tune, and in turn, how each singer's rendition influences the way we hear the text.

II

Richard Rodgers cast the song "I Didn't Know What Time It Was" (see Example 3) in a standard thirty-two-bar AABA form with a not-so-standard four-bar coda.[7] The song's division into four-bar phrases results from several related factors: motivic parallelism, the placement of long rhythmic values every fourth measure, the rhyme scheme, and the closure of sense units in the text. Furthermore, in each A

section, the song's harmonic progression combines with additional motivic parallelisms, internal rhymes, and the partial closure of sense units to further articulate these phrases into two-bar subgroupings.

While this regularity of phrase articulation lends rhythmic

predictability, most ideal to a song headed for reincarnation as a danceband arrangement, in itself such uniform marching of phrases would bore us. The song succeeds in holding our interest by virtue of its unstable tonal design, which counteracts the stabilizing effect of the song's phrase structure. In its persistent unwillingness to settle on either the major form of the key or its relative minor, the harmony weaves a delightfully ambivalent tonal path and keeps us wondering until that four-bar coda whether or not the song's ending will delivery happy resolution. The tonal design also explains why the coda is both unexpected and logical. Each eight-bar section ends on the dominant, which leaves all of them, including the last, tonally unresolved. Thus in order to satisfy the need for closure created by the tonal design, the song requires extra measures. The coda restates the melody from the opening two measures, with new harmonies.

Hart's lyrics render the chiaroscuro of Rodgers's unsettled tonality through the voice of a narrator that vacillates between past and present, pain and pleasure, loneliness and love. As each successive A section nearly duplicates its antecedent musically, so too does each begin with the textual formula "I didn't know what X it was."[8] The song's high degree of rhythmic, melodic, and textual redundancy thus presents an ideal backdrop against which the relationship between a song's lyrics and a jazz singer's phrasing may emerge.

Comparison of each of the A section's opening measures, as sung by Billie Holiday in her first chorus (see Example 4), reveals an important difference between Holiday's and Rodgers's approach to melodic form: for Holiday, each A section differs from the one that precedes it via subtle rhythmic alterations. To begin, we notice that each time the word "I" recurs, it falls earlier in the measure. It also gets progressively longer at each recurrence, in order that "know" will fall on the downbeat. Later we shall consider a consequence of increasingly emphasizing the pronoun "I."

In the tune as written (see Example 3), each occurrence of the words "time it was," at m. 2 and at m. 6, receives a similar treatment rhythmically. In Holiday's reading, however, each new context produces a different rhythmic

treatment and a shift in emphasis. Hear how in m. 2 she delays these words slightly, partly in order to enunciate the repeated consonant between "what" and "time." (In the later A statements at m. 10 and m. 26 the substitution of "day" and "year" respectively after the word "what" eliminates the repeated consonant, and hence the delay.) Further back in m. 2 we discover that the delay begins even earlier, when Holiday expands the word "know" beyond the second beat, deferring what follows. That "know" occurs with a relatively long rhythmic value on the downbeat intensifies its metric accent, and shorter values on the preceding upbeat further strengthen this accent by leading "didn't" agogically to "know." Thus in the opening statement of the tune, Holiday has shifted the focus of the phrase from the word "I" to the word "know," accomplishing this mainly via rhythmic means.

With regard to pitch, Holiday waits until the words "time it was" to depart from Rogers's version, and the resulting changes in the melody, while subtle, nonetheless affect the words' accentuation. Despite a change in pitch at the word "it," Rodgers's original melody deemphasizes this word, by giving it a short rhythmic value, and the resulting "escape-tone" places emphasis on the word "was" by leaping down to it. In contrast, Holiday's melodic changes use the ascending move to create emphasis; she anticipates the ascent by one note, which shifts it to the word "time," and she gives it a longer note value. The rhythmic break after the word "what" further draws our attention to this ascent. As in Rodgers's melody, "it" receives a short rhythmic value, but because it now falls on a passing tone between "time" and "was," it receives even less emphasis than in the original, in spite of its falling *on* the beat, rather than after it.

Significantly, Holiday retains Rodgers's pitch on the downbeat of m. 2. By obscuring the harmonic motion to the relative minor with the uneasy arrival on a dissonant eleventh, Rodgers's melody literally undermines the verb "know." This musical gesture is so integral to the sound and emotion of the song that most performers retain it, even when dramatically reshaping many other elements.[9]

Contrast the above description with the recurrence of the words "time it was" in m. 6 (see Example 5). We immediately notice that Holiday does not delay it (see arrows); in fact, she anticipates it. The long vowel /iy/ of the preceding word, "lovely," allows her to move the rhythm forward to the word "time" by affording a smooth transition to the /t/ sound; and Holiday exploits the phonetic environment here by giving the word "lovely" shorter note values than in the original tune. Increased rhythmic activity on the downbeat weakens metric stress on the adjective "lovely," and sets it in motion to its goal—the noun "time." In addition to placing an agogic accent on "time," Holiday's rhythm speeds its arrival.

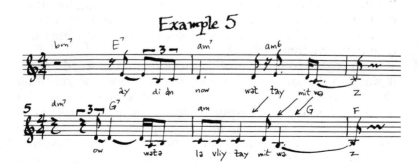

Keeping Rodgers's melodic shape here, which does not change pitch on "time," further smooths the transition through the word "lovely." Notice in m. 6 that the word "it" falls on the beat, rather than between beats. Recall that in m. 2 "it" likewise falls on the beat, in this case the fourth beat of the measure. On paper both instances seem to accent an unaccented word; to the ear, however, Holiday's syncopations, as well as her dynamic inflections, conform to the prosody. A later examination of these syncopations will reveal how they help to produce Holiday's swing.

In response both to the meaning and the sound of the word "lovely," and to a lesser degree the melodic (but not harmonic) arrival on the tonic, Holiday anticipates and then stretches out the words "time it was." In so doing she evokes the sensation of rushing to a lover and then lingering there, a gesture which echoes warmly against the hesitations of the opening line. Although her changes of Rodgers's melody undermine the musical parallelism between these two passages, Holiday deepens their connection by allowing the speech rhythms and the emotional development of the words to reshape the music; by making musical choices which differentiate the sense units and the meaning of each passage, she helps us to understand their meaning. To see how truly effective and expressive are Holiday's subtle digressions from the original, we need only reverse the two settings (see Example 6). Phonetic similarity between two passages does not necessarily generate a new rhythmic

Example 6

treatment, despite a change in meaning. For example, m. 2
("know what") and m. 5 ("Oh, what") both share the sounds
/owhwət/ (see Example 5). Yet in spite of a difference in
meaning the durations are comparable. The recurrences of
these sounds, at m. 10 and again at m. 26 (see Example 4),
with their corresponding rhythmic parallels suggest that the
long-short vowel sequence usually generates long-short
rhythmic values accordingly, unless overriding factors pre-
vail (when a short vowel occurs on the final syllable of a
phrase, for example). Listening to similar sequences in
Holiday's performance reveals a general consistency, regardless of whether the short vowel falls on or off the beat. Her
respect for this aspect of prosody contributes to the intelligibility of her performance.

Holiday modifies Rodgers's motivic parallelism between
mm. 9–10 and mm. 13–14, in order to accommodate
important linguistic differences at these places in the lyrics
(see Example 7). Consider the several factors which distinguish these two passages. In m. 9 the word "I" receives a
single, sustained pitch, as it did previously; but in m. 13
Holiday capitalizes on the voiced /r/ of the word "warm," by
giving it a descending slide.[10] Holiday lingers on this word,
too; so much, in fact, that she rhythmically displaces what
immediately follows. Compared to m. 9, where Holiday
retained the anacrucic quality of the word "didn't," in m. 13
she delays the word "like," which in turn makes "the" fall on
the downbeat and form a dissonant ninth with the harmony.
In addition, although the words "like the" and the word

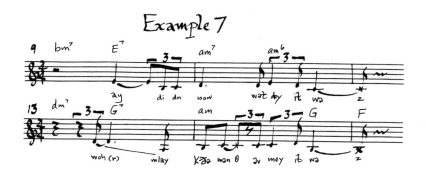

Example 7

"didn't" both consist of two syllables, the sounds /laykɜə/ are more complex phonetically than the sounds /didn/, and therefore require more time to sing. Note that, as in m. 1 and later in m. 25 (see Example 4), Holiday simplifies "didn't," clipping off the final /t/ so it elides with the /n/ of "know," thereby allowing even greater flow through this word.

At first glance Holiday's rhythm in mm. 13–14 seems to damage the prosody by giving "the" a metric accent. The metric accent is weakened, however, by the melodic shape, in which "the" functions as a passing tone; by the rhythm, in which "like the" leads agogically to "month"; and by the dynamic nuancing, with which "the" is uninflected. One important result of this approach is to bring her barline (on the word "month") into direct conflict with the band's. We will come back to this. Notice, finally, that the sliding and lingering on the word "warm" produce a highly expressive touch of word-coloring, which increases her identification with the song's narrator.

Other rhythmic accommodations to phonetic content may be found in Example 7, by comparing m. 10 to m. 14. Whereas the long /ow/ sound of "know" dictates the word's rhythmic elongation m. 10, at the corresponding moment in m. 14, the short /ə/ vowel of "month" shortens its rhythmic value. As in m. 2, the word "know" flows smoothly into "what," because of the shared /w/ (/nowwət/), which provides a transitional rounding between the two words. In contrast, the caesura after "month" groups the fricative ending, /Θ/, with what precedes it (/mən/) and articulates it from what follows (/əv/), thus averting the possibility of hearing the non-sensical /mən/ - /Θəv/. As one might expect, the internal rhymes "day it was" and "May it was" receive nearly identical treatment. Nevertheless, "what" is slightly longer than "of." Holiday does this in order to accommodate the unvoiced alveolar cluster between "what" and "day" (/td/) in m. 10; the /vm/ between "of" and "may" requires less time to enunciate, because both of the voiced elements, /v/ and /m/, are produced at the lips.

The two analogous passages at mm. 25–26 and mm. 29–30 resemble each other more than other passages we have heard (see Example 8). Holiday's virtually identical rhythmic,

Example 8

metric, and motivic treatment of these two passages combines with the rhyme scheme to create the strongest moment
of musical parallelism in her performance, yet even here
there are subtle differences which underline her interpretation. A slight upward bending of pitch on the word "know"
in m. 26 intensifies the third statement of the lyric's "hook"
by lending this word a yearning quality. What a different
effect the sudden, almost disdainful falling-off of pitch on the
word "love" creates in m. 30, an effect we will consider
again. If we recall how the sound /ə/ in the syllable /ləv/ at m.
6 (see the word "lovely" in Example 5) helped to quicken the
rhythmic activity on the downbeat of that measure, then the
way this same sound in m. 30 (see Example 8) acts to truncate
the syllable will come as no surprise. The way Holiday treats
the same sound in the syllable /wəz/ throughout the song,
however, lengthening the vowel at phrase endings, and
quickening it within phrases, suggests that her main purpose
in abandoning the word "love" almost as soon as it begins in
m. 30 is to color it with irony.

After members of the band solo on the tune, Holiday sings
the song a second time. Her second "chorus" reveals that she
improvises only in a narrow sense, for the two choruses differ
only in the subtlest ways (see Example 1). Nevertheless,
certain details in the second chorus suggest that she intends
for it to build upon the emotion of her first chorus. In
Example 9, we hear one such detail, with which Holiday sets
the final statement of the A material apart from all previous
A sections. At m. 26[II] (a roman numeral "II" after the

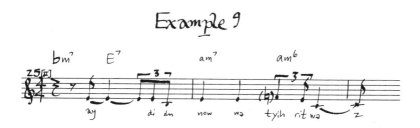

Example 9

measure number indicates that the measure is located in the second chorus), she uses the words "know," "what," "year," and "was" to stress each beat of the measure, contrasting significantly with the way Holiday has woven her rhythms around the beat earlier in the song; the word "didn't" stands out because of its fresh pitch shape; the word "year" rises yearnfully to an f-natural, creating a cross relation with the f-sharp in the am6 chord. Holiday keeps the falling major-third that extends from "I" to "was," but because she replaces the intervening d-natural that occurred previously on "know" in all of the preceding A sections, with an insistent e-natural, the fall to c-natural happens suddenly, at the final two words. All of these features conspire to make this last statement of the A material the most expressive.

The general trend of increasing variation and intensity with each statement of A over the period of two choruses suggests that Holiday sought to extend the formal shape of her performance beyond the confines of a single chorus. Her use of the song's verse as an introduction (excluded in Example 1 and Example 3) contributes to this effect, and two other factors add to this impression.

First, unlike the sheet music, which closes all but the first A section with the fifth scale degree, Holiday closes only the very last A section in the second chorus with the fifth scale degree (see Example 1). In doing so, she delays the effect of a rising line, e-f-g-a, that Rodgers concealed in the song, starting at the first note of the song and proceeding through the endings of the first two A sections, to the beginning of the bridge (see Example 3).[11] Holiday's change sacrifices the

formal integrity and melodic development of the song, as
Rodgers intended it. Instead she saves the g-natural for the
crucial moments in the song's form at the end of the bridge
and at the close of the final statement of A. In the former
case, which occurs in both choruses, she immediately slides
down from it, which weakens its impact. It figures more
prominently at the end of the second chorus, when she
compresses the ascent e-(f-)g into the last A section. The
pitch variations at the beginning of the final A section (see
Example 9) may now be heard as preparatory to this
sustained g-natural, lending a climactic quality to the entire
eight-measure section from m. 25[II] to m. 32[II], and giving
a destination to the entire performance. By touching upon
this important pitch in the second coda, Holiday effects a
summary of the performance's defining vocal compass (see
Example 10).

Second, the coda of the second chorus creates a greater
feeling of closure than does the coda of the first chorus.
Holiday creates partial closure in the first coda by singing the
tonic on the downbeat of the third measure of the phrase, a
rhythmic location that his hitherto received no emphasis. In
effect this phrase closes two measures too soon, leaving
vacant a full measure and a half of established phrase time in
the vocal line. The vocal line's disappearance here acts as the
traditional "break" before the next chorus, which makes way
for the coming horn solos. By disrupting the established
phrasing and by dropping out early in the four-bar time span

Example 10

Holiday signals that more will follow. Thus Holiday's phrasing prepares the listener for the instrumental chorus to come, and contributes to the coda's incomplete quality.

Contrast the above with the second coda. A different chord progression, an increased vocal range, and a new rhythmic placement for the melodic line within the four-bar time span, which emphasizes the last measure of the phrase (m. 36[II]), all create a stronger feeling of closure this time, and precipitate the arrangement's codetta (not included in the example). Listeners who know Holiday's other performances will recognize the final two notes of the second chorus (a 2-1 appoggiatura) as her signature ending. Thus, through her approach to the successive A sections and to the two codas, Holiday achieves a compelling design to her entire performance. Despite intervening solos, her subtle variations act to increase consistently the emotional intensity throughout both choruses and to keep the listener attuned to her every nuance of expression.

The musical gesture Holiday employs to color the word "love" in the last A section of both choruses, discussed above (see Example 8, m.30) reflects the general character of this rendition. Holiday's overall air of detachment lends the performance an almost cynical tinge. In *The Swing Era,*[12] Gunther Schuller mentions Holiday's unsentimental delivery, and here it conditions our perception of the narrator's persona, by enabling her to amplify the nostalgic quality of the song without inviting pity. The casually withdrawn mood, due partly to the choice of tempo, is broken only occasionally by flashes of expression which stand in direct relief against the hard-edged backdrop. These nuances betray an emotional undercurrent which is all the more intense because it lies scarcely beneath the surface.

As mentioned before, Holiday's treatment of the word "I" takes on added significance as her performance unfolds; because this word is embedded in the textual formula discussed earlier, it occurs frequently in the lyrics. Holiday emphasizes it and keeps it fresh each time it occurs by increasing its duration and by changing its placement within the measure. She further stresses the word by syncopating many of its entrances, thereby setting them against the metric backdrop of the supporting ensemble. The syncopated entrances stand out all the more because the song and each successive A section begin with it.

Example 11 presents another instance of the word "I," and we notice that Holiday inverts the original rhythmic relationship between the words "then" and "I" in m. 3. Little surprise that the short-long rhythmic design here conforms to the vowel length. Contrasting this passage to the same passage in the sheet music further demonstrates Holiday's focus on the "I" word.[13]

Holiday's tendency to emphasize the word "I" over the course of the song has a two-fold effect: it lends a self-absorbed persona to the song's narrator, and it heightens Holiday's identification with her material, making the song seem autobiographical. Lorenz Hart built the narrator's persona into the song by his choice of words and by their placement in the melody, but Rodgers's tune does not allow for many nuances in the dramatic development of this feature, because of the strict formal demands of the AABA song-form; the persona therefore remains somewhat static throughout the song. Here Holiday's unique musical contribution steps in to create the singer's personal identification with the song's narrator, lending the song a confessional quality that several of her performances share. The impression that "Holiday doesn't sing a song; she lives it," which echoes throughout the writings about Holiday, grows from just such musical choices, which act to turn a song into a personal testimony. Her choice of this particular song may

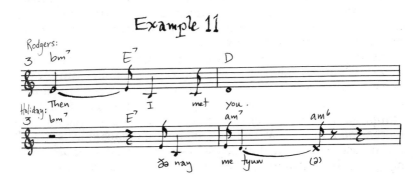

Example 11

not have grown directly from the song's existentialist narrative, but she exploits its intimate revelations to maximum dramatic effect.

A performer's stylization of a song derives as much from her limitations as her assets, but the best performers use even their weaknesses to good effect. While Holiday's choice of key, for example, puts the song comfortably within her low range, transposing the song thus also darkens the general timbre of the song and lends the lowest pitches a "growly" quality. Her choice of material and key suits her dark tone color well, and although "I Didn't Know What Time It Was" (insert, Example 1) ends on an affirmative note, Holiday's vocal timbre gently shades the song with sadness throughout.

Lack of adequate breath support also poses a problem for Holiday; yet instead of spoiling her phrasing in this song, her shortness of breath somehow enhances it, creating gaps in the line which set each thought in relief against the steady pulse and harmonic support of the band. By "airing" out the phrases in this way she also allows the obbligato lines of the horn players to be heard. Her complex approach to beat and meter is the source of her swing, and it requires that the clear rhythmic foundation provided by the supporting ensemble emerge distinctly. This is accomplished superbly by her approach to phrasing, which also is the key to her dramatic timing.

The coda (see Example 10) provides a wonderful moment when phrasing and dramatic timing coalesce. Earlier we noted the striking absence of harmonic and melodic closure in the final measure of the last A section (just before the coda), a moment which typically serves to close an AABA song form. This moment underscores the narrator's indecisiveness and precipitates the coda musically. In addition, unlike any other phrase in the song, Rodgers's coda begins with an upbeat, and, as though provoked by the new rhythmic impulse, the narrator changes from past to present tense. The mood also switches from one of recollection to one of action. The change in grammatical tense points to the transformation in the narrator's outlook and serves as the turning point of the text. The fact that Rodgers reharmonizes the coda's melodic reference to the beginning of the song (see mm. 33–4 in Example 1) now takes on extramusical significance.

Like Rodgers, Holiday waits until the coda to change to an anacrucic rhythmic impulse, but the change impresses us all the more now, because we have heard each A section begin with a delayed entrance. Her approach to the phrase structure also spares us the tedium of hearing e-natural persistently fall on the downbeat beginning all three A sections, and keeps it fresh for the downbeat beginning the coda.

Compare the rhythm of the words "(I) know what time it (is now)" as they appear in the coda with the broken rhythm of their earlier appearance, "(I didn't) know what time it (was)" (see Example 4). The change in feeling at the coda motivates a smoother delivery, which sacrifices the enunciation of the repeated /t/. This suggests that while Holiday may capitalize upon specific phonetic elements in order to amplify the word's expression, she is willing to dispense with them when rhythmic factors accomplish this expression better.

Holiday's swing, while less overtly dramatic than her phrasing, fills no less essential a place in her style. Her willingness to use speech accents to contradict the song's regular meter produces a delightful interplay between the rhythms of the vocal line and the meter as stated by the band. Example 12 shows the beginning of Holiday's vocal line, rebarred so the barlines fall on textual downbeats (i.e. before "I," "know," "then," and "you"). In the original line the textual downbeats correspond to the metric downbeats, yet in her performance they often contradict them, creating wonderfully complex polymeters. The resulting measures in the vocal line consist of a variable number of beats, expanding and contracting according to where the singer wishes to place emphasis. Holiday's swing results from superimposing these unequal measures over the regular metric template generated by the supporting ensemble. Hear in m. 4 how the agogic stress of the word "you" sets up a downbeat in the vocal line which conflicts with the metric downbeat, while the shorter value of "met" weakens the metric downbeat by leading agogically to "you." We noted other instances of this phenomenon back in m. 2 and m. 6 (see Example 5) and in mm. 13–14 (see Example 7). To

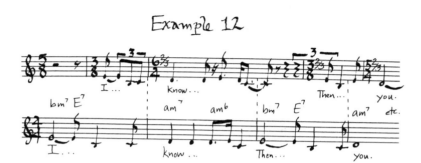

listeners who know the song in its original form, as Holiday's audience members undoubtedly did, and who focus their attention almost exclusively on the melody and the words, the effect of these variable measures is to accelerate and retard the song, creating fulfillment and suspense.

Hear in Example 12 how freely the additive measures[14] of irregular length in the vocal line float above the regular metric foundation of the accompaniment, unhindered by the accompaniment's vertical regularity of downbeats. While Holiday relates her rhythmic designs to the accompaniment by referring to the band's tempo, beat, and subdivisions, only one of her four downbeats shown in Example 12 corresponds to the band's downbeats. In the vocal line's relationship to and independence from the meter we may hear the meeting of two rhythmic worlds.

Holiday's swing arises from the linguistic impulse of the lyrics, which acts in turn to stall or propel the melodic line in order to suspend or fulfill the meaning of each sense unit in the text. The additive meter of the vocal line amplifies the effect of agogic accents, which work in conjunction with speech accent to produce syncopations (see note 4). Holiday's swing liberates the rhythms of her vocal line from reinforcing the vertical template of the meter. The resulting horizontal flow makes her vocal line a remarkably effective vehicle for the setting of English prosody.[15]

Holiday's swing, phrasing, vocal compass and tone color, formal and melodic judgment, and diction all contribute to project her characteristic reading of the text, and brand the performance as hers. To be sure, the stylization of a single Holiday performance cannot be fully understood without reference to her other performances, which would indicate her musical style in a larger sense, and to the performances of other jazz singers, which would establish those traits shared by the community within which she creates. Questions remain as to whether she made certain musical decisions for reasons specific to that performance or on larger stylistic grounds. Nevertheless, while patterns that emerge from a single performance can only hint at some of her distinguishing habits, we may begin to approach a sense of how distinctively Billie Holiday communicates her image of a song by hearing how differently Better Carter handles the same material.[16]

III

Betty Carter's version of "I Didn't Know What Time it Was" (insert, Example 2) bears little resemblance to Billie Holiday's. We know that each singer's performance takes the same song by Rodgers and Hart as its point of departure, mainly due to the obvious similarities both in text and chord changes that each has to the original; yet the two performances differ from each other in so many other respects, in tempo and rhythmic feel,[17] in supporting ensemble, in melodic design, and in overall form, that only by some considerable stretch of the imagination can we hear them in relation to one another.[18] Carter's bold departure from the original standard assumes that at least a few members of the audience already know the tune in some form, and, judging from their grateful response to the first measures of her singing, she assumes correctly. As we consider how Carter's response to the lyrics influenced her musical choices, and how these choices in turn effect the text's delivery, we will begin to hear important relationships between the two performances.

On first hearing, each appearance of the song's hook reveals striking rhythmic departures from the original (see Example 13). Perhaps more striking still, Carter departs from Rodgers's tune nearly as much melodically as she does rhythmically. Instead of approaching the word "know" from

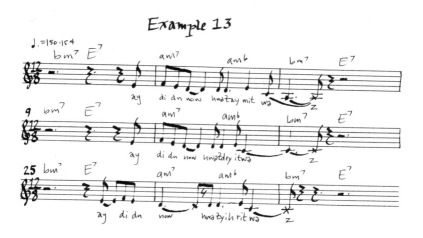

Example 13

below, as the original tune does (see Example 3), Carter inverts the melodic direction of the first four pitches. Studying the example carefully reveals that she retains the pitch motion from e-natural, through d-natural to c-natural, around which the original hook is built; however, her elaborations disrupt our immediate sense of the connection between the original tune and her performance, especially when we rely solely upon our ears.

The low a-natural she sings at the end of the hook's first occurrence, in m. 4, further undermines the connection between the two versions, partly because we now hear the preceding c-natural as an elaboration of this new note, rather than as the structural ending of the phrase. By singing the word "was" on the root of a tonicized a-minor chord, Carter strengthens the word's tonal stability, and gives the song's opening statement greater definition. We immediately identify Carter's narrator as an altogether different character from Holiday's: one who projects a sense of assurance in her convictions.

As in Holiday's version, subtle rhythmic alterations distinguish each A section from the one that preceded it. The words "know" and "was," both verbs, receive agogic accents that get amplified in different ways with each recurrence.

Carter syncopates "know" against the beat the first two times we hear it, and lengthens it the third time; she always syncopates "was" across the barline, whether she begins it on the fourth beat, as in m. 10, or after it, as in m. 2 and m. 26; and her slurring of the word "was" going into m. 3 further accents it. The noun substitutions "time," "day," and "year" also get agogic stresses, but to a lesser degree; and despite surrounding rhythmic displacements she consistently sings these nouns on the third beat of the measure, as if to anchor each phrase to them.

Coming off the bridge (at m. 25) Carter sings the word "I" a beat earlier in the measure. She also lengthens this word slightly, but not enough to keep the word "didn't" from advancing into this measure now, and enhancing the anacrucis to the downbeat of m. 26. In so doing she keeps the word "I" rhythmically connected to "didn't know." Shortly we will hear how this connection contrasts with the effect Rodgers's melody has on Hart's lyrics.

Almost as a response to the subtle emphasis Carter gives to the word "I" this last time, she lengthens the word "know" too. These metric displacements cause the word "know" to fall on the ensemble's downbeat, and its greater length strengthens the metric accent in this measure. If we recall that the rhythmic activity on the downbeats of m. 2 and m. 10 tended to weaken the metric stress in those measures, then we become aware that the ways in which the last A section of the first chorus differs from its earlier counterparts amplify the urgency in the narrator's reminiscence, especially in light of what she has revealed in the bridge.

Notwithstanding the effect of the rhythm on the word "didn't," the slight rise in pitch and volume on each occurrence of this word does produce a gentle stress. In Rodgers's melody this word also receives an accent (see Example 3), but Carter's accentuation differs significantly, both in method and effect. Instead of assertively leaping down a fourth to a syncopation, which, in conjunction with the long note that preceded it, acts to disconnect "didn't" from "I," Carter gently leans on the word "didn't" by an expressive half-step, linking it to the word "I" with shorter rhythmic values. The fast tempo enhances the linking effect of these short values. Thus, by altering the original tune, both through changes in pitch and in rhythm, Carter regroups Hart's words, now binding them more closely together with quicker rhythmic values and stepwise melodic movement, at other times separating them with durations, silences and leaps; new relationships unfold among the words with each alteration.

Carter's driving tempo invests the song's phonetics with even greater effect on the rhythmic propulsion and articulation than they had in Holiday's performance. Compare the noun substitutions in Example 13. In m. 2 the rhythmic value of the words "time it" exceeds the rhythmic value of their counterparts in m. 10 and m. 26 (at the words "day it" and "year it"). In the first instance longer rhythmic values allow time for the voiced consonant /m/ to resonate. In each of the latter two cases, however, the semi-vowel glides (/y/ and /r/, respectively) generate a smoother rhythmic flow and hence require shorter rhythmic values. Because of the faster tempo, Carter also has less time to enunciate as carefully, or in as mannered a fashion, as Holiday. Thus, moments in the song that Holiday articulates, such as between the words "what" and "time," in m. 2, Carter tends to connect.

Each A section's second half offers more striking examples of Carter's melodic freedom (see Example 14). While we

Example 14

could still faintly discern elements of Rodgers' melody in the first two measures of each A section (see Example 13), albeit with the mnemonic aid of the transcription, we can barely hear the passages represented by Example 14 in relation to the same passages in the original tune, even when looking closely at the notes. In the fifth and sixth measures of each A section, Carter completely recomposes Rodgers's tune. In so doing, she not only weakens her version's association with the original but also weakens the parallel function these measures once had in relation to one another and to other passages in the song. Nevertheless, Carter's motivation for such freedom is not arbitrary, nor is it strictly musical.

Recall that Rodgers repeats the opening motive a step lower in each of these passages. While this descending sequence creates a melodic parallelism with the beginning of each A section, it also produces a subtle drop in energy. As we noticed earlier regarding Holiday's rendition (see Example 5 and Example 6), however, the lyrics continue a dramatic development that goes against this musical effect. Not content to adapt the lyrics to Rodgers's melody via rhythmic adjustments (as Holiday does in her performance), Carter allows the lyrics' development to distort Rodgers's line, even at the expense of his melodic parallelism. As a result, she not only redirects the emphasis of the song but also entirely transforms its emotional thrust.

By rising a third on the second word of the phrase beginning in m. 5, for example, she places a tonic accent on the word "what," thus echoing and exceeding the stress placed on the corresponding word, "didn't," at m. 1 (see Example 15). Also, the appoggiatura on "lovely" and the drawing out of its second syllable (/liy/) combine to add weight and expressiveness to this adjective. Significantly, despite the similarities between Carter's singing of the words "time it was" in both phrases, the second phrase has a feeling of growth, due largely to the different way Carter approaches these words.

The way Carter obliterates the parallel relationship mm. 14–15 had to mm. 5–6 (see Example 14), by almost completely inverting the earlier phrase's melodic shape and by delaying the whole passage nearly half a measure,

Example 15

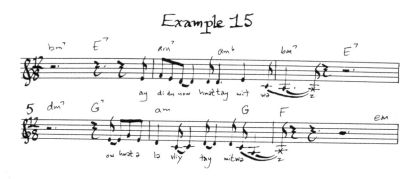

damages the original song's formal design even more overtly. Carter makes the former change in order to shift the word accents from the second word of the phrase, "like," to the first word of the phrase, "warm." With this shift she again emphasizes the adjective, despite its new location in the line.

In order to understand the deeper motivation for such extreme changes, however, we need to contrast the duration of each syllable in m. 14 with each corresponding syllable in the parallel measure from the preceding phrase, at m. 10 (see Example 16). By listening closely to how Carter sings each syllable, we can hear now that she draws out the rhythm at the words "warm like the month" to make room for the many and complex phonetic sounds they contain. The words "I didn't know" in m. 10 required less time to sing, so for them Carter used quick rhythmic values. In addition, separating the words "like the month of May it was" slightly from the word "warm" clarifies their grammatical function. In the original tune (see Example 3) the leap down and the rhythmic delay made an even greater separation here, and this may explain why, despite strong rhythmic and melodic disparities between them, Carter's pitch shape in m. 14 approaches the original tune's more closely (at m. 13) than other analogous passages in the song. We will hear Carter amplify this separation considerably in the second chorus. Like Holiday, Carter wishes to expressively color the word "warm," and she too allows the word's expressiveness to influence what follows, but to a far greater degree.

Example 16

Syllabic alignment of note values

Combined with the delay mentioned above, for example, the longer rhythmic values at the beginning of the phrase in m. 14 force her to squeeze the words "of May it was" into rhythmic values that are significantly shorter than their rhyming counterpart in m. 10. Comparing m. 14 to m. 6 and m. 30 (see Example 14) we learn that the phonetic structure of the words "May it was," which hinges on the semi-vowel glide /y/ makes this transformation possible, and thus allows for the effect of an accelerando.[19] The phonetics in the parallel passages before and after are not conducive to the rapid delivery of text demanded by such an acceleration. Here in m. 14 the lyrics' sound and meaning conspire to provoke Carter's extreme musical changes.

While Carter's rhythmic nuances may stem from a sense of dramatic timing that prompts her to savor certain words and animate others, they have a significant impact on the song's musical development as well. Her delaying of the phrase beginning in m. 14, for example, causes the phrase that follows, "and I'll swear it was grand," to extend into the beginning of the bridge at m. 17 (see Example 17). A unique formal tension gets generated by the overlapping here, owing to the clash between two different kinds of phrases: vocal phrases that result from the rhythmic cohesion Carter gives the lyrics' sense units, and formal divisions such as the one that marks the bridge's beginning, which result from the song's chord changes. This formal tension reveals how much Carter understands Holiday's swing and how far she has gone

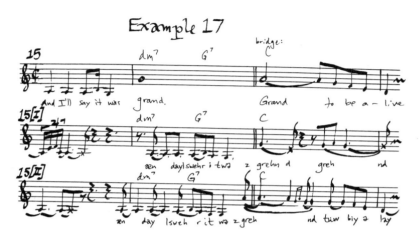

Example 17

beyond it—far past the rhythmic level of beat and measure, to the level of phrase itself. Carter's swing allows whole vocal phrases to come into direct conflict with the song's formal divisions, thereby exploiting the song's stable phrase structure in order to create a volatile rhythmic dynamic that is nonetheless formally coherent.

Due to the phrase overlap here at mm. 16–17, the time between the last word of the phrase and its echo at the beginning of the next phrase gets concentrated, with both now happening in the course of a single measure. On a grander scale, this concentration prepares the listener for the fuller expression that the word will receive in the second chorus (see Example 17), where its echo collapses into a single climactic statement and where two vocal phrases dramatically merge into one. The performance's climax in the second chorus most vividly demonstrates how Carter uses her swing as a powerful expressive tool, a tool with which she often propels her material well beyond the limits of recognizability. Ironically, her second-chorus bridge quotes Rodgers's melody more closely than any other moment in the song; yet because of the way she disrupts rhythm, phrase, and section, and their interrelation, we no longer hear these pitches in relation to the original tune.

Going back to the first chorus, notice how Carter gives the

adjective, "grand," a prominent position in the measure and in the phrase, by singing it on the first downbeat of the bridge (see m. 17 in Example 2). She further draws our attention to this moment by singing the words that come before, "and I'll swear it was," as an extended anacrucis to "grand." Furthermore, for the very first time in the song, a downbeat in the vocal line marks the beginning of a formal division. Carter will use the same approach to phrasing in both codas as well. Recall that Holiday reserved this phrasing technique solely for each of her codas, where it highlighted the song's turning point. Future investigations of jazz vocalism might consider whether either of the singers in question, or other singers as well, use the technique of singing "behind the beat," and indeed behind the phrase, as a means of establishing a rhythmic foil, against which the singing of a song's climax, or crucial moments in the text, may stand out. Jazz writers generally assume that this technique of "airing out" phrases serves a strictly musical/stylistic function, but some jazz singers may also be using it to rhythmically punctuate certain passages, by establishing a backdrop of silences against which they set these moments in relief.

Carter also sets certain pitches in relief, by saving them for crucial moments in the song's overall form. Recall that Rodgers embeds a stepwise melodic line in the first half of the song that travels from the starting note, e-natural, through the final pitch of each A section, f-natural and g-natural, to arrive at the song's highest point, the a-natural that begins the bridge (see Example 3 and note 11). Until the coda, Carter avoided emphasizing a-natural, only using it to coyly elaborate the g-natural that serves as the first-chorus's uppermost limit. She carefully reserves the a-natural for three important moments in her performance, moments in when she gives the pitch special weight: at the first-chorus coda, where it serves to introduce the transition to her upper register (see Example 2); in the second chorus at the end of the first A section (mm. 8–9 [II]), where it elides with the beginning of the second A section, and thus sustains the intensity of the second chorus while preparing us for the disrupted phrasing of the bridge; and at the song's climax in the second-chorus bridge, where the emotion of the entire performance crystallizes.

In terms of short term formal factors, Carter's transition to her upper register in the coda of the first chorus acts to deny the coda its function as the song's ending. Carter's treatment of the coda's lyrics, her shift of register, her phrasing and her dynamics all lend the beginning of second chorus the character of an interruption; and because it has the character of an emotional outburst, Carter's second chorus goes even further to disrupt Rodgers's melodic line (see Example 18). She begins the opening phrase of the second chorus on the highest pitch we've heard so far, and within two measures drops to the lowest, she picks up the tempo and has the bass "walk," she intensifies accents and increases the general dynamic level. She also replaces the subtle tonic accent and slight metric shift we heard earlier on "didn't" (see Example 13), with an agogic accent, upon which she heavily leans. The verb "know" now falls squarely on the downbeat of m. 2 [II], with a longer duration than it had earlier; instead of the eleventh of the chord resolving to the tenth, the ninth now resolves to the root. These factors generate a feeling of urgency and yearning which distinguishes this chorus dramatically from the one before it.

Example 18 reveals some of the ways that Carter steadily increases the energy level of the second chorus up to the bridge and then decreases the energy level after it: she gives the first sections of this chorus greater weight and breadth by drawing each phrase out; on the downbeat of m. 10 [II] she amplifies the metric accent of the word "know" with a tonic accent, lengthening the c-natural here, and slurring it to b-natural to give greater feeling to the word than it received m. 2; she also curtails the lyric here to "I didn't know the day." Only until m. 25 does she begin to draw back from the emotion of this chorus, reversing the process by decreasing the dynamic level, shortening the phrases and putting the word "know" on a lower pitch. Nevertheless, the slightly flattened fifth degree of a-minor on "know" and the curtailed lyric "I didn't know the year" help to accomplish a smooth transition to the ending by preventing the intensity from

Example 18

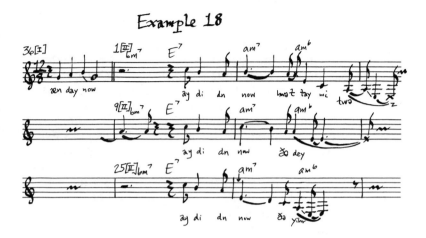

dropping too suddenly. The interested reader can find other examples of how Carter shapes the energy of the second chorus in Example 2 (insert).

Carter's shaping of the song's formal development over two choruses owes something to the place these choruses fill in the overall form of the performance, which, as it turns out, includes more than this one standard: the second-chorus coda segues directly into another standard, "All The Things You Are," and the performance ultimately ends with the standard "If They Asked Me, I Could Write A Book," thus rounding out a medley of compositions by Richard Rodgers. The jazz listener generally does not expect a typical performance to exceed the presentation of a single tune. With this medley, Carter challenges that expectation, so that the listener will hear each successive song as a response to the one that preceded it. Medleys such as this one have served throughout her career as one of several ways in which she has sought to exceed the expressive scope of the jazz standard, and deal with questions of long-term form. While such an approach in itself breaks no new ground, Carter goes beyond the typical arbitrary approach to medleys.

Carter has yoked these particular songs together for dramatic reasons. Their juxtaposition, and especially the relationship between the first two, amplifies the shift in the narrator's perspective that occurred in the coda(s) of the first song, from the negative to the positive, and from the past to the present. The second song continues the dramatic trajectory begun in the first by maintaining the present tense and positive tone that the coda initiated, while shifting from first to second person (from "I Didn't Know" to "You Are"). Thus, although the climax of her performance of the song "I Didn't Know What Time It Was" occurred at the second-chorus bridge, the dramatic turning point for the entire medley occurs at the second-chorus coda.

The way that the second-chorus coda resonates against our memory of the first-chorus coda reveals that Carter intended the first coda to do more than avoid short-term closure. In addition to the function it served in relation to what immediately followed it, we can now hear that she also meant for the first-chorus coda to prepare us for the role the coda has in effecting the song's nonclosure at the end of the second chorus. By having the first-chorus coda refer rhythmically to the way she began the bridge, Carter had already hinted at the role this first coda will play in the song's larger form.

Recall how the silence after the words "I'm wise" in mm. 34–5 (see Example 2) hung uncertainly when the clarifying rejoinder "and I know (what time it is now)" did not immediately follow. At the end of the second chorus, the words "I'm wise" are now put in closer relation to the words "and I know," suggesting that we may yet hear the full realization of the title's transformation "I know what time it is now," which was denied us the first time around; but after singing this phrase (twice this time) Carter again interrupts the line, not with another chorus now, but with another standard. As in the first chorus, the second-chorus coda accomplishes nonclosure textually, by deleting the words "what time it is now" from the final line of lyrics. Carter reinforces the coda's lack of closure this time by substituting a dominant pedal for the standard changes. In recalling the tune's brief introduction, this dominant pedal pulls both choruses together, and places them within the medley's larger framework.

Carter also uses her vocal compass to help create the performance's larger form, and, as we discussed earlier, she

gives certain pitches a specific role in the development of her
melodic ideas. She limits the vocal compass of the first chorus
to the major ninth from g-natural to a-natural; but especially
in the A sections, most of her singing sits within the fifth
between a-natural and e-natural, which acts to reinforce the
minor tonality in the song. In Example 19 we may hear the
pitches Carter uses to organize her vocal line placed within
the vocal compass of each chorus. (The single occurrence in
mm. 7–8 of g-sharp does not stand out beyond its ornamental
function.) Carter generally sings the pitches above f-natural
with either short rhythmic values, or a descending slide, both
of which tend to de-emphasize their occurrence. The pitch b′
occurs at the very end of the first chorus, exceeding this
range, but because Carter delays its occurrence until the last
measure of the coda, after a two-measure pause in the vocal
line, we tend to hear it more in relation to the second chorus
than the first. This seems appropriate, as it helps to
accomplish the registral shift into the second chorus.

The range expands dramatically in the second chorus to a
minor thirteenth, from e to c″, and the pitch collection
expands to include f-sharp, g-sharp, b-flat, and a-flat.
Although the chromatic pitches receive slightly more prominence than the g-sharp did in the first chorus, they still serve
an ornamental function, with none of them receiving substantial duration. (The instability of the pitches in mm.
27–8[II] does lend the words "life was no prize" a touch of
irony.) The pitch b′ receives special emphasis in the second

Example 19

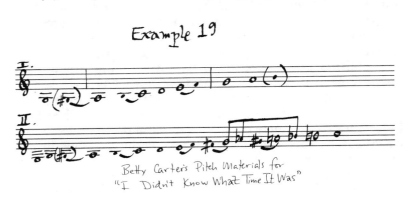

Betty Carter's Pitch Materials for
"I Didn't Know What Time It Was"

chorus. Where the first-chorus coda led upwards from this pitch, we now hear the second-chorus bridge as a downward resolution of this pitch; and where the first chorus gently elaborated the e'-d'-c' tessitura, the second emphasizes the c''-b'-a' tessitura, each in their own way dramatizing the song's inherent tonal suspense.

Carter's melodic approach over both choruses increases the importance of the a-minor tonality, by giving it more melodic stability. This would lend the coda's resolution of the song's tonal ambiguity even greater surprise value than it had in Rodgers's version if Carter allowed the coda to bring resolution. As we discussed earlier, she does not, and thus she provides a musical equivalent for her truncation of the lyric's closing sentiment. This approach weakens the structural importance of the coda, which allows Carter to shift the formal weight to the second chorus bridge.

The simplified pitch collection of the melodic line begins essentially as a pentatonic one ([g];a;c';d';e';g';[a']), with a minor second, f-natural, above the fifth scale degree of a-minor, and a minor second, b-natural, below the tonic degree of c-major. While the f-natural takes on slightly more melodic importance in the bridge, in general the tones used to elaborate the pentatonic collection help to create the tonal anticipation for a-minor and c-major resolutions. The a-minor/c-major polarity of this song make this malleable pitch collection especially appropriate, since either pitch of the major second pair g-natural/a-natural is available both at the bottom and at the top of the compass, and depending upon the harmonic context may be used as a structural tone (fifth degree of c-major/tonic of a-minor).

Carter makes effective use of this feature in the first bridge, where she ornaments the g-natural as a fifth degree to c-major, first in its upper form at parallel locations, m. 17 and m. 21, and then in its lower form to close the bridge. Unlike the original, which ends the bridge with an ascent to the upper g-natural (see m. 24 in Example 3), Carter keeps this pitch and register fresh by taking this moment down into the bottom of this chorus's compass. Significantly the descent here produces a greater feeling of closure than most of her other phrase endings. The counterpart to this passage in the second chorus elaborates the upper g-natural with pitches borrowed from the parallel minor. In sum, a close examination to Carter's treatment of pitch reveals her extreme sensitivity to the harmonic and expressive possibilities of the tone/semitone distinction.

Given how much Carter digresses from the original tune's pitches, the ones she does choose to retain warrant attention. We have already noted how much the beginning of the second-chorus bridge resembles the bridge in the original. At key moments in the first chorus Carter refers to specific shapes from the original, distilling these shapes into momentary allusions to Rodgers's melody (see Example 3). For example, the beginning of each A section refers to the falling major third (e'-c') with emphasis on the intervening d-natural (see Example 13). Like Holiday she simplifies the third and fourth measures of each of Rodgers's A sections to an e'-d' descent (see Example 2). The fifth and sixth measures of each A section seem the most transformed, but when we approach the end of each A section, Carter reconnects with the original pitches. Similarly, while the first four measures merely hint at the original melody, the bridge's second half bears a stronger resemblance to it. Recall that the rising minor seventh (g-f') at the end of the first A section, which prepared us for the return of the e-natural that begins the next A section, was elevated to motivic importance in Holiday's version. Carter sings it once, in m. 8, and thereafter dispenses with it.

By destroying many of the melodic parallelisms within the original, Carter gives her performance the character of a through-composed line, in the manner of a recitative or chant. Eliminating the "jingle" produced by many of the rhymes contributes to this character. In the absence of the original melody's rather extreme formal logic, we may wonder what holds her performance together.

On one level, Carter's melodic simplifications may be interpreted as a way of allowing the flow of speech rhythms to direct the melodic line. In this respect they shift our attention from the music to the words, and they give the lyrics more importance in shaping the music's development. On another level her melodic approach, which emphasizes the repetition and variation of little pitch shapes, recalls the melodic approach of Sonny Rollins. The accumulation and development of these fragments replace the periodic, and somewhat static, coherence of the original with a less predictable, more flexible organization. Carter's unpredictable melodic approach makes her performance seem spontaneous, which lends greater immediacy to her delivery of the song's lyrics, but comparison with her earlier performance of this song (see discography) reveals that a very detailed plan lies behind the the apparent freedom of her performance.

When we listen closely to Carter's performance, we become aware that its apparent freedom conceals a formal logic that keeps Carter's melodic choices from seeming arbitrary. For example, despite the fact that the pitch choices in m. 14, at the words "warm like the month" contrast strongly with mm. 5–6, as well as with other phrase beginnings in the performance, we may understand them in terms of what we heard earlier, in m. 10 at the words "day it was" (Example 13 and Example 14), and in terms of the general role of the descending second, e'-d' as a melodic point of reference (see note 13). At mm. 29–30 (see Example 14) Carter combines melodic elements from the beginning of mm. 5–6 and the ending of the mm. 13–14, this time emphasizing the word "love," and to a slightly lesser degree, the word "want."

By comparing the second chorus to the first (see Example 20) we may further understand how Carter's formal logic works. In the bridge the persistent minor third, g'-e', that Carter sang in mm. 19–20[I] to the adjectives "young" and "mad" becomes in mm. 18–19[II] a descending second that gets increasingly higher, a motivic transformation that contributes powerfully to the climactic character of the bridge. In the first chorus, the word "love" in m. 30[I] echoed the word "lovely" in m. 6[I] (see Example 14). In the second chorus (see Example 2), Carter reiterates the d'-c' appoggiatura at m. 6[II]; but the echo occurs sooner this time, at m. 13[II] where the word "warm" now gets placed more prominently in the phrase. At m. 28[II] Carter now substitutes lower pitches, in part because the expressive potential of this motive has been exhausted. From these

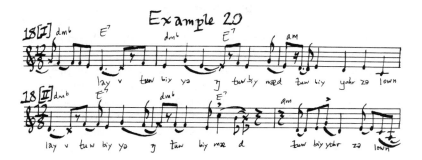

examples and others we can hear how Carter builds her
two-chorus solo by taking a melodic fragment, and expanding upon it rhythmically and melodically, in order to
transform its expressive function. In fact, Carter embeds
enough of the first chorus in the second, that we may hear the
second chorus as an intensified paraphrase of the first. In the
closing measures of the second chorus (see Example 2),
Carter refers to the motive e-g-e-d-c which has provided a
point of reference for the entire performance, having
occurred in both choruses at mm. 5–6 and mm. 29–30. This
choice reveals the consistency of Carter's formal logic; by
ending her rendition of this standard with the two passages
that most violently distort Rodgers's melody, she makes it
truly hers.[20]

Carter's approach to the overall form of the two choruses
now emerges more clearly. The reader will recall that back in
mm. 25–32 of the first chorus she began an intensification
that grew out of the first chorus's bridge. At that point, one
felt the music's formal character begin to evolve, changing
from an expository to a developmental nature. The intensification, begun so subtly then, continued through the first
coda, and into the second chorus to culminate in the bridge of
the second chorus. In the course of this progression, the
mood grew from an urgency that had its roots in the tempo
Carter has chosen to a desperation that gets revealed in the
increased dynamic and higher pitch. Before resolving the
emotion of this song into the calm determination that
characterizes her rendition of "All The Things You Are,"

Carter draws back in the final A section of the second chorus, starting at m. 25 [II]. The way she sings "I wanted love" the second time, in m. 29[II], now eliminating the expressive appoggiatura from before, modulates the energy of the motive from the first chorus to a lower level. Carter does this to prepare us for the second inconclusive coda that now serves as a transition to "All The Things You Are."

If we consider Carter's use of vocal register and dynamics to communicate her emotions as the song's narrator, we may then hear the overall shape of her performance as a direct product of modes of nonverbal expression. Thus, Carter's emotional response to the lyrics generates not only the many nuances of expression that color every word, but the performance's entire formal design as well.

In this light, Carter's interpretation of Rodgers and Hart's song seems unrelated to the meaning intended by its authors. By reducing the song's persistent emphasis on the word "I," for example, she minimizes the narrator's self-absorbed quality, so strongly implied by the lyrics. Carter also replaces the wistful tempo marking in the sheet music with a lively one that lends the narrator's persona a vitality and involvement with the moment that the original narrator lacks. In the process of reinterpreting this tune, she exposes an irony in the authors' original conception: that although the text is about the awakening of a person by the power of love, the emotional state suggested by the original version seems to derive from before the narrator's transformation.

IV

A stylistic gulf separates the two performances of "I Didn't Know What Time It Was" under consideration. Besides the obvious difference in tempo, the two performances generate an entirely different rhythmic feel. While both singers replace the two-step feel of the original version's cut time (see Example 3) with a steady four-to-the-bar, Billie Holiday's line grows out of a predominantly binary subdivision of the beat (or two eighth notes to the beat), whereas in Betty Carter's line a ternary subdivision (or three eighth notes to the beat) prevails (see note 17). Unlike many of their differences, this one does not come from their individual responses to the lyrics, but results mainly from each singer's participation in a different jazz tradition. While Holiday's swing-era roots influence the rhythmic feel of her arrangement, Carter's approach owes its feel to the bebop tradition.

We may also attribute other differences between Holiday's and Carter's arrangements, such as choice of ensemble and the use of chord substitutions and extensions, largely to each singer's allegiance to different jazz styles. The way Holiday uses the horns, for example, and the character of her harmonic support grow directly out of the swing era approach to making a small ensemble vocal arrangement. On the other hand, Carter's trio consists of players schooled in hard bop and bop styles. Significantly, Carter feels no need for horns, as her line has effectively replaced a solo horn line.

We may not conclude from these general stylistic factors that textual considerations do not influence a jazz singer's arrangement. Only upon examining a singer's repeated performances of the same song, accompanied by a new ensemble each time, may we discover the role of a song's text upon a singer's arrangement. As Holiday did not record this song before or after the performance currently under discussion, in her case the question will await further inquiry. Carter did record this tune within a year before the performance discussed here, but the supporting ensemble and the arrangement were identical. The minor differences between these performances reveal a lot about Carter's approach to improvisation, but they do not indicate to what extent the arrangement originates in her reading of the lyrics. The analysis undertaken here has thus been limited to each singer's vocal line and to how the line relates to the accompaniment.

The most revealing dissimilarity between the two different approaches is the way they diverge from one another in their interpretation of the formal and dramatic weight of the coda and the bridge. While Holiday's approach makes her rendition turn upon the song's coda, Carter's transitional coda shifts the emphasis of the lyrics to the bridge of the second chorus, where her performance climaxes. In the bridge, verbs about sensing predominate ("to be," "to see," "to touch" and "to hear"), and by climaxing here Carter reinforces the emotional intensity and vividness of the narrator's character. Another instance of this reinterpretation may be found in the importance Carter gives to adjectives, which gives more weight to the narrator's response to her past than to her description of it.

While the performances display a strong conflict in approaches, both singers nevertheless agree upon some values. If only on this basis alone, these areas of concurrence deserve consideration. The most obvious consensus lies in the way they break the line: both singers agree that musical phrases should generally segment the text into grammatical units. Because of this overall agreement, the few passages in which they break the line differently have relevance to the study of each singer's personal style.

As Hart's lyrics unfold in the second half of the bridge, at mm. 21–24, ambiguity emerges about how the narrator will continue the thought "(it was) Grand to . . . hear your voice" (see Example 3). This ambiguity results in part because of the way the bridge grows out of the lyrics "and I'll say it was grand," and because of the way it refers back to them. In addition, the phrase "hear your voice" parallels the phrases "see your face" and "feel your touch," and the expectation created by this parallelism sets up a sense of completeness. Yet in m. 23 we are also vaguely aware that the thought remains unfinished, if only because the song's rhyme scheme and phrase lengths lead us to expect a rhyme in m. 24 for the word "alone" in m. 20. When the bridge ends, fulfilling this formal expectation, we realize that the thought "(it was) Grand . . . to hear your voice say: I'm all your own," has also emerged. The extended meaning turns on the verb "say," which frames the words that follow, as though they were in quotation marks. Each singer has a distinctive way of handling this complex grammatical structure.

Turning to their performances, we notice that during the first chorus each singer breaks the line differently at the words "hear your voice say I'm all your own," in m. 23 (see Example 21). At this point Holiday breaks the line before the verb "say," while Carter breaks the line after it. As we

observed in the original song, Hart used this verb to connect two thoughts by defining the grammatical function of the words that ensue. Holiday's way of breaking the line tends to weaken the relationship between the verb and the words that precede the verb, by grouping the verb with the words that follow it. In the entire passage above, Holiday emphasizes the nouns "face," "touch," and "voice," and deemphasizes the verb, "say." Sung in this fashion, the words "hear your voice" reinforce the parallelism, and the melodic repetition of the preceding phrases "see your face" and "feel your touch," and therefore serve mainly a musical purpose. Her approach is so musical, in fact, that we don't even notice the resulting damage it causes to the sentence's structure and to its logic.

In contrast, Carter accents the verb, and groups it with the words that precede it. The accent stands out all the more precisely because she so eagerly disrupts the parallelism that Holiday strives to reinforce. By doing this she sets apart the words that follow, thereby clarifying their grammatical function. In her second chorus, the significance of Carter's approach takes on greater proportions. By singing this same passage in even note values, thus eliminating the line break altogether, and to the tune of an ascending scale, Carter further communicates the words' complex inter-connections and the sense of excitement the narrator feels.

In each of the singer's first chorus A sections, the procedure for articulating the grammatical units is to delay the beginning of each two-measure phrase, producing gaps between phrases of roughly two beats in length. Carter lays back more than Holiday to provide a foil for her second chorus, where the gaps are shortened. She also relates the bridge to the coda by beginning both on the downbeat of the four-bar section and by accenting both downbeats with a descending slide. As mentioned earlier, Holiday reserves this phrasing solely for the coda.

In the second chorus, Carter alters line breaks from before, in order to increase the emotional intensity to the climax. She makes a rhythmic and registral break after the phrase "how sublime it was," at the word "too" (meaning "also") in m. 8[II], making it almost sound as if she means "too" (meaning "excessively"). The separation here, and the word's rhythmic placement, cause it to sound like an anticipated downbeat at the beginning of the next phrase. These factors combine with the word's pitch to cause this passage to anticipate the performance's climax. In m. 13[II] the word "warm" now occurs much earlier in the phrase and gets connected to what preceded it, "you held my hand," so that we now associate the warmth more directly with the lover's hand. The phrase structure of Carter's first chorus weakened this association, and perpetuated a vagueness inherent in the original song's break in the line (between "hand" and "warm"). Despite Carter's greater freedom with phrase articulations, varying them substantially in her second chorus to express the development in the narrator's emotional state, she never damages the sentence structure.

Both singers share certain phonetic habits. They generally respect the prosody, by assigning short-long rhythmic values to short-long vowel lengths. More specifically, a comparison of the way each singer differentiates m. 10 from m. 14 (see Example 7 and Example 16) reveals that they both allow the consonant's placement in the front or back of the mouth to affect the rhythmic articulation and flow. The tiny break after the word "month" in m. 14, provides another example of this phenomenon. Compare the way Holiday and Carter both give the fricative, /Θ/, a moment to resonate (see Example 7 and Example 14). A corresponding moment in m. 2 (see Example 7 and Example 13) required no such articulation, owing to the semi-vowel glide /w/ which connected "know" and "what." The moments that both singers vary in the second chorus display the same responsiveness to the phonetic demands of the text, regardless of the degree of variation. In addition, both singers use final consonants to articulate the beat (as indicated by the x that appears at the end of many words and all phrases notated in the transcriptions).

Both singers agree upon the importance of giving the performance an overall shape, and both agree that the second chorus provides an opportunity for growth. Holiday makes fewer overt changes in her second chorus, partly because she must work within the limitations of the swing-era style. Nevertheless, her more static conception of the narrator's persona requires less development during the course of her two choruses. For Carter, the first chorus lays the foundation for the second, providing the basis upon which she will expand upon the first motivically, registrally, dynamically, rhythmically, and emotionally. Neither chorus would make sense without the other. In addition, both singers transpose the tune down a fifth. Among other effects, this change places the song in each singer's chest voice, which gives the song a mature, voice-of-experience quality.

Finally, within a framework that makes syncopation the norm, both singers emphasize the beat to build intensity. For Holiday, the strongest example of this may be found in the final statement of A (see Example 9); for Carter, it occurs throughout the second chorus. Because Carter "airs out" the phrases less in the second chorus than in the first, references to the beat in the vocal line keep her rhythms explicitly grounded in the band's support. That both singers choose to delay the entry of the phrases in the first chorus can be seen as a mechanism of swing, and not as a textually motivated decision.

The phenomenon of swing lends the jazz vocal line a

melodic freedom most appropriate to the setting of American English, enabling the singer to duplicate the flow and articulation of speech in her rhythmic choices. As used by both Holiday and Carter, speech accent becomes an ideal vehicle for the musical cross-accentuation essential to swing. On the other hand, because consonants and vowels define the envelope of each pitch, the more the jazz singer concerns herself with intelligibility, the more the sounds of the language will influence the melodic line. Gerald Abraham stated in *The Tradition of Western Music:*

> . . . owing to the hybrid nature of our language, ambiguities remain, and the result of this hybridism has perhaps been to deprive the language of any obvious positive formative influence on English and American music, though it offers a rich variety of phonetic raw materials.[21]

At least in the case of American popular song this description does not apply, especially in light of the performance practice of jazz singers. Analysis of this repertoire must account for the improvisations of jazz singers and the new vocal lines that result from these improvisations, if it seeks to reflect the musical results accurately. Clearly, the jazz vocal lines in these two performances bear the distinct mark of having evolved in direct response to the demands of linguistic factors. The implications of this fact may extend beyond vocal music, for some jazz instrumentalists, such as Lester Young, have stressed the importance of knowing the words to the tune, and many of them, including Louis Armstrong and Jack Teagarden, gained recognition as singers in their own right. An examination of the actual performances of other genres of English and American music may reveal that native speech inflections have played more of a "formative" role than Abraham suspects.

Nevertheless, the way the jazz vocal line balances textual values against musical ones sets jazz singing apart from other genres of music. We owe this to the subtle play in a jazz singer's performance between improvisation and paraphrase, a play which enables a singer's own speech rhythms and inflections to shape the vocal line even while she performs it. The musical-verbal balance that each jazz singer arrives at must therefore be counted among her stylistic features, for it can do much to reveal her personal conception of a song. Jazz singing appears in this light as a richly layered process, in which the sounds of the text color the musical line as it emerges, while the musical line, in turn, colors the meaning of the text as it unfolds. Music's subtle degrees of accentual differentiation afford the singer a means to lend the words greater nonverbal implications than speech itself allows; and the rhythms and timbres of the text give the singer/improviser a unique means to set her line in relief against the many levels of rhythm which constitute her backdrop.

What is more, even the large-scale form may be affected by nonverbal considerations. Betty Carter literally "raises her voice" in her second chorus. From the panic and urgency that develops in her voice we may infer the desperation of a woman begging her lover not to leave her, trying to convince him that she's different now, that she's changed. From an actor's standpoint, which Carter claims to adopt,[22] Carter's nonverbal expression projects a subtext, or hidden motivation "to grasp," or "to hold onto at any cost," and from her persistent emphasis on verbs and adjectives we sense the intense vitality and powerful sensuality of the character she plays in this rendition. Holiday's version has a wholly different meaning, one which has less overt drama but no less impact. Even the fact that she refuses to "raise her voice" has its roots in the nonverbal expression of withheld emotion and irony that characterize her rendition. While her version conveys a quality of resignation or withdrawal, ultimately she exposes less overt emotion than Carter.

Thus do we listen to the performance of a jazz standard through the filter of personality. From examining Holiday's and Carter's idiosyncratic approaches to one song, we have determined that the ways in which a song varies from one performer to the next result at least as much from what a singer wishes to say about the text as from any of her musical/stylistic attributes. Future research will reveal if patterns of interpretation and technique may emerge from the application of these analytic methods to a larger body of jazz vocal performances. Nevertheless, this study demonstrates that we arrive at a deeper understanding of a how a jazz singer realizes her intentions by confronting how the singer's emotional response to the text and her musical decisions resonate against one another.

NOTES

1. The research for this paper was partly supported by an award from the Carter-Berger Fund at the Institute of Jazz Studies, Rutgers University. This article benefited from the helpful suggestions of Lewis Porter. Comments by Howard Brofsky, Leo Treitler, and my wife, Marge, have also guided the paper's revisions. I would also like to thank the staff of the Institute of Jazz Studies for their assistance.

2. Cases in which improvisation ultimately proves absent show that some performers may work out arrangements in advance, performing them from memory; for those who analyze jazz performances from a formulaic standpoint, improvisation itself proves less spontaneous than it seems on first hearing. Nevertheless, even within a style that maintains very clearly defined stylistic constraints both in vocabulary and syntax (e.g., when playing bop), a jazz player's execution inevitably warrants less attention than her ideas.

3. King Oliver acknowledged this threat when he discouraged Louis Armstrong from straying too far from the melody. At the other end of the spectrum, Miles Davis's famous Philharmonic Hall performance of "My Funny Valentine" from 1964 challenges us with extreme distortion. Davis seems to paraphrase the tune at times, but he consistently blurs the line between paraphrase and improvisation. This results in part because he omits a formal "head," or complete paraphrase of the tune. Classical musicians cannot allow their personal styles to distort a work this much; accusations of self-indulgence at the expense of the composer would follow.

4. Of the phonetic elements given above, accent shares musical and linguistic functions, a fact which comes into play later in this paper. In music, accent heightens expression; in the English language accent conveys meaning (for example, distinguishing the verb "[to] perfect" from the adjective "[it's] perfect"). Yet we achieve accent in language via the musical

means of pitch, duration, and dynamics. Thus by using these musical means to define the specific nature of the accent at any given point in the text, the musical setting of words fixes their nonverbal content into the vocal line to create a stylized reading of the lyrics.

5. For example, when Ella Fitzgerald retains the lyrics to a standard and improvises a new melodic line, she sometimes will sacrifice intelligibility, placing musical concerns above textual ones. On the other hand, her paraphrases sometimes quote the tune more faithfully than one might expect. (For an example of this last point listen to her rendition of the tune discussed below, done with the Buddy Bregman Orchestra in 1956. This recording also warrants attention because Billie Holiday's recording falls roughly nine months later.) Like Holiday and Carter, Lorez Alexandria respects the song's lyrics when generating new melodic lines (see discography). This paper continues the sad neglect of her remarkable work, solely for space considerations.

6. A phonetic chart of the Trager-Smith phonetic symbols appears in the Appendix.

7. Richard Rodgers and Lorenz Hart. From "Too Many Girls," New York, N.Y. (Chappel & Co., 1939). I have transposed the tune from its original key of G-major for the sake of comparison.

8. Hart employs this lyricist's tool, often called a "hook," in many of the lyrics he wrote. The construction "Grand to . . ." in the bridge of this song serves a similar function, unifying the lyrics within the bridge and relating the bridge lyrically to what precedes it. Note that the customary approach of most songwriters at the time involved writing the lyrics *after* the music was composed. (See Oscar Hammerstein II, *Lyrics,* Hal Leonard Books (Milwaukee, 1985, p. 5.)

9. See discography for other important performances.

10. The term "voiced" refers to a consonant's ability to carry pitch.

11. Alec Wilder gets the credit for observing this hidden ascent. See *American Popular Song,* p. 213.

12. Gunther Schuller. *The Swing Era.* New York, N.Y. (Oxford University Press, 1989), pp. 530 and 543. Schuller's discussion of Billie Holiday (pp. 527–547) warrants reading.

13. In m. 4 (see Example 11), and later, in m. 12 and m. 28 (see insert, Example 1), Holiday replaces Rodgers's passing-tone c-natural with a return to the e-natural. That she does this

consistently throughout both choruses, despite differences in phonetic content, strongly suggests that her reasons are musical and not motivated by the lyrics. If we relate her pitch changes in m. 2 and m. 10 to this phrase ending, we may hear the new line's persistent repetition of the e'-d' descent as a tendency to reduce Rodgers's original melody to something akin to a reciting tone with occasional melodic extensions, at least at these key moments in the song. This explanation may also help us to understand her elimination of the chromatic descent in m. 20, on the words "yours alone" (see Example 1), which allows her to hearken back to the descending major third e-c that serves as a point of reference for much of the song.

14. As opposed to proportional meter, in which measures divide into equal, regularly occurring beats, additive meter results from the accumulation, and regrouping of the shortest rhythmic value into beats and measures of irregular size. Examples include Eastern European folk music, Indian *talas*, and the music of Bartok and Stravinsky. Because Holiday derives the smallest rhythmic unit for regrouping from the subdivision of the beat, her additive measures sometimes include fractions of the beat. To describe this phenomenon, I suggest the term "irrational measures." Lewis Porter has drawn my attention to another perspective on the rhythmic conflict between a jazz vocal line and its accompaniment, which places them each in different tempi. I have not been able to locate a copy of the paper that Hao and Rachel Huang delivered at the 1987 National Conference of the College Music Society in New Orleans, which presents this approach.

15. Significantly, the flowering of seventeenth century English song occurred in the context of a premetric rhythmic vocabulary which gave the prosody room to flow forward according to the demands of phonetic and metric considerations. See Elise Bickford Jorgens, *The Well Tun'd Word.*

16. This author's Ph.D. dissertation in progress, *Betty Carter: Style and Expression in the Jazz Singer's Art*, treats the subject more thoroughly.

17. I have transcribed Carter's line in $\frac{12}{8}$ because of this, even though the band clearly feels *four* beats to the measure. She so consistently uses a ternary subdivision of the beat, and so frequently regroups these subdivisions to form longer values that the standard approach of using triplets would have done more to obscure than to reveal her rhythmic approach. Notice,

for example, in mm. 22–4[II], how she introduces a new metric feel in each measure (see insert, Example 2). Specifically she changes from feeling four dotted quarter notes to the measure in m. 22[II] to six quarter notes to the measure in m. 23[II] to three half notes to the measure in m. 24[II]. I entertained the notion of using different time signatures in measures such as these, where she changes from the original metric feel. I chose the $\frac{12}{8}$ approach, however, because she still feels the original four-to-the-bar as well. However, standard jazz notation (which uses swung eight notes) cannot capture these metric transformations (which happen throughout Carter's performance) without looking unnecessarily complicated. On the other hand, Holiday does not consistently swing her eighth notes and sometimes performs them evenly. Therefore the distinction between triplet and eighth note in my transcription truly reflects her rhythmic approach. Again, standard jazz notation does not distinguish between even and swung eighths very well. The notational difference in the two transcriptions thus articulates in tangible form the difference between the singers rhythmically.

18. Leo Treitler has raised important questions on the relationship between the performance of Gregorian chant and its notation, and on how chant singers generated melodic variants. Some of his observations seem relevant to jazz singing because they address questions about improvisation. Treitler's work hints at some of the difficulties inherent in trying to learn what significance the sheet music may have for jazz singers, specifically with regard to the making of their own distinctive renditions. How much other singers' versions of the same song influence them (even versions from which they learned the tune) will also remain hard to ascertain. These difficulties become even more apparent when we try to account for other elements such as chord extensions and substitutions, and the bass line, which may further distance the singer's arrangement from one suggested by the sheet music. Thus, instead of considering a jazz vocal performance as an attempt to realize the notated version of a song, hearing it as merely one instance of a conceptual model's manifold expressions may provide a more useful understanding. Listening to Billie Holiday struggle to produce a composer-approved take of Bernstein's "Big Stuff," supports the notion that Holiday generally did not want simply to realize the song's notation. The previously unissued rehearsals have recently become available on *Billie Holiday:*

The Complete Decca Recordings, MCA Records, (NY, NY: 1991).

Keep in mind that transcriptions may mislead us, because without our noticing, we can easily begin to think of them in the same way we often think of sheet music (i.e. synoptically). Unless one is attempting to recreate a jazz performance literally, however, its transcription serves a purely descriptive function. To adapt an image of Jan LaRue's, it traces the path left behind by the unfolding of the music. On the other hand, the sheet music prescribes and hence remains incomplete until someone realizes it in some way. It acts as a blueprint for the sounds that we are to make and as such has served as a point of reference for this study.

What importance may we give, then, to the observation that the transcription of Carter's performance bears less overt a resemblance to the sheet music than the transcription of Holiday's performance? Given the extreme difference in function between the sheet music and the transcription, we can more fruitfully compare apples and oranges than these superficially similar musical notations. Don't we mean, rather, that we hear Holiday's performance in relation to a literal realization of the sheet music, such as the ones produced by the swing band singers (for examples of the latter see the discography) more easily than we do Betty Carter's? As noted earlier, however, in the context of jazz performance, literal realizations have no inherent value as jazz. The matter awaits fuller consideration.

19. Imagine the difficulty of singing the words "time it was" in this rhythmic configuration.
20. This motive consists of the closing pitches of Holiday's performance. Could Carter be paying homage to one of her self-proclaimed models?
21. Gerald Abraham. *The Tradition of Western Music.* Oxford University Press. California: 1974, p. 79.
22. Carter has emphasized the dramatic implications of her job in numerous published interviews and several conversations with me.

DISCOGRAPHY

(Bold face indicates recordings discussed in this article.)

Bob Eberle (with Jimmy Dorsey), Decca, NY 7/16/39

Louise Tobin (with Benny Goodman), Jazum 41; Tax m-8021, NY 9/13/39

Louise Tobin (with Benny Goodman), Phontastic 7606, NY 9/13/39

Mildred Bailey (with Benny Goodman), unreleased air check, "Camel Caravan" NBC Radio Network, NY 11/4/39

Helen Forrest (with Artie Shaw), Bluebird; Montgomery Ward; His Master's Voice, NY 11/9/39

[Charlie Parker (instrumental with strings), Verve 833268-2; 837141-2; NY 11/30/49]

Ella Fitzgerald (with Buddy Bregman), Verve MGV 4002-2; MGV 4023, Verve 821580 LA 8/29/56

Billie Holiday, Verve MGV 8257; Verve 817.359-1, Verve 513.859 (complete Verve set) LA 1/4/57
Produced by Norman Granz
Personnel: Harry "Sweets" Edison, trumpet
              Ben Webster, tenor saxophone
              Jimmy Rowles, piano
              Barney Kessel, guitar
              Red Mitchell, bass
              Alvin Stoller, drums

Frank Sinatra (with M-G-M studio orchestra), Capitol W912, LA 9/25/57

Lorez, Alexandria, King LP676, Chicago 1959

Betty Carter, "Finally," Roulette SR5000, at Judson Hall, NY 12/6/69 (Stuart Nicholson gives this date in the CD notes to the 1991 EMI reissue, which draw upon a discussion he had with Ms.

Carter. According to Nicholson, Betty Carter recorded the next entry, "Betty Carter," "just a few days later.")

Betty Carter, "Betty Carter," Bet-Car MK 1001, NY 1970
Recorded live at the Vanguard, possibly on Ms. Carter's Birthday, May 16, or in December 1969, (see above entry) Same trio as on "Finally."
Personnel: Norman Simmons, piano
Lisle Atkinson, bass
Al Harewood, drums

Sarah Vaughan (with Joe Pass), Pablo Today 2312137, Hollywood 3/1-2/82

Ernestine Anderson (with Hank Jones), Concord CJ214, San Francisco 2/83

Cassandra Wilson (with Mulgrew Miller), JMT 834419-1, NY 2/88

APPENDIX

Modified Trager-Smith phonemes

VOWELS

<u>short</u>

pit	/i/		put	/u/
pet	/e/	cut /ə/	Paul[1]	/oh/
pat	/æ/	pale[2] /eh/	pot	/a/

<u>long</u>

beat	/iy/	dispute /yuw/	boot /uw/
bait	/ey/	boy /oy/	boat /ow/
bite	/ay/		about /æw/

SEMI-VOWELS

yes /y/   hat /h/   with /w/

CONSONANTS

pop /p/		tight[3] /t/		kick[4] /k/
Bob /b/		did /d/		gag /g/
			church /č/	
			judge /j/	
	fife[5] /f/	thin /θ/	sass /s/	shush /š/
	valve /v/	this /ð/	zebra[6] /z/	measure /ž/
mum /m/		nun /n/		sing /ŋ/
		lull /l/	rear /r/	

The above layout of consonants indicates their vocal placement; those on the left of the chart get produced toward the front of the mouth, and those on the right of the chart get produced toward the back of the mouth.

---

[1] Also paw

[2] Trager-Smith notation does not account for this vowel sound, except before /r/, as in the word "where."

[3] Also stopped

[4] Also cat and pique

[5] Also phase and rough

[6] Also xylem

AN ANNOTATED BIBLIOGRAPHY OF NOTATED CHARLIE CHRISTIAN SOLOS

By Clive G. Downs

INTRODUCTION

My aim in this paper is to give details of all publications containing notated solos of Charlie Christian, and to identify every solo included in them. Several authors have already listed published transcriptions, for example Summerfield (1978), Voigt (1978), Koger (1985), Kernfeld (1989), and Hitchcock et al. (1986), but all are incomplete, and are not intended to be comprehensive. Most list only five or so sources.

As a discography lists deleted records, so this bibliography gives details of out-of-print books and periodicals. This will be of value for those who study Christian's music. Christian recorded several versions of certain compositions, and some records contain solos spliced from different performances or takes. Most published transcriptions do not give full discographical data, so the aim here is to provide that information, so each notation can be readily identified.

There are few bibliographies of solo transcriptions; Koger (1985) lists solos published in *Down Beat* from 1939 to 1985; Downs (1986) is an earlier attempt to document Christian solos; and Downs (1989) deals with Eric Dolphy solos. A related genre, the solography, which gives discographical information and discusses all solos by a specific artist (but does not list published notations), was pioneered by Jan Evensmo, and Evensmo (c. 1976) documents all known Christian solos.

As Kernfeld (1989) points out, it is accepted that jazz

153

musicians use solo transcriptions to develop their art, yet there is little discussion of the history or process in the literature. Notated solos began to be published in the 1920s and more frequently in the 1930s in such journals as *Melody Maker* and *Down Beat,* and in the 1940s collected albums of transcriptions appeared; jazz education flourished in the 1970s and 1980s, and with it the number of published transcriptions increased.

Charlie Christian played, it is reported, in a number of local bands during his youth, but was never recorded then. It is said he was heard by the impresario John Hammond, who in 1939 arranged for him to audition with Benny Goodman, with whom he then played until his hospitalization in 1941, shortly followed by his death from tuberculosis in 1942.

His brief recording career, from 1939 to 1941, comprises mainly tunes with the Goodman small groups, where Christian usually plays short solos of one chorus or less. He recorded also with Lionel Hampton and Edmond Hall; further recordings with Jerry Jerome and at Minton's have more extended solos. He is generally acknowledged to be a major influence on jazz guitar playing ever since.

METHOD USED TO COMPILE BIBLIOGRAPHY

My personal collection was the starting point for the bibliography, supplemented by inquiries to many publishers, periodicals, libraries, correspondence with jazz educators, and checking of reference books. In addition, I learned of some sources through responses to my earlier published bibliography, which included a request for information.

PUBLICATIONS CONTAINING SOLO
TRANSCRIPTIONS

Each publication is followed by a summary of the notated solos it contains, in alphabetical order of title. Some sources contain photographic reproductions of previously published notations, and these are indicated. In some cases, sources include notations which have been transcribed from previous publications, and these too are identified where possible. In order to avoid undue repetition in this section, only such comments that apply to *all* notations in a compilation are noted. For publications consisting of a single solo notation, or where only *some* solos in a compilation are not original transcriptions, this fact is noted in the next section, a listing of notations in alphabetical order of solo title.

Some publications do not acknowledge that notations have been copied from previous sources, and in such cases they have been compared with other transcriptions and a judgment formed of the most likely source.

Details of each solo are followed by brief discographical information showing where it was issued. Wherever possible, the most recent US issue on CD (or CD available in the USA as an import) is cited, except where notations are clearly transcribed from particular LP issues with tracks containing solos spliced from various master takes. If a track has not been issued on CD, details of a representative LP issue are provided, or if never issued on LP, the 78 catalog number.

Almo (1978a). *World's Greatest Jazz Solos: Flute.* Hollywood: Almo,

(———) (1978b). *World's Greatest Jazz Solos: Guitar.* Hollywood: Almo,

(———) (1978c). *World's Greatest Jazz Solos: Saxophone.* Hollywood: Almo,

(———) (1978d). *World's Greatest Jazz Solos: Trumpet.* Hollywood: Almo.

Note: All the above publications notate the same solo, transposed for the instrument in question.

Solo Flight March 4 1941 Columbia CL652

Antonich, Mark E. (1982). *The Jazz Style and Analysis of the Music of Charlie Christian.* Thesis, Duquesne University.

Note: All notations in this thesis are transcribed from previously published sources.

Air Mail Special March 13 1941 Columbia CL652
Boy Meets Goy April 16 1940 Columbia CK 40846
Breakfast Feud December 19 1940/January 15 1941 Columbia CL652
Guy's Got to Go May 1941 Vogue 600135
I Can't Give You Anything But Love December 19 1940 Columbia CK 40379
I Found a New Baby *(take 2)* January 15 1941 Columbia CG30779
Lip's Flip May 1941 Vogue 600135
Profoundly Blue February 5 1941 Blue Note B-6505
Rose Room October 2 1939 Columbia CK 40846
Seven Come Eleven November 22 1939 Columbia CK 40846
Six Appeal June 20 1940 Columbia CK 40846
A Smo-o-o-oth One March 13 1941 Columbia Co 36099
Solo Flight March 4 1941 Columbia CK 40846
Swing to Bop May 12 1941 Vogue 600135
Till Tom Special February 7 1940 Columbia CK 40846
Up on Teddy's Hill 8 May 1941 Vogue 600135

Ayeroff, Stan (ed.) (1979). *Charlie Christian.* New York: Consolidated Music Publishers.

As Long as I Live November 7 1940 Columbia CG30779
Dinah December 16 1939 Vintage Jazz Classics VJC 1021
Good Morning Blues December 24 1939 Vanguard VCD2-47/48
Guy's Got to Go May 1941 Vogue 600135
Honeysuckle Rose November 22 1939 Columbia CG30779
Honeysuckle Rose December 24 1939 Vanguard VCD2-47/48
Honeysuckle Rose November 19 1940 Vintage Jazz Classics VJC 1021
I Can't Give You Anything but Love December 19 1940 Columbia CK 40379
Ida Sweet as Apple Cider April 14 1941 Vintage Jazz Classics VJC 1021
I Found a New Baby *(take 1)* January 15 1941 Columbia CK 40846
I Found a New Baby *(take 2)* January 15 1941 Columbia CG30779
I Surrender Dear April 16 1940 Columbia CK 40379

Lip's Flip May 1941 Vogue 600135
Pagin' the Devil December 24 1939 Vanguard VCD2-47/48
The Sheik of Araby April 10 1940 Columbia CK 40379
The Sheik of Araby April 12 1940 Vintage Jazz Classics VJC
  1021
Stardust September 24 1939 Columbia CG30779
Stardust October 2 1939 Columbia CK 40379
Swing to Bop May 12 1941 Vogue 600135
Up on Teddy's Hill 8 May 1941 Vogue 600135

Bell, Anne M. (n.d.). *Styles Lessons: Charlie Christian.* Boston: Freelance Music.

Note: This publication consists of loose leaf, photocopied sheets.

Air Mail Special March 13 1941 Columbia CG30779
Boy Meets Goy April 16 1940 Columbia CK 40846
Breakfast Feud January 15 1941 Columbia CG30779
Breakfast Feud January 15 1941 Columbia CG30779
I Found a New Baby January 15 1941 Columbia CG30779
I Got Rhythm September 24 1939 Columbia CG30779
On the Alamo January 15 1941 Columbia CK 40379
Stardust September 24 1939 Columbia CG30779
Waitin' for Benny March 13 1941 Columbia CK 40846

Berklee School of Music (n.d.). *Transcriptions Library Archive.* Boston: Freelance Music.

Note: This source consists of photocopied, loose leaf sheets.

Air Mail Special March 13 1941 Columbia CL652
As Long as I Live November 7 1940 Columbia CG30779
Benny's Bugle November 7 1940 Columbia CK 40846
Boy Meets Goy April 16 1940 Columbia CK 40846
Breakfast Feud December 19 1940/January 15 1941 Columbia
  CL652
Flying Home October 2 1939 Columbia CK 40379
Gone with "What" Wind February 7 1940 Columbia CG30779
Honeysuckle Rose November 22 1939 Columbia CG30779
I Can't Give You Anything but Love December 19 1940
  Columbia CK 40379
I Found a New Baby January 15 1941 Columbia CG30779
I Got Rhythm September 24 1939 Columbia CG30779

I Surrender Dear April 16 1940 Columbia CK 40379
Memories of You*(take -A)* November 22 1939 Columbia CK 40379
Memories of You*(take -B)* November 22 1939 Columbia CG30779
Poor Butterfly April 10 1940 Columbia CK 40379
Profoundly Blue February 5 1941 Blue Note B-6505
Rose Room October 2 1939 Columbia CK 40846
Seven Come Eleven November 22 1939 Columbia CK 40846
The Sheik of Araby April 10 1940 Columbia CK 40379
A Smo-o-o-oth One March 13 1941 Columbia CL652
Solo Flight March 4 1941 Columbia CK 40846
These Foolish Things June 20 1940 Columbia CK 40379
Wholly Cats November 7 1940 Columbia CL652

Birkett, James (transcr.) (1987). *Jazz Guitar*. Woodford Green, England. International Music Publications.

I Got Rhythm September 24 1939 Columbia CG30779

Britt, Stan (1984). *The Jazz Guitarists*. New York: Sterling.

I Can't Give You Anything but Love December 19 1940 Columbia CK 40379

Carter, Rich (1979). *Jazz Guitar Masterpieces*. Flat Five Publishing.

I Found a New Baby January 15 1941 Columbia CG30779

Down Beat (1940, April 15), p. 17. "Charlie Christian's Guitar Get-Offs on 'Flying Home'. "

Flying Home October 2 1939 Columbia CK 40379

(———)(1943, January 15), p. 22. "By the Late Charlie Christian."

Rose Room October 2 1939 Columbia CK 40846

(———)(1950, February 10), p. 16. "Charlie Christian Solo: 'I've Found a New Baby'."

I Found a New Baby January 15 1941 Columbia CK 40846

(———)(1950, August 25), p. 12. "Jazz off the Record," Russo, B., & Lifton, L.

Rose Room October 2 1939 Columbia CK 40846

(———)(1961, July 20), pp. 25–28. "Up beat: Charlie Christian," Berklee School of Music.

Boy Meets Goy April 16 1940 Columbia CK 40846
Honeysuckle Rose November 22 1939 Columbia CG30779
I Found a New Baby January 15 1941 Columbia CK 40846
On the Alamo January 15 1941 Columbia CK 40379
Profoundly Blue February 5 1941 Blue Note B-6505
A Smo-o-o-oth One March 13 1941 Columbia Co 36099

(———)(1968, October 31), pp. 36–37. "Gone with What Wind."

Gone with "What" Wind February 7 1940 Columbia CG30779

(———)(1969, July 10). "Charlie Christian Solo on Rose Room."

Rose Room October 2 1939 Columbia CK 40846

(———)(1970, June 11), p. 36. "A Charlie Christian Blues Solo."

Boy Meets Goy April 16 1940 Columbia CK 40846

(———)(1991, May), pp. 56–57. "Charlie Christian's Solo on 'I Got Rhythm'."

I Got Rhythm September 24 1939 Columbia CG30779

Duchossoir, René (1987). *Jazz Guitar True Notes. Vol 1.* Paris: Behar.

Stardust October 2 1939 Columbia CK 40379

Edmonds, Hank, and Prince, Bob (transcr.) (1958). *The Swingingest Charley Christian.* New York: Charles Colin.

Guy's Got to Go May 1941 Vogue 600135
Lips Flips May 1941 Vogue 600135
Swing to Bop May 12 1941 Vogue 600135
Up on Teddy's Hill May 8 1941 Vogue 600135

Feather, Leonard (1957). *The Book of Jazz*. New York: Horizon.

Up on Teddy's Hill May 8 1941 Vogue 600135

Fox, Dan (ed.) (1964). *The Art of the Jazz Guitar: Charley Christian*. New York: Regent Music. [reprinted, 1988].

Air Mail Special March 13 1941 Columbia CL652
Benny's Bugle November 7 1940 Columbia CK 40846
Boy Meets Goy April 16 1940 Columbia CK 40846
Breakfast Feud December 19 1940/January 15 1941 Columbia CL652
Gone with "What" Wind February 7 1940 Columbia CG30779
Seven Come Eleven November 22 1939 Columbia CK 40846
Shivers December 20 1939 Columbia CK 40379
Six Appeal June 20 1940 Columbia CK 40846
A Smo-o-o-oth One March 13 1941 Columbia CL652
Solo Flight March 4 1941 Columbia CK 40846
Till Tom Special February 7 1940 Columbia CK 40846
Wholly Cats November 7 1940 Columbia CL652

Guitar Extra (1990, Summer), p. 15. "Analyzing Charlie Christian."

Seven Come Eleven November 22 1939 Columbia CK 40846

Guitar Player (1982, March), pp. 56–57. "Charlie Christian's Solo Style: 'Honeysuckle Rose'," Obrecht, Jas.

Honeysuckle Rose November 22 1939 Columbia CG30779

Guitar World (1982, January), p. 73. "Charlie Christian Takes Off." Dave Steen (transcr.)

Breakfast Feud January 15 1941 Columbia CG30779

Hitchcock, H. Wiley, & Sadie, Stanley (eds.) (1986). *The New Grove Dictionary of American Music, Vol. 1*. New York: Macmillan. (Thomas Owens, "Charlie Christian.")

Breakfast Feud December 19 1940/January 15 1941 Columbia CL652

Ingram, Adrian (1980). *Modern Jazz Guitar Technique.* Northampton, England: Hampton.

Boy Meets Goy April 16 1940 Columbia CK 40846
I Found a New Baby January 15 1941 Columbia CG30779

Jazz Educators Journal (1979, Dec./Jan.), p. 38.

Seven Come Eleven November 22 1939 Columbia CK 40846

Jazz Hot (1972, May), p. 283. "Charlie Christian: From Swing to Bop."

Swing to Bop May 12 1941 Vogue 600135

Kernfeld, Barry (ed.) (1989). *The New Grove Dictionary of Jazz.* New York: Macmillan. (Thomas Owens, "Charlie Christian.")

Breakfast Feud December 19 1940/January 15 1941 Columbia CL652

Mairants, Ivor (1988). *Famous Jazz Guitar Solos 2.* London: International Music Publications.

Flying Home [unidentified date]
Solo Flight March 4 1941 Columbia CK 40846

Martin, Henry (1986). *Enjoying Jazz.* New York: Schirmer.

I Found A New Baby (take 1) January 15 1941 Columbia CK 40846

Matzner, Antonín, and Wasserberger, Igor (1969). *Jazzové Profily.* Prague: Supraphon.

Up on Teddy's Hill May 8 1941 Vogue 600135

Melody Maker (1947, August 23), p. 3. "Theme—and extemporisation," Mairants, I.

I Surrender Dear April 16 1940 Columbia CK 40379

Mongan, Norman (1983). *The History of the Guitar in Jazz*. New York: Oak Publications.

Swing to Bop May 12 1941 Vogue 600135

Owens, Thomas (see Hitchcock, Kernfeld).

Petersen, Jack (1979). *Jazz Styles & Analysis: Guitar*. Chicago: Down Beat.

> **Air Mail Special** March 13 1941 Columbia CL652
> **Boy Meets Goy** April 16 1940 Columbia CK 40846
> **Rose Room** October 2 1939 Columbia CK 40846
> **Solo Flight** March 4 1941 Columbia CG30779

Polillo, Arrigo (1979). *I Grandi Del Jazz: Gli Stilisti*. Milan: Fabbri.

> **On the Alamo** January 15 1941 Columbia CK 40379

Schiff, Ronny S. (ed.) (1988). *Solos for Jazz Guitar*. New York: Carl Fischer.

> **Air Mail Special** June 20 1940 Columbia CK 40379
> **Air Mail Special** March 13 1941 Columbia CG30779

Schuller, Gunther (1989). *The Swing Era*. New York: Oxford University Press.

> **Breakfast Feud** December 19 1940/January 15 1941 Columbia CG30779
> **I Found a New Baby** January 15 1941 Columbia CK 40846
> **Memories of You** December 24 1939 Vanguard VCD2-47/48
> **Rose Room** October 2 1939 Columbia CK 40846
> **Stardust** October 2 1939 Columbia CK 40379
> **Stompin' at the Savoy** May 12 1941 Vogue 600135

Smith, Earl, & Tharp, Paul (transcr.) (1958). *Hot Jazz Guitar Solos*. Pueblo: Smith Tharp Publishing.

> **Boy Meets Goy** April 16 1940 Columbia CK 40846
> **Rose Room** October 2 1939 Columbia CK 40846
> **These Foolish Things** June 20 1940 Columbia CK 40379

Spaces IV Jazz Fake Book

Note: All notations are transcribed from previously published sources. A notation of "I Got Rhythm" is included that is attributed to Charlie Christian, but it does not appear to correspond to the only known performance of September 24, 1939.

Gone with "What" Wind February 7 1940 Columbia CG30779
Profoundly Blue February 5 1941 Blue Note B-6505
Rose Room October 2 1939 Columbia CK 40846

Spring, Howard A. (1980). "The Improvisational Style of Charlie Christian." MFA Thesis, York University.

AC-DC Current December 2 1939 Vintage Jazz Classics VJC 1021
AC-DC Current June 1940 Vintage Jazz Classics VJC 1021
Ad-Lib Blues October 28 1940 Jazz Document va-7997
Air Mail Special June 20 1940 Columbia CK 40379
Air Mail Special March 13 1941 Columbia CG30779
Air Mail Special March 17 1941 Vintage Jazz Classics VJC 1021
All Star Strut February 7 1940 Columbia CG30779
As Long as I Live November 7 1940 Columbia CG30779
Benny's Bugle November 7 1940 Columbia CK 40846
Benny's Bugle November 19 1940 Vintage Jazz Classics VJC 1021
Benny's Bugle May 28 1941 Vintage Jazz Classics VJC 1021
Boy Meets Goy April 16 1940 Columbia CK 40846
Breakfast Feud December 19 1940 Columbia CL652
Breakfast Feud January 15 1941 Columbia CG30779
Charlie's Dream October 28 1940 Vintage Jazz Classics VJC 1021
Dinah December 16 1939 Vintage Jazz Classics VJC 1021
Flying Home August 10 1939 Jazz Archives JA-23
Flying Home March 10 1941 Vintage Jazz Classics VJC 1021
Gone with "What" Wind February 7 1940 Columbia CG30779
Gone with "What" Wind April 6 1940 Vintage Jazz Classics VJC 1021
Good Morning Blues December 24 1939 Vanguard VCD2-47/48
Guy's Got to Go May 1941 Vogue 600135
Honeysuckle Rose November 22 1939 Columbia CG30779
Honeysuckle Rose November 19 1940 Vintage Jazz Classics VJC 1021

I Can't Give You Anything but Love December 19 1940 Columbia CK 40379
Ida Sweet as Apple Cider April 14 1941 Vintage Jazz Classics VJC 1021
I Found a New Baby January 15 1941 Columbia CG30779
I Got Rhythm September 24 1939 Columbia CG30779
I Never Knew October 28 1940 Vintage Jazz Classics VJC 1021
Lester's Dream October 28 1940 Vintage Jazz Classics VJC 1021
Lips Flips May 1941 Vogue 600135
Memories of You October 23 1939 Vintage Jazz Classics VJC 1021
Memories of You November 22 1939 Columbia CG30779
On the Alamo January 15 1941 Columbia CK 40379
Rose Room October 2 1939 Columbia CK 40846
Rose Room October 9 1939 Vintage Jazz Classics VJC 1021
Royal Garden Blues November 7 1940 Columbia CG30779
Seven Come Eleven November 22 1939 Columbia CK 40846
The Sheik of Araby April 12 1940 Vintage Jazz Classics VJC 1021
Six Appeal June 20 1940 Columbia CK 40846
Six Appeal June 22 1940 Vintage Jazz Classics VJC 1021
Stompin' at the Savoy May 12 1941 Vogue 600135
Till Tom Special December 31 1939 Vintage Jazz Classics VJC 1021
Till Tom Special February 7 1940 Columbia CK 40846
Up on Teddy's Hill May 8 1941 Vogue 600135
Wholly Cats October 28 1940 Vintage Jazz Classics VJC 1021
Wholly Cats *(take 3)* November 7 1940 Columbia CG30779
Wholly Cats *(take 4)* November 7 1940 Columbia CG30779
Wholly Cats November 19 1940 Vintage Jazz Classics VJC 1021
Wholly Cats April 7 1941 Jazz Archives JA-23

(———) (1991). "The Use of Formulas in the Improvisations of Charlie Christian." *Jazz Research/Jazzforschung,* 22, pp. 11–51.

Note: All notations transcribed (some are extracts) from Spring (1980).

Air Mail Special March 13 1941 Columbia CG30779
Air Mail Special March 17 1941 Vintage Jazz Classics VJC 1021
All Star Strut February 7 1940 Columbia CG30779
Benny's Bugle November 7 1940 Columbia CK 40846
Benny's Bugle November 19 1940 Vintage Jazz Classics VJC 1021

Benny's Bugle May 28 1941 Vintage Jazz Classics VJC 1021
Boy Meets Goy April 16 1940 Columbia CK 40846
Breakfast Feud January 15 1941 Columbia CG30779
Dinah December 16 1939 Vintage Jazz Classics VJC 1021
Flying Home August 10 1939 Jazz Archives JA-23
Flying Home March 10 1941 Vintage Jazz Classics VJC 1021
Gone with "What" Wind April 6 1940 Vintage Jazz Classics VJC 1021
Guy's Got to Go May 1941 Vogue 600135
Honeysuckle Rose November 22 1939 Columbia CG30779
Honeysuckle Rose November 19 1940 Vintage Jazz Classics VJC 1021
Lips Flips May 1941 Vogue 600135
Memories of You October 23 1939 Vintage Jazz Classics VJC 1021
Royal Garden Blues November 7 1940 Columbia CG30779
Seven Come Eleven November 22 1939 Columbia CK 40846
The Sheik of Araby April 12 1940 Vintage Jazz Classics VJC 1021
Stompin' at the Savoy May 12 1941 Vogue 600135
Up on Teddy's Hill May 8 1941 Vogue 600135
Wholly Cats October 28 1940 Vintage Jazz Classics VJC 1021
Wholly Cats*(take 3)* November 7 1940 Columbia CG30779
Wholly Cats*(take 4)* November 7 1940 Columbia CG30779
Wholly Cats November 19 1940 Vintage Jazz Classics VJC 1021
Wholly Cats April 7 1941 Jazz Archives JA-23

Takayanagi, Masayuki. (1975). *Charlie Christian Jazz Improvisation.* Tokyo: Nichion.

As Long as I Live November 7 1940 Columbia CG30779
Gone with "What" Wind February 7 1940 Columbia CG30779
Honeysuckle Rose November 22 1939 Columbia CG30779 (*note: complete score*)
I Can't Give You Anything but Love December 19 1940 Columbia CK 40379
I Found a New Baby January 15 1941 Columbia CG30779
I Surrender Dear April 16 1940 Columbia CK 40379
Memories of You *(take -A)* November 22 1939 Columbia CK 40379
Memories of You *(take -B)* November 22 1939 Columbia CG30779
Royal Garden Blues November 7 1940 Columbia CK 40846

The Sheik of Araby April 10 1940 Columbia CK 40379
Stardust September 24 1939 Columbia CG30779
Stardust October 6 1939 Collectors' Classics CC18

Tempo (1947, March), p. 8. "By the Late Charlie Christian."

Rose Room October 2 1939 Columbia CK 40846

Wise (1987a). *Jazz Transcriptions for the Alto Saxophone.* New York: Wise Publications.

I Surrender Dear April 16 1940 Columbia CK 40379

(———) (1987b). *Jazz Transcriptions for the Guitar.* New York: Wise Publications.

Stardust September 24 1939 Columbia CG30779

Gridley (1978) reports that the publisher Giant Steps produced transcriptions of Charlie Christian solos, but it has not been possible to obtain a copy of these. A bibliography of jazz guitar notations published in *Jazz Hot* (1972) lists an item which appears to include Christian material, but this could not be traced; although it is not clear from the bibliography, the publication may also include notations of Barney Kessel, and Chuck Wayne, and appears to be titled *Manuscript series of recorded jazz chorusses* [sic]. No publisher or date of publication is given.

ANALYSIS OF PUBLISHED SOLO TRANSCRIPTIONS

Each recorded solo of Christian for which a transcription is published is listed in alphabetical order of title. The date of recording is noted, and the catalog number of a familiar LP issue. Relevant details of the transcription are noted, such as its completeness, inclusion of annotations, chord symbols, and the key in which it is notated, if there is inconsistency between multiple versions. The format of entries is based on that used in Koger (1985).

AC-DC Current December 2 1939   Vintage Jazz Classics VJC 1021

Spring (1980). Chords unidentified; notates only 2 solos of 4 bars; annotated.

AC-DC Current June 1940   Vintage Jazz Classics VJC 1021

Spring (1980). Chords unidentified; complete (3 solos of 4 bars); annotated.

Ad-Lib Blues October 28 1940   JazzDocument va-7997

Spring (1980). Chords identified; complete (2 choruses); annotated; this includes a 4-bar notation of the false start guitar solo.

Air Mail Special June 20 1940   Columbia CK 40379.

Schiff (1988). Chords identified; complete; annotated; referred to in text as "Air Mail Special (I)."

Spring (1980). Chords identified; complete; annotated.

Air Mail Special March 13 1941   Columbia CG30779.

Note: This L.P. issue has two guitar solos spliced from the same takes as Columbia CL652 (see below), except that the second solo has the first 8 bars omitted (details in Callis, 1978, p. 41).

Bell (n.d.). Chords unidentified; notates only the first 13 bars of the first solo; not annotated; referred to in text as "Good Enough to Keep."

Schiff (1988). Chords identified; complete (i.e. first solo of 32 bars, second of 24 bars); annotated; referred to in text as "Air Mail Special (II)."

Spring (1980). Chords identified; complete; annotated.

(———)(1991). *Adapted from Spring (1980);* notates 1st 11 bars of first chorus, then bars 18–25 (i.e. starting at 2nd bar of bridge) of 2nd chorus

Air Mail Special March 13 1941   Columbia CL652.

Note: This L.P. issue has two guitar solos (each a 32-bar chorus) spliced from separate takes (details in Callis, 1978, p.41).

Antonich (1982). *Transcribed from Fox (1964); annotated.*

Berklee School of Music (n.d.). Chords identified; complete (i.e. both solos); not annotated.

Fox (1964). Chords identified; complete (i.e. both solos); annotated.

Petersen (1979). Chords identified; notates only the second guitar solo; annotated.

Air Mail Special March 17 1941 Vintage Jazz Classics VJC 1021.

Spring (1980). Chords identified; complete; annotated.

(————)(1991). *Adapted from Spring (1980);* notates from bar 24 to end; annotated.

All Star Strut February 7 1940 Columbia CG30779.

Spring (1980). Chords identified; complete; annotated.

(————) (1991). *Transcribed from Spring (1980); annotated.*

As Long as I Live November 7 1940 Columbia CG30779.

Ayeroff (1979). Chords identified; complete; annotated.

Berklee School of Music (n.d.). Chords identified; complete; not annotated.

Spring (1980). Chords identified; complete; annotated.

Takayanagi (1975). Chords identified; complete; annotated (in Japanese).

Benny's Bugle November 7 1940 Columbia CK 40846.

Berklee School of Music (n.d.). Chords identified; complete; not annotated.

Fox (1964). Chords identified; complete; annotated.

Spring (1980). Chords identified; complete; annotated.

(————) (1991). *Transcribed from Spring (1980); annotated.*

Benny's Bugle November 19 1940 Vintage Jazz Classics VJC 1021.

Spring (1980). Chords identified; complete; annotated.

(————) (1991). *Transcribed from Spring (1980); annotated.*

Benny's Bugle   May 28 1941   Vintage Jazz Classics VJC 1021

Spring (1980). Chords identified; complete; annotated.

———— (1991). *Transcribed from Spring (1980); annotated.*

Boy Meets Goy   April 16 1940   Columbia CK 40846

Antonich (1982). *Transcribed from Fox (1964); annotated.*

Bell (n.d.). Chords identified; notates first chorus and two bars of second chorus; not annotated; referred to in text as "Goy."

Berklee School of Music (n.d.). Chords identified; complete; not annotated.

Down Beat (1961). Chords identified; complete; annotated.

Down Beat (1970). *Reproduced from Down Beat (1961).*

Fox (1964). Chords identified; complete; annotated.

Ingram (1980). Chords identified; notates only 4 bars from bar 11, first chorus; annotated; untitled in text, transcription 2.

Petersen (1979). Chords identified; complete; annotated.

Smith & Tharp (1958). Chords unidentified; complete; not annotated.

Spring (1980). Chords identified; complete; annotated.

(————) (1991). *Transcribed from Spring (1980); annotated.*

Breakfast Feud

Table 1 shows which takes of the composition "Breakfast Feud," recorded on December 19, 1940 and January 15, 1940, have been notated. Some of the notations were taken from earlier LP issues, which included tracks with solos from different takes, spliced together in various combinations. Full details of this splicing are given in Callis (1978, p. 40), and Evensmo (n.d., p. CC18–20). Principal LPs concerned are Columbia CL 652 and CG30779.

Antonich (1982). *Transcribed from Fox (1964); annotated.*

Bell (n.d.). Chords identified; notates first 12 bars of first spliced solo from take 29512-Y; annotated; referred to in text as "Feud" (page 1).

Table 1: Notations of "Breakfast Feud" solos

Source Matrix	December 19, 1940 29259-1	January 15, 1941			
		29512-1	29512-2	29512-X	29512-Y
Bell (n.d.)				(2)	(1)
Fox (1964)	(1)		(3)	(2)	
Guitar World (1982)					(1)
Schuller (1989)	(1)	(5)	(4)	(3)	(2)
Spring(1980)	(1)	(4)	(3)	(2)	(1)
Spring(1991)		(4)	(3)	(2)	(1)

Notes:
1. Take numbers are those supplied by Evensmo (c. 1976).
2. Numbers in brackets show the order in which solos are notated in the source.

(———). Chords unidentified; notates 8 bars from start of solo from take 29512-X; not annotated; referred to in text as "Feud" (page 2).

Berklee School of Music (n.d.). Chords identified; not annotated; notation of solos is similar to Fox (1964).

Fox (1964). Chords identified; notates take 29259-1 (sections I and J), then 29512-X (sections K, and first chorus of L), then 29512-2 (sections L (second chorus) and M); annotated.

Guitar World (1982). Chords unidentified; notates take 29512-Y; annotated.

Hitchcock et al. (1986). Chords identified; notates three fragments from take 29259-1; annotated.

Kernfeld (1989). *Reproduced from Hitchcock et al. (1986);* annotated.

Schuller (1989). Chords unidentified; notates take 29259-1 from December 19, 1940, and takes 29512-1, -2, -X, and -Y from January 15, 1941; annotated.

Spring (1980). Chords identified; notates all solos from same takes as transcribed by Schuller (1989); annotated;

(———) (1991). *Adapted from Spring (1980);* notates solos only from January 15, 1941, takes as follows: 29512-Y (complete), -X (first 8 bars), -2 (first 8 bars), -1 (last 12 bars); annotated.

Charlie's Dream   October 28 1940   Vintage Jazz Classics VJC 1021.

Spring (1980). Chords identified; complete; annotated.

Dinah   December 16 1939   Vintage Jazz Classics VJC 1021.

Ayeroff (1979). Chords identified; complete; annotated; key A^b.

Spring (1980). Chords identified; complete; annotated; key B^b.

(———) (1991). *Adapted from Spring (1980);* notates up to bar 23; annotated.

Flying Home   August 10 1939   Jazz Archives JA-23.

Spring (1980). Chords identified; complete; annotated.

(———) (1991). *Transcribed from Spring (1980);* annotated.

Flying Home   October 2 1939   Columbia CK 40379.
(take - A)

Berklee School of Music (n.d.). Chords unidentified; complete; not annotated.

Down Beat (1940). Chords unidentified; complete; not annotated.

Flying Home   March 10 1941   Vintage Jazz Classics VJC 1021.

Spring (1980). Chords identified; complete; annotated.

(———) (1991). *Adapted from Spring (1980);* notates first 11 bars only; annotated.

Flying Home   date unknown

Mairants (1988). Chords identified; annotated; the text suggests this transcription is from the 78 Parlophone Pa R2917, but it does not appear to correspond to the equivalent CD issue (Columbia CK 40379), nor to the alternate take (Nost. 7610), and not to other well known LP issues.

Gone with "What" Wind   February 7 1940   Columbia CG30779.

Berklee School of Music (n.d.). Chords identified; complete; not annotated.

Down Beat (1968). *Reproduced from Fox (1964).*

Fox (1964). Chords identified; complete; annotated.

Spaces IV (n.d.). *Similar to transcription in Fox (1964).*

Spring (1980). Chords identified; complete; annotated.

Takayanagi (1975). Chords identified; complete; annotated (in Japanese).

Gone with "What" Wind   April 6 1940   Vintage Jazz Classics VJC 1021.

Spring (1980). Chords identified; complete; annotated.

(———) (1991). *Transcribed from Spring (1980);* annotated.

Good Morning Blues   December 24 1939   Vanguard VCD2-47/ 48.

Ayeroff (1979). Chords identified; complete; annotated; this solo is attributed to Eddie Durham in the text.

Spring (1980). Chords identified; complete; annotated.

Guy's Got to Go   May 1941   Vogue 600135.

Antonich (1982). *Transcribed from Ayeroff (1979);* annotated.

Ayeroff (1979). Chords identified; complete; annotated.

Edmond & Prince (1958). Chords identified; complete; not annotated.

Spring (1980). Chords identified; complete; annotated.

(———) (1991). *Adapted from Spring (1980);* notates from bar 32 (last bar) of 1st chorus, until 1st bar of middle eight; annotated.

Honeysuckle Rose   November 22 1939   Columbia CG30779.

Ayeroff (1979). Chords identified; annotated; referred to in text as "Honeysuckle Rose (I)."

Berklee School of Music (n.d.). Chords unidentified; complete; not annotated.

Down Beat (1961). Chords unidentified; complete; annotated.

Guitar Player (1982). *Reproduced from Ayeroff (1979).*

Spring (1980). Chords identified; annotated.

(———) (1991). *Adapted from Spring (1980);* notates only first 24 bars; annotated.

Takayanagi (1975). Chords identified; annotated (in Japanese); includes complete score of the arrangement.

Honeysuckle Rose   December 24 1939   Vanguard VCD2-47/48.

Ayeroff (1979). Chords identified; complete; annotated; referred to in text as "Honeysuckle Rose (III)."

Honeysuckle Rose   November 19 1940   Vintage Jazz Classics VJC 1021.

Ayeroff (1979). Chords identified; omits half-bar lead-in; annotated; referred to in text as "Honeysuckle Rose (II)."

Spring (1980). Chords identified; complete; annotated.

(———) (1991). *Adapted from Spring (1980);* notates first 13 bars only; annotated.

I Can't Give You Anything but Love   December 19 1940   Columbia CK 40379.

Antonich (1982). *Transcribed from Ayeroff (1979).*

Ayeroff (1979). Chords identified; complete; annotated.

Berklee School of Music (n.d.). Chords identified; complete; not annotated.

Britt (1984). Chords identified; notates first 8 bars; annotated.

Spring (1980). Chords identified; complete; annotated.

Takayanagi (1975). Chords identified; complete; annotated (in Japanese).

Ida Sweet as Apple Cider   April 14 1941   Vintage Jazz Classics VJC 1021.

Ayeroff (1979). Chords identified; complete; annotated.

Spring (1980). Chords identified; complete; annotated.

I Found a New Baby   January 15 1941   Columbia CK 40846.
(*take -1*)

Ayeroff (1979). Chords identified; complete; annotated; referred to in text as "I've Found a New Baby (I)."

Down Beat (1950). Chords identified; complete; annotated.

(———) (1961). *Reproduced from Down Beat (1950)*.

Martin (1986). Chords identified; complete; annotated.

Schuller (1989). Chords unidentified; notates bars 4 to 6, and bar 8; annotated.

I Found a New Baby   January 15 1941   Columbia CG30779.
(take - 2)

Antonich (1982). *Transcribed from Ayeroff (1979); annotated.*

Ayeroff (1979). Chords identified; complete; annotated; key F; referred to in text as "I've Found a New Baby (II)."

Bell (n.d.). Chords identified; notates only first 12 bars of first chorus; not annotated; key F; referred to in text as "Baby."

Berklee School of Music (n.d.). Chords identified; complete; not annotated; key G^b.

Carter (1979). Chords identified; complete; annotated; key F; untitled in text.

Ingram (1980). Chords identified; notates first 4 bars only; annotated; key F.

Spring (1980). Chords identified; complete; annotated; key F.

Takayanagi (1975). Chords identified; complete; annotated (in Japanese); key G^b.

I Got Rhythm   September 24 1939   Columbia CG30779

Note: This L.P. issue is spliced from separate recordings; details are given in Callis (1978, p. 2).

Bell (n.d.). Chords identified; notates first 8 bars of first chorus only; not annotated; key B; referred to in text as "Rhythm."

Birkett (1987). Chords identified; complete; annotated; key B^b.

Down Beat (1991). Chords identified; notates first chorus, then middle eight of 2nd spliced chorus; annotated; key B^b.

Spring (1980). Chords identified; complete; annotated; key B.

I Never Knew   October 28 1940   Vintage Jazz Classics VJC 1021.

Spring (1980). Chords identified; complete; annotated.

I Surrender Dear   April 16 1940   Columbia CK 40379.

Ayeroff (1979). Chords identified; complete; annotated.

Berklee School of Music (n.d.). Chords identified; complete; annotated.

Melody Maker (1947). Chords identified; complete; annotated.

Takayanagi (1975). Chords identified; complete; annotated (in Japanese).

Wise (1987a). Chords identified; complete; not annotated.

Lester's Dream   October 28 1940   Vintage Jazz Classics VJC 1021.

Spring (1980). Chords identified; complete; annotated.

Lips Flips   May 1941   Vogue 600135.

Antonich (1982). *Transcribed from Ayeroff (1979); annotated.*

Ayeroff (1979). Chords identified; complete; annotated; key D^b.

Edmonds & Prince (1958). Chords identified; complete; not annotated; key C; final 15 bars of notation are not guitar solo.

Spring (1980). Chords identified; complete; annotated; key D^b.

(———) (1991). *Adapted from Spring (1980);* notates 1st chorus, and 1st 16 bars of 2nd chorus; annotated.

Memories of You   October 23 1939   Vintage Jazz Classics VJC 1021.

Spring (1980). Chords identified; complete; annotated; key E.

(———) (1991). *Transcribed from Spring (1980); annotated.*

Memories of You   November 22 1939   Columbia CK 40379.
(take - A)

Berklee School of Music (n.d.). Chords identified; complete; not annotated; key E^b; first item on page.

Takayanagi (1975). Chords identified; complete; annotated (in Japanese); key E^b; p. 16.

Memories of You   November 22 1939   Columbia CG30779
(take - B)

Berklee School of Music (n.d.). Chords identified; complete; not annotated; key E^b; second item on page.

Spring (1980). Chords identified; complete; annotated; key E^b.

Takayanagi (1975). Chords identified; complete; annotated (in Japanese); key E^b; p. 19.

Memories of You   December 24 1939   Vanguard VCD2-47/48.

Schuller (1989). Chords identified; notates only final 4 bars; annotated; key E^b.

On the Alamo   January 15 1941   Columbia CK 40379.

Bell (n.d.). Chords unidentified; complete; annotated; referred to in text as "Alamo."

Down Beat (1961). Chords identified; complete; annotated.

Polillo (1978). Chords unidentified; complete; annotated (in Italian).

Spring (1980). Chords identified; complete; annotated.

Pagin' the Devil   December 24 1939   Vanguard VCD2-47/48.

Ayeroff (1979). Chords identified; complete; annotated; solo attributed to Eddie Durham in text.

Poor Butterfly   April 10 1940   Columbia CK 40379.

Berklee School of Music (n.d.). Chords identified; complete; not annotated.

Profoundly Blue   February 5 1941   Blue Note B-6505.
Note: First take (i.e. not "Profoundly Blue No. 2").

Antonich (1982). *Transcribed from Down Beat (1961);* annotated.

Berklee School of Music (n.d.). Chords identified; complete; not annotated; key F; referred to in text as "Profoundly Blue #1."

Down Beat (1961). Chords unidentified; complete; annotated; key E^b.

Spaces IV (n.d.). *Similar to transcription in Berklee (n.d.)*

Rose Room   October 2 1939   Columbia CK 40846.

Antonich (1982). *Transcribed from Spaces IV (n.d.);* annotated.

Berklee School of Music (n.d.). Chords identified; complete; not annotated; key A^b.

Down Beat (1943). Chords identified; complete; not annotated; key A^b.

(———) (1950). *Transcribed from Down Beat (1943).*

(———) (1969). *Reproduced from Down Beat (1950).*

Petersen (1979). Chords identified; complete; annotated; key A^b.

Schuller (1989). Chords identified; notates bars 1 to 29 only; annotated; key A^b.

Smith & Tharp (1958). Chords identified; complete; not annotated; key A^b.

Spaces IV (n.d.). *Similar to transcription in Berklee (n.d.).*

Spring (1980). Chords identified; complete; annotated; key A^b.

Tempo (1947). *Reproduced from Down Beat (1943).*

Rose Room   October 9 1939   Vintage Jazz Classics VJC 1021.

Spring (1980). Chords identified; complete; annotated; key B^b.

Royal Garden Blues   November 7 1940   Columbia CK 40846. *(take - 1).*

Takayanagi (1975). Chords identified; complete; annotated (in Japanese).

Royal Garden Blues   November 7 1940   Columbia CG30779. *(alternate take).*

Spring (1980). Chords identified; complete; annotated.

(———) (1991). *Transcribed from Spring (1980);* annotated.

Seven Come Eleven   November 22 1939   Columbia CK 40846.

Antonich (1982). *Transcribed from Fox (1964);* annotated.

Berklee School of Music (n.d.). Chords identified; complete; not annotated.

Fox (1964). Chords identified; complete; annotated.

Guitar Extra (1990). Chords identified; complete; annotated.

Jazz Educators Journal (1979). *Reproduced from Fox (1964).*

Spring (1980). Chords identified; complete; annotated.

(———) (1991). *Adapted from Spring (1980);* notates first 24 bars only; annotated.

The Sheik of Araby   April 10 1940   CBS CK 40379.

Ayeroff (1979). Chords identified; notates complete solo chorus, omits four bar exchanges; annotated; referred to in text as "The Sheik of Araby (I)."

Berklee School of Music (n.d.). Chords identified; notates complete solo, omits 4-bar exchanges; not annotated.

Takayanagi (1975). Chords identified; complete; annotated (in Japanese).

The Sheik of Araby   April 12 1940   Vintage Jazz Classics VJC 1021.

Ayeroff (1979). Chords identified; complete; annotated; referred to in text as "The Sheik of Araby (II)."

Spring (1980). Chords identified; complete; annotated.

(———) (1991). *Adapted from Spring (1980);* notates first 7 bars only; annotated.

Shivers   December 20 1939   CBS CK 40379.

Fox (1964). Chords identified; complete; annotated.

Six Appeal   June 20 1940   Columbia CK 40846

Antonich (1982). *Transcribed from Fox (1964);* annotated.

Fox (1964). Chords identified; complete; annotated.

Spring (1980). Chords identified; complete; annotated.

Six Appeal   June 22 1940   Vintage Jazz Classics VJC 1021
Spring (1980). Chords identified; complete; annotated.

A Smo-o-o-oth One   March 13 1941   Columbia CL 652
(take -1).

Berklee School of Music (n.d.). Chords identified; complete; not annotated; key G^b.

Fox (1964). Chords identified; complete; annotated; key G^b.

A Smo-o-o-oth One   March 13 1941   Columbia Co 36099
(take -2)

Antonich (1982). *Transcribed from Down Beat (1961);* annotated.

Down Beat (1961). Chords identified; complete; annotated; key F.

Solo Flight   March 4 1941   Columbia CK 40846.
(take - 1)

Antonich (1982). *Transcribed from Fox (1964);* (omits non guitar passage, section E).

Berklee School of Music (n.d.). Chords unidentified; follows same pattern as Fox (1964); not annotated; key C.

Fox (1964); Chords identified; complete—from the clarinet solo (E), an earlier section of the solo (almost all of section D) is repeated, and before the final section of the solo is a passage not heard on the record; annotated; key C.

Mairants (1988). Chords identified; notates only the first two 32-bar sections; annotated; key C.

Petersen (1979). Chords identified; complete; annotated; key D^b.

Solo Flight   March 4 1941   Columbia CL652
(take - 2)

Almo (1978a). Chords identified; complete; annotated; key C.

(———) (1978b). Chords identified; complete; annotated; key C.

(———) (1978c). Chords identified; complete; annotated; key (transposed) A.

(———) (1978d). Chords identified; complete; annotated; key (transposed) D.

Stardust   September 24 1939   Columbia CG30779.

Ayeroff (1979). Chords identified; notates first chorus only; referred to in text as "Stardust (I)."

Bell (n.d.). Chords identified; notates first 12 bars only; annotated; referred to in text as "Dust."

Takayanagi (1975). Chords unidentified; notates first 32 bars only; annotated (in Japanese).

Wise (1987b). *Reproduced from Ayeroff (1979).*

Stardust   October 2 1939   CBS CK 40379.

Ayeroff (1979). Chords identified; complete; annotated; referred to in text as "Stardust (II)."

Duchossoir (1987). Chords identified; complete; annotated (in French).

Schuller (1989). Chords identified; notates only bars 1 to 25; annotated.

Stardust   October 6 1939   Collectors Classics CC18.

Takayanagi (1975). Chords identified; complete; annotated (in Japanese).

Stompin' at the Savoy   May 12 1941   Vogue 600135.

Schuller (1989). Chords identified; notates only bars 9 to 25 of first chorus of first solo; annotated; untitled.

Spring (1980). Chords identified; complete; annotated.

(———) (1991). *Adapted from Spring (1980);* notates first 5 bars, then first 7 bars of fifth chorus; annotated.

Swing to Bop   May 12 1941   Vogue 600135.

Antonich (1982). *Transcribed from Edmonds & Prince (1958)* (chorus 1 until bridge, transposed to B^b minor), then from *Ayeroff (1979)* (to end); annotated.

Ayeroff (1979). Chords identified; omits first section until first middle eight; annotated; key B^b minor.

Edmonds & Prince (1958). Chords identified; complete; not annotated; key A minor.

Jazz Hot (1972). Chords identified; notates second and third complete choruses only; not annotated; key B^b minor.

Mongan (1983). Chords identified; notates only first three choruses of first solo; annotated; key B^b minor; notates each note as though twice its correct length (e.g. eighth-note as quarter-note).

These Foolish Things   June 20 1940   Columbia CK 40379.

Berklee School of Music (n.d.). Chords identified; complete (includes 4-bar guitar introduction); not annotated.

Smith & Tharp (1958). Chords identified; omits introduction; not annotated.

Till Tom Special   December 31 1939   Vintage Jazz Classics VJC 1021.

Spring (1980). Chords identified; complete; annotated.

Till Tom Special   February 7 1940   Columbia CK 40846.

Antonich (1982). *Transcribed from Fox (1964);* annotated.

Fox (1964). Chords identified; complete; annotated.

Spring (1980). Chords identified; complete; annotated.

Up on Teddy's Hill   May 8 1941   Vogue 600135.

Antonich (1982). *Transcribed from Edmonds & Prince (1958);* (first section until 2 bars before first bridge, transposed to D^b), then from *Ayeroff (1979),* to end; annotated.

Ayeroff (1979). Chords identified; omits first 10 bars of solo; annotated; key D^b.

Edmonds & Prince (1958). Chords identified; complete; not annotated; key C.

Feather (1961). Chords identified; notated from bar 17 to end of third chorus; annotated; key D^b.

Matzner & Wasserberger (1969). *Similar to transcription in Feather (1961);* annotated.

Spring (1980). Chords identified; complete; annotated; key D^b.

(————) (1991). *Adapted from Spring (1980);* notates bar 8 to 17 of first chorus, then bars 19 to end of 3rd chorus, and bars 12 to 17 of fourth chorus; annotated.

Waitin' for Benny   March 13 1941   Columbia CK 40846.

Bell (n.d.). Chords unidentified; notates 12 bars from bar 14 of audible start of solo; not annotated; referred to in text as "Wait'n."

Wholly Cats   October 28 1940   Vintage Jazz Classics VJC 1021.

Spring (1980). Chords identified; complete; annotated.

(————) (1991). *Adapted from Spring (1980);* notates bars 2 to end of second chorus, and entire second chorus; annotated.

Wholly Cats   November 7 1940   Columbia CL652.
(take -1)

Berklee School of Music (n.d.). Chords identified; complete; not annotated.

Fox (1964). Chords identified; complete; annotated.

Wholly Cats   November 7 1940   Columbia CG30779.
(take - 3)

Spring (1980). Chords identified; complete; annotated.

(————) (1991). *Transcribed from Spring (1980);* annotated.

Wholly Cats   November 7 1940   Columbia CG30779.
(take - 4)

Spring (1980). Chords identified; complete; annotated.

(————) (1991). *Adapted from Spring (1980);* notates only first chorus; annotated.

Wholly Cats   November 19 1940   Vintage Jazz Classics VJC 1021.

Spring (1980). Chords identified; complete; annotated.

(————) (1991). *Transcribed from Spring (1980);* annotated.

Wholly Cats   April 7 1941   Jazz Archives JA-23.

Spring (1980). Chords identified; complete; annotated.

(———) (1991). Adapted from Spring (1980); notates first chorus only; annotated.

COMMENTS ON NOTATIONS OF CHRISTIAN PERFORMANCES

Boukas (1977) does not contain any Christian notations, although Voigt (1978) indicates that it does.

An important research question concerns the proportion of Christian's solo performances which have been notated and published. To assess this, the author counted all solo passages that have been issued on commercial recordings, defining "solo passages" to include solo choruses, introductions, obbligatos, and accompaniments. Evensmo's (c. 1976) solography was used as a database, updated to include certain more recent issues. This survey indicated a total of 142 solo passages, as defined above. Of these, published transcriptions are available for 78, just 55 percent.

Not included in this article is a cross-referenced index of all known solos, annotated to show sources of published notations and indicating solos that remain untranscribed. Such an index is useful and has been prepared by the author.

DISCUSSION

In his analysis of Charlie Parker's technique, Owens (1974, p. 271) suggests that the literature of jazz contains little technical discussion of the style of individual performers. For example, it is difficult, Owens notes, to find any documentation of the favorite melodic phrases used by a jazz soloist. Similarly, Spring (1980) observed that there had been no detailed study of the style of Charlie Christian. Certainly there are a number of brief discussions of his improvisational style, including the sleeve notes by Al Avakian and Bob Prince on Columbia CL652, annotations to the transcriptions in Fox (1964), an interesting analysis (mainly of the rhythmic features) of the "Seven Come Eleven" solo by Collier (1981) (but without any notations), and Schuller's (1989) recent analysis. Spring (1980) provides the first extended study of Christian, including the largest single collection of solo transcriptions.

The body of transcriptions identified here is a resource, which may save much of the laborious task of transcribing for future research, and should serve as the basis for further studies of his technique. Some 233 solo notations, and 49 published sources have been identified here. One of the major problems in this task has been in locating material, most of which is published in books or collections of transcriptions and thus cannot be found by computerized literature searches or in most catalogues. This is clearly a significant issue for information scientists and librarians.

Although this study focuses on *published* notations, we should note that Leo Valdes of El Paso, Texas, has transcribed nearly all Charlie Christian's solos, riffs, and introductions. Also, Patrick Zemb of Lorient, France, has notated the bulk of Christian's recorded legacy.

ADDITIONAL REFERENCES

Boukas, R. (1977). *Jazz Riffs for Guitar*. New York: Amsco.

Callis, J. (1978). *Charlie Christian 1939–1941: A Discography*. London: Tony Middleton.

Collier, J. L. (1978). *The Making of Jazz*. Boston: Houghton Mifflin.

Downs, C. G. (1986, Jan.). "Charlie Christian: A guide to published solo transcriptions." *Names & Numbers, 3*, pp. 15–17.

Downs, C. G. (1989). "An Annotated Bibliography of Eric Dolphy Solo Transcriptions." *Jazz Research/Jazzforschung, 21*, pp. 49–54.

Evensmo, J. (c. 1976). *The Guitars of Charlie Christian, Robert Normann, Oscar Aleman*. Oslo: Author.

Gridley, M. C. (1978) *Jazz Styles*. (1st Ed.) Englewood Cliffs: Prentice-Hall.

Jazz Hot (1972, May). "Joe Viera: Bibliographie," p. 81.

Koger, T. S. (1985). "Fifty years of Down Beat solo jazz transcriptions: A register." *Black Music Research Journal*, pp. 43–79.

Owens, T. (1974). *Charlie Parker: Techniques of Improvisation*. Ph.D Dissertation, University of California.

Summerfield, M. J. (1978). *Jazz Guitar: Its Evolution and its Players.* Ashley Mark. Gateshead, England.

Voigt, J. (1978). *Jazz Music in Print.* (2nd ed.). Hornpipe Music. Boston.

COMPACT DISCS

1941 Historical Performances. Vogue 600135.

The Benny Goodman Sextet 1939–1941 Featuring Charlie Christian. Columbia CK 40379.

Charlie Christian: The Genius of the Electric Guitar. Columbia CK 40846.

Solo Flight. Vintage Jazz Classics VJC 1021.

Spirituals to Swing. Vanguard VCD2-47/48.

LP RECORDS

The Alternate Goodman: Vol. II. Nostalgia NOST 7610.

B.G., His Stars and His Guests. Queen-disc Q-016.

Charlie Christian with the Benny Goodman Sextet and Orchestra. Columbia CL652.

Charlie Christian with Benny Goodman and the Sextet (1939–1941). Jazz Archives JA-23.

Jazz Classics: Celestial Express. Blue Note B-6505.

The Rehearsal Sessions: Benny Goodman 1940. JazzDocument va-7997.

Solo Flight—The Genius of Charlie Christian. Columbia CG30779.

ACKNOWLEDGEMENTS

I am grateful to the following people who have been most helpful in supplying information and giving access to certain publications: Judith Barnes, Christopher Beeston, Thierry Bruneau, Gary Carner, Lubomír Dorůžka, Mark Gridley, Nancy Huntress, Wolfram Knauer, Elisabeth Kolleritsch, John Kuzmich Jr., Ivor Mairants, Thomas Owens, Jack Petersen, Howard Spring, Maurice Summerfield, Mike Sutcliffe, Fred Turco, Leo Valdes, Martin Williams, and Patrick Zemb. In particular, I am indebted to Gail L.

Freunsch and the Music Specialist staff of The Library of Congress for their patient assistance and to the staff of Reading Public Libraries for their continued help.

Also I am grateful to my reviewers and to Leo Valdes for their helpful comments and suggestions on earlier drafts of the paper. For her tolerance and support, I am indebted to Maureen Stallard.

FURTHER INFORMATION

I should be most grateful for information on any other published solos not listed in this paper. Please contact me with any details which you have available: 2 Ennerdale Road, Reading, Berks, England RG2 7HH.

CHARLIE CHRISTIAN, BEBOP, AND THE RECORDINGS AT MINTON'S

By Jonathan Finkelman

Charlie Christian (1916–1942) has been acknowledged by his contemporaries as well as by jazz historians as a pivotal figure in the formation of the music that came to be known as "bebop." Yet the fact that he did not live to see the style come into its first maturity, and the fact that nearly his entire recorded legacy lies within the context of Benny Goodman's group (one of the foremost "swing" bands of the time), make it difficult to assess fully the nature and extent of his contribution.

While Christian's recordings with Goodman reveal a tremendously creative and innovative talent, the circumstances under which Christian recorded were severely restrictive. Of the forty or so studio sides on which he played solos with Goodman (not including alternate and composite takes), Christian is given as much as a full chorus on only about half of them, and he takes more than one chorus only on fast 12-bar blues numbers (where he is usually given two choruses). The lone exception is "Solo Flight," a big band recording which features Christian almost all the way through but which is so dense in orchestration that he does not really get a chance to "stretch out." In the "live" airchecks that survive, the soloing formats generally follow those of the studio recordings, with little or no additional solo space added, even in the small group recordings.

As an antidote to this confining situation, Christian began participating regularly in after-hours sessions at Harlem clubs, most notably Minton's, on West 118th Street, and Clark Monroe's Uptown House on West 133rd Street. Minton's and Monroe's were two of the most important venues where experimentation by younger musicians such as Thelonious Monk, Kenny Clarke, Dizzy Gillespie, and Charlie Parker led to the formation of bebop. Jerry Newman, a young jazz enthusiast who recorded Christian and many others on his portable disc recorder in New York in 1941, recalls:

> He [Christian] would bring his guitar and amplifier uptown to sit in at Minton's, where he was treated as a "maestro." Charlie never disappointed his listeners, and if he knew that people were paying attention he really improvised. . . . the paying customers paid tribute by standing still in front of the stand and just listening while Charlie played the same exciting jazz that was driving the whole Goodman band.[1]

Christian began spending more and more time at Minton's, eventually leaving a spare amplifier there so that he could travel uptown quickly and easily after a night with Goodman.[2]

There exist six known recordings of Charlie Christian made by Newman at Minton's and Monroe's (a selected discography is appended to this article.) They capture Christian in loose, after-hours jam sessions far removed from the restrictions of the Goodman band. Three of them feature bop innovators Monk and Clarke, who, along with trumpeter Joe Guy and bassist Nick Fenton, comprised the house band at Minton's. Recorded in May 1941, these are also among the last recordings Christian made. Gunther Schuller describes them as marking "a new stylistic departure" for Christian.[3]

For this essay, I have chosen to focus on two of the Minton's recordings, "Charlie's Choice" (based on the chords of "Topsy" and also issued as "Swing to Bop") and "Stompin' at the Savoy." These recordings feature the most extended Christian solos on record and also represent some of his greatest, most exciting playing.

TRAITS AND INFLUENCES

Ross Russell, in his article "Bebop," writes: "Christian's playing . . . actually foreshadowed bebop line phrasing and harmony."[4] Such assertions are common in jazz histories but are rarely substantiated beyond such general descriptive terms. Hesitancy to go beyond this point in analysis is understandable, since it is difficult to state precisely *how* Christian's playing "foreshadowed bebop." While mature swing and mature bebop are easily distinguishable and the differences between them relatively easily described, a transitional figure like Christian tends to exemplify the commonality and continuity between the styles more than their radical differences (and both commonality and radical differences exist at the same time). Through studying these solos, I hope to be able to describe more precisely what has generally been perceived as Christian's shift towards the emerging bop style. In order to provide a frame of reference for discussion of the recordings at Minton's, it may be helpful to discuss, in a general way, some of Christian's stylistic traits and influences.

Charlie Christian, growing up in the musically rich and varied environment of Oklahoma City, was exposed to many kinds of music, including jazz, southwestern blues, country, western swing, and classical, and he absorbed many of these influences.[5] When asked about specific early musical models, Christian never named any particular musician,[6] but there can be little doubt that one of the most important was Lester Young, whom Christian was said to have heard in Oklahoma City when Young passed through there in 1929 and 1931.[7] In attempting to define Christian's style, particularly in terms of his "modernist" tendencies, it is probably best to begin by looking at Young's influence on Christian. Lewis Porter, in his study of Young, thoroughly documents many aspects of Young's style. His analysis warrants close inspection as it relates to Christian's style.

One important component which defines a player's style is what Porter calls "formulas:"

> A formula—called a "lick" by jazz musicians—is a brief idea that is functional rather than compositional. It is, for example, a pattern that fits a particular chord, chord sequence, or cadence. Formulas recur in similar contexts regardless of the song.[8]

A player's collection of formulas is in large part what makes his style unique and recognizable. At the same time, excessive reliance on those formulas contribute to routine and predictable playing. Several of the formulas cited by Porter as characteristic of Young are also found frequently in Christian's playing.

Of course, Christian used many other formulas which were very much his own. As Schuller points out, Christian's "recurrent use of formulaic motivic figures"[9] are a central component of his style, which would become monotonous without frequent variations and alternating nonformulaic passages. In some of Christian's Goodman recordings (for example, "Shivers" and "Six Appeal"), his use of formulas is so extensive that his playing borders on predictability.

Porter makes other observations about Young's style which bear comparison to Christian's. He points out Young's frequent use of the major sixth scale degree in both major and minor keys.[10] Although the sixth was commonly used in the Swing Era, both Young and Christian used it extensively, often as a repeated, stressed note. A favorite device employed by Young to emphasize the sixth was the repetition of the note using alternate fingerings to vary its timbre.[11] Christian also often accentuated the sixth scale degree, sometimes emulating Young's technique and effect by playing the same note on adjacent strings. According to Porter, Young did not use many ninths in his solos until after 1942.[12] In contrast, Christian used the ninth and other higher chord tones throughout his entire recording career, often as stressed notes.

Porter cites Young's penchant for "long, flowing eighth-note lines."[13] Christian adopted this characteristic and extended it further, as we shall see later. Christian was also one of the first players to incorporate Young's approach to the beat (which divided the quarter note between two eighth notes more evenly than was the norm) into his style. If anything, Christian's eighth notes were sometimes *more* even than Young's. As Schuller suggests, Christian may also have been influenced in this regard by the single-string guitar soloists (such as Leon McAuliffe) of the western swing bands.[14]

Asymmetrical phrasing is another significant feature of Young's style. "Lester's musical thought flowed, not within the accepted confines of two- or four-bar sections, but more freely," writes Ross Russell.[15] Christian's playing exhibits a similar freedom, which developed further as his style evolved.

Then there is the matter of sound. Christian's sound—cool, vibratoless, relaxed, detached (compare it to the fiery, passionate sound of Django Reinhartdt)—is a perfect parallel to Young's distinctive voice on the tenor saxophone. It is perhaps easiest to hear the link between Young and Christian in the area of pure sound.

Many of the above characteristics shared by Young and Christian are those often cited by those who view Young as a forerunner of the bop style: the introduction of stressed nonchord tones or higher chord intervals, the use of relatively even eighth notes, extended eighth-note passages, asymmetrical phrasing, and reduced vibrato. We have seen how Christian adapted these traits and in some cases extended them further. Like Young, when Christian began recording, his style was already fully formed and mature. Since we do not have documentation of his early development, we can only guess at the precise nature of Young's or others' influence. But in terms of Christian's connection to bebop, Young's influence must be considered the most important.

THE MINTON RECORDINGS

I will next examine the recordings at Minton's in the context of the larger body of Christian's recorded work in order to discover how he further developed these "modernistic" tendencies.

From his earliest recorded solos, Christian tended to construct longer, more complex lines over the B section of an AABA 32-bar song form while playing simpler figures over the A sections. Christian's solo on "Seven Come Eleven," recorded November 22, 1939, provides a good early example of this tendency. The A sections consist mainly of short, blues-inflected phrases which are largely diatonic or in the "blues pentatonic" mode. In the bridge (Example 1), Christian plays longer, more flowing eighth-note lines which demonstrate many of the hallmarks of Christian's style: accented chromatic passing tones, harmonic anticipations, and extensive use of upper-chord tones (sometimes dispensing with the root altogether).

Example 1: Seven Come Eleven, mm. 16–25

These characteristics appear more extensively in the bridge sections of "Stompin' at the Savoy" and "Charlie's Choice." For example, while the "Seven Come Eleven" bridge does contain long eighth-note runs, the phrases correspond more or less to the harmonic rhythm; that is, Christian plays two-measure phrases (enlivened by harmonic anticipations) which relate to each chord. This type of phrasing is typical of his playing style with Goodman. In contrast, the first bridge of "Stompin' at the Savoy" consists of an almost unbroken flow of eighth notes (see Example 2). This continuity is achieved by an intensified use of chromatic passing tones in conjunction with a profusion of harmonic anticipations. As a result, the melodic line seems to "float" over the chords. Also, the consistent use of harmonic anticipation leads to a heightened sense of tension between the improvised line and the underlying harmony.

Example 2: Stompin' at the Savoy (1st solo) mm. 17–24

In addition to actual anticipations of chord changes, Christian plays notes which can be heard as functioning in two harmonic areas simultaneously. For example, the B and C# in the triplet figure on the third beat of m. 22 in Example 2 at first sound like the fifth and sixth (or thirteenth) degrees of E. The G-natural which follows on the fourth beat antici- pates the A7 in m. 23. Then in m. 23, the notes of the last half of m. 22 are repeated over the A7 harmony, but now clearly arpeggiating a rootless A9 chord. Thus, in retrospect, we hear the B and C# in m. 22 as the third and ninth of the approaching A7 chord.

The omission of the root (or its placement on a weak part of the beat) during the bridge is pervasive throughout these solos and is another difference between them and Christian's

recordings with Goodman. A survey of the bridges of
Christian's solos with Goodman reveals that, while Christian
often omits the root of a chord or plays it only on the weak
part of a beat, many other times he comes down firmly and
repeatedly on the root. Emphasis of the root in dominant
seventh progressions is much rarer in the Minton's solos,
contributing to their feeling of increased harmonic freedom.

Other harmonic devices which appear in earlier solos are
expanded upon. In the bridge of "I Found a New Baby"
(master take from January 15, 1941), Christian plays the
figure in Example 3.

Example 3: I Found a New Baby, mm. 21–23

Here, Christian uses an accented chromatic passing tone
(G^b) in conjunction with the following D to imply a
momentary interpolation of D-major, the dominant of the
underlying chord, which is then immediately "resolved" to
G7 by the tritone F-B. This device, used occasionally in
Christian's earlier recordings, appears extensively throughout "Charlie's Choice" and "Stompin' at the Savoy." In
Example 4, Christian uses this idea to further intensify the
sense of increased harmonic activity. Here, he plays three
consecutive tritones, implying two descending parallel chromatic lines (A^b—G—G^b; D—D^b—C) which outline the
progression B^b7—E^b7—A^b7 (with an eighth-note harmonic
anticipation of A^b7).

Example 4: Charlie's Choice (1st solo, 4th chorus), mm. 20–21

In general, chromatic lines appear more frequently in the
Minton's recordings than they do previously. The use of

tritones to connect dominant seventh chords also becomes more common.

There is, however, another set of recordings in which Christian's playing at times approaches the harmonic and rhythmic adventurousness of the recordings at Minton's. Significantly, these recordings, made with a pickup group in Minneapolis in 1939 or 1940 (the date is disputed),[16] also take place in an informal setting outside of the context of the Goodman band. Here, Christian plays extended solos on "I Got Rhythm," "Stardust," and "Tea for Two." Although Christian's approach to the bridge sections on these recordings is generally comparable to his playing on "Seven Come Eleven" (largely consisting of two-measure phrases which closely follow the underlying harmony), on "I Got Rhythm" he plays one extraordinary bridge (Example 5) which is the equal of any on the Minton's recordings in terms of innovative harmony and phrasing.

Example 5: I Got Rhythm (3rd solo), mm. 17–25

Additionally, on "Tea for Two," Christian plays a three-against-four whole-tone run in augmented triads (Example

6) that is remarkably similar to a Dizzy Gillespie formula which first appears on another 1941 Minton's recording.

Example 6: Tea for Two (last solo), mm. 17–20

Dizzy Gillespie: Kerouac (1941) (2nd solo), mm. 13–15

This pattern was later incorporated into the 1946 Gillespie big band arrangement of "One Bass Hit."

Many motives and formulas which appear in earlier solos recur throughout the Minton's recordings. In some cases, Christian developed them further. Beginning at m.10 of his first solo on "Charlie's Choice," Christian plays a repeated three-note figure. This figure also appeared at the beginning of Christian's solo on the alternate take of "I've Found a New Baby," though here he extends it much further. As he repeats the figure, he shifts its placement, resulting in occasional accented passing tones. The figure is extended in mm. 17–18 and mm. 19–20, and finally expanded further into an even longer figure in mm. 21–23. Christian relates every figure in the entire complex of phrases from m.10 through m.23 by ending each one on an off-beat, accented D^b. Here Christian has created a unified yet varied statement which arises out of the simplest of materials.

Another Christian formula which is transformed on the Minton's recordings is a rootless arpeggiation of a dominant thirteenth chord (Example 7).

Example 7: I Found a New Baby (1/15/41—alternate take), m. 32

Christian plays variations of this formula several times in "Charlie's Choice," each time over the final chord of the bridge (always in a less symmetrical way than in Example 7). In Christian's first use of the figure (Example 8), he places it rhythmically in such a way that he creates a two-beat anticipation of the dominant seventh chord, while the thirteenth, the most harmonically "distant" note, lands on the downbeat of the measure in which the chord actually appears.

Example 8: Charlie's Choice (1st solo, 1st full chorus), m. 23

The next time the figure occurs (Example 9), Christian begins it half a beat later, embellishing it with a descending chromatic run, and ending it with a striking and unusual exposed major seventh leap up to the thirteenth, an uncharacteristic turn for Christian or any other swing player.

Example 9: Charlie's Choice (1st solo, 3rd chorus), m. 24

Christian evidently liked this variation, for he repeats it note for note in the following bridge.

STRUCTURAL ARTICULATION

Due to the sheer length of Christian's solos, we can hear in these recordings an approach to form that could only be hinted at in the Goodman recordings. (Since Christian rarely played more than one chorus with Goodman, he obviously didn't get much of a chance to experiment with form.) On the Minton's recordings, Christian brings the aforementioned contrast between A and B sections of a 32-bar form into even sharper relief and uses it over the course of several choruses to build an effective dramatic structure. Saxophonist James Moody recalls hearing Christian at Minton's:

> I used to remember that tune "Savoy." They used to play it, and I remember Charlie Christian would be playing on it, and he'd start playing, and on the outside of it he would just be going along slowly, and as soon as he came to the difficult part, the bridge, he would tear it up, he would dive in. Now I know that was intentional, it was beautiful.[17]

The third chorus of Christian's second solo on "Charlie's Choice" provides a striking example of this type of structural articulation. Christian repeats a single spare, riff-like motive throughout the A section. This contrasts sharply with the following bridge, which consists of a highly chromatic exploration of the chord changes in continuous eighth notes. The continual contrast between A and B sections provides an overarching structure which builds anticipation and tension through the A sections and finds release in the outbursts of eighth notes at the bridges.

The blurring of form is another characteristic which distinguishes bop from swing. On a localized scale, Christian achieves this through the increased use of harmonic anticipations. On a larger scale, Christian sometimes connects one chorus with another by playing across the "seam" between two choruses (for example, mm. 30–34 of "Stompin' at the Savoy" and mm. 15–18 of "Charlie's Choice").

RHYTHMIC VITALITY

On the Minton's recordings, Christian exhibits a new, aggressive approach to the beat which derives from Young's propulsive, streamlined style, but is more relentless and driving and seems to look forward to the rapid-fire eighth-note feel of bop. Additionally, Christian connects his eighth notes more fluidly, contributing to the sense of forward momentum. This increased legato is also discernible on some of Christian's later Goodman sessions, notably the privately issued March 13, 1941, rehearsal (which fortuitously caught the Goodman sextet warming up while waiting for the leader to arrive).

An important factor in the increased rhythmic vitality of Christian's playing on the Minton's recordings is the presence of Kenny Clarke. Clarke is generally acknowledged to be the founder of bop drumming, and his playing here provides a fascinating glimpse of his style at a transitional stage. In his dissertation on jazz drumming, Theodore Brown includes an extended discussion of Clarke's playing on "Charlie's Choice." According to Brown, Clarke uses a combination of swing and bop techniques, sometimes playing the bass drum on all four beats in the swing style, and at other times using the bass drum for off-beat punctuations (also known as dropping "bombs").[18]

Although Clarke displays these modern tendencies throughout the recordings, his playing with Christian is even more interactive than with the other soloists, as Brown acknowledges:

> It is important to note that Clarke's playing consistently depends upon the ideas presented by Christian, for the interaction between soloist and drummer is an essential part of bop. This type of interaction . . . is an indication of the intense concentration Clarke applied to his playing.[11]

The close rapport between guitar and drums can be heard as Clarke takes up Christian's rhythmic motives and incorporates them into his accompaniment. At one point, this give-and-take results in Clarke and Christian playing the same figure simultaneously (Example 10).[20]

Example 10: Charlie's Choice, last 3 mm. of 1st chorus
and mm. 1–3 of 2nd chorus

The interaction between Clarke and Christian is one of the most exciting aspects of the Minton's recordings and, as Brown indicates, is an important step towards a bop conception. Clarke's role as rhythmic catalyst is crucial, particularly in the increased incidence of asymmetrical phrasing in Christian's solos.

In sum, Christian's playing on the Minton's recordings does not represent a dramatic stylistic departure from the rest of his recorded output. Rather, certain tendencies that were already present are developed more fully. The formulas and patterns that help to define Christian's style are sill there, but in the freer atmosphere of Minton's, and spurred on by the incipient bop rhythm section of Clarke, Monk, and Fenton, they begin to undergo a transformation.

Christian's eighth-note lines become even more elongated, incorporating a greater degree of chromaticism than before. There is an increased use of harmonic anticipations, particularly in the use of tritones to anticipate dominant seventh chords. Tritones are also used to imply interpolated dominant seventh chords. At the same time, a further de-emphasis of the root in dominant seventh progressions contributes to a greater sense of harmonic freedom. Asymmetry is increased through harmonic anticipations and by the blurring of the divisions between choruses. Rhythmically, Christian's eighth notes become more connected, resulting in a more dynamic sense of swing. The presence of Clarke provides a new rhythmic impetus, and the interplay between Clarke and Christian prefigures the spontaneous interaction between soloist and drummer that is typical of bop.

Although many important elements of mature bop are not in place here (for example, chord substitutions, phrasing and syntax, double-time runs), the Minton's recordings provide ample evidence of a bop sensibility emerging from Christian's established style.

NOTES

1. Jerry Newman, liner notes to *The Charlie Christian Memorial Album* (Vox VSP 302).
2. Rudi Blesh, *Combo USA* (Philadelphia: Chilton, 1971), p. 180.
3. Gunther Schuller, *The Swing Era* (New York: Oxford University Press, 1989), p. 577.
4. Ross Russell, "Bebop," in Martin Williams, ed., *The Art of Jazz: Essays on the Nature and Development of Jazz* (New York: Oxford University Press, 1959), p. 193.
5. Schuller, p. 563.
6. Ibid., p. 566.
7. Blesh, p. 171.
8. Lewis Porter, *Lester Young* (Boston: G. K. Hall, 1985), p. 57.
9. Schuller, p. 573.
10. Porter, p. 66.
11. Ibid., p. 68.
12. Ibid., p. 66.
13. Ibid., p. 87.
14. Schuller, p. 564.
15. Russell, p. 209.
16. Bruyninckx (p. C315) dates these sessions "early March 1940," while Jan Evensmo (p. CC3) dates them as either from September 24, 1939, (a date "which has turned up recently") or early March 1940. John Callis (p. 2) leans toward the 1939 date, as Goodman had been in St. Paul the night before, but

says the date is not certain. Schuller (p. 576) does not mention
a date, but implies a later date, associating these sessions with
the Minton's recordings stylistically.
17. Ira Gitler, *Swing to Bop* (New York: Oxford University Press,
    1985), p. 41.
18. Theodore Dennis Brown, "A History and Analysis of Jazz
    Drumming to 1942." (Ph.D. dissertation, University of Michi-
    gan, 1976), p. 489.
19. Ibid., p. 490.
20. Ibid., p. 492.

BIBLIOGRAPHY

Ayeroff, Stan, ed. *Charlie Christian.* Jazz Masters Series. New
    York: Amsco, 1979 [transcribed solos].
Blesh, Rudi. *Combo USA.* Philadelphia: Chilton, 1971.
Brown, Theodore Dennis. "A History and Analysis of Jazz
    Drumming to 1942." Ph.D. dissertation, University of
    Michigan, 1976.
Bruyninckx, W. *Sixty Years of Recorded Jazz, 1917–1977.* Issued
    in looseleaf form. Belgium: various dates.
Callis, John. *Charlie Christian 1939–41.* Lewisham, London:
    Middleton, 1977 [discography].
Connor, D. Russell and Warren Hicks. *Benny Goodman on the
    Record.* New Rochelle, N.Y.: Arlington House, 1969.
DeVeaux, Scott Knowles. "Jazz in Transition: Coleman Hawkins
    and Howard McGhee 1935–1945." Ph.D. dissertation,
    University of California at Berkeley, 1985.
Evensmo, Jan. *The Guitars of Charlie Christian, Robert Norman,
    Oscar Aleman (in Europe).* Jazz Solography Series, no. 4.
    Oslo: Jan Evensmo, n.d.
Feather, Leonard. *From Satchmo to Miles.* New York: Stein &
    Day, 1972.
Fox, Dan, ed. *The Art of the Jazz Guitar: Charlie Christian.* New
    York: Regent Music, 1964 [transcribed solos].
Gitler, Ira. *Swing to Bop.* New York: Oxford University Press, 1985.
Hennessey, Mike. *Klook: The Story of Kenny Clarke.* New York:
    Quartet Books, 1990.
McKinney, John Francis. "The Pedagogy of Lennie Tristano."
    Ph.D. dissertation, Farleigh Dickinson University, 1978.
Morgan, Alun and Raymond Horricks. *Modern Jazz: a Survey of
    Developments Since 1939.* London: Victor Gollancz, 1956.
Porter, Lewis. *Lester Young.* Boston: G. K. Hall, 1985.

Russell, Ross. "Bebop." *The Art of Jazz: Essays on the Nature and Development of Jazz.* Edited by Martin Williams. New York: Oxford University Press, 1959, pp. 187–214.

Schuller, Gunther. *The Swing Era.* New York: Oxford University Press, 1989.

Shapiro, Nat and Nat Hentoff, eds. *Hear Me Talkin' To Ya.* 1955. Reprint: New York: Dover Publications, 1966.

Spring, Howard. "The Use of Formulas in the Improvisations of Charlie Christian." *Jazzforschung* 22 (1990): 11–52.

Stone, Rick, ed. "Stompin' at the Savoy." Unpublished manuscript [transcribed solo].

Strunk, Steven. "The Harmony of Early Bop—A Layered Approach." *Journal of Jazz Studies* 6 (1979): 4–53.

Wang, Richard. "Jazz Circa 1945—A Confluence of Styles." *Musical Quarterly* 59 (1973): 531–546.

SELECTED DISCOGRAPHY

I have tried to list the most recent issues available. The long-playing records may be out of print. Most of the cited recordings have been available on other issues.

Christian, Charlie. *Charlie Christian.* Vols. 1 and 2. Masters of Jazz 3024, 3029 (CD), 1939–1941.

———. *Charlie Christian Live 1939–1941.* Music Memoria 34009 (CD).

———. *Genius of the Electric Guitar.* Sony/CBS 40846 (CD), 1939–1941.

———. *Live Sessions at Minton's.* Accord Jazz 550012 (CD), 1941.

———. *Solo Flight: Charlie Christian with the Benny Goodman Sextet.* Vintage Jazz Classics VJC-1021-2 (CD), 1939–1941.

Goodman, Benny. *The Un-heard Benny Goodman.* Blu-Disc T1006 (LP), 1941. Contains rehearsal of March 13, 1941.

Guy, Joe, and Oran "Hot Lips" Page. *Joe Guy and Hot Lips Page: Trumpet Battle at Minton's.* Xanadu 107 (LP), 1941. Contains one title, "Rhythm-a-ning," with Christian.

LATIN JAZZ, AFRO-CUBAN JAZZ OR JUST PLAIN OL' JAZZ?

By Vernon W. Boggs

In a recent issue of *Latin Beat* magazine, Max Salazar, the writer, mildly rebuked bandleader Ray Barretto for implying that Afro-Cuban jazz does not exist. Salazar noted that Barretto asserted that just because some musicians have played jazz with an accompanying Afro-Cuban rhythm section does not mean that it is no longer purely jazz.[1] To understand this debate fully, we must first conceptualize it musically and then review its history to determine whether the term *Afro-Cuban/Latin jazz* is a misnomer or an accurate statement.

Perhaps the most appropriate musical conceptualization for this genre of music is the one provided by Fernando Ortiz between 1952 and 1956 in his many discussions of Afro-Cuban music: *musical transculturation*.

> . . . The Negro's music first passes on to the dances of the lowest classes of the whites . . . and the *musical transculturation* is begun. Little by little, the exotic dances pass on, undoubtedly with readjustments, to the customs of the underworld . . . and the poor who live together with the Negroes . . .; there comes a time in which, now generalized and naturalized for the common people, the folk, the new dances . . . continue climbing . . . to the highest levels of society . . . (italics added).[2]

Although his emphasis is seemingly on Afro-Cuban dances, Ortiz was addressing the bicultural nature of all Afro-Cuban music. He argued that Cuban popular music stemmed from the "fusion" of Spanish and African roots. In essence, his argument suggests that musical "purity" would not explain

Afro-Cuban musical traditions. This notation of "purity" lies implicitly at the center of the Salazar v. Barretto debate. Therefore, we must turn our attention to the American history of Latin jazz in order to draw an informed conclusion about its nature.

More than thirty years ago, Marshall Stearns's *The Story of Jazz* devoted one chapter to "Afro-Cuban Music":

> The powerful and largely rhythmic influence of Afro-Cuban music on jazz . . . reached a peak in the winter of 1947 when bandleader Dizzy Gillespie hired the Cuban drummer, Chano Pozo, for a Town Hall concert. . . .[3]

Stearns added that Cuban music had had a tremendous influence on American jazz since the late nineteenth century, but "the final blending proceeded at different speeds, in different places, and at different times".

The blending of jazz and Afro-Cuban rhythms was not stable until the 1940s:

> Perhaps the most stable pattern in this blending of blends was established by Machito and his Afro-Cubans. Organized in 1940, this band slowly but surely assimilated the jazz idiom—they grew up in the Cuban idiom—and created a new blend of both. . . . The key to the pattern was Mario Bauza, Machito's brother-in-law, who organized the band, arranged the music, and played lead trumpet.[4]

Stearns felt that, with the exception of Tito Puente's and Machito's efforts, much of what passed for Afro-Cuban jazz was an imperfect blending of two musical genres. But he added:

> . . . Afro-Cuban music brought a large and enthusiastic audience along with it in the process of blending with jazz . . . and it made many jazz [fans convert] to Latin music. The demand was genuine, the support consistent, and the combination self-propelled.[5]

John Storm Roberts further clarified the impact of Cuban music on American jazz:

. . . the first half of the 1940s saw Latin music become an established style and influence within mass popular music. During the second half of the decade, two major creative movements developed that were to reach maturity during the 1950s. One—the mambo—belonged to the central core of U.S. Latin music, the other—Afro-Cuban jazz, or Cubop—was a fusion style; but both were extremely tightly intertwined, especially during the 1940s.

Though its impact was sudden and dramatic, Cubop did not spring fully armed from anybody's head. It was one flowering of a fusion process that had been going on ever since the days of the habañera, and has continued ever since. Many of the swing bands of the early 1940s had dabbled in jazz-Latin fusion. Though most of the these were fairly superficial, they were also increasingly Latin. . . .[6]

Roberts argued that many of the efforts to "marry" Cuban rhythmic patterns with jazz harmonies did not work out too well at first despite the common roots of the two. But in time, they were successfully merged.

Though much of the Latin music of the 1940s was frankly silly, it was also a decade of enormous creativity. Above all, it was the first decade in which Latin elements began to move below the surface of U.S. music, so to speak, and establish themselves as an integral part of it. . . .[7]

Another informed source, Dizzy Gillespie, stated that collaboration with Chano Pozo "was really the fusion between Afro-Cuban music and jazz." This required effort on the part of composers and arrangers because their time signatures were different, but, more importantly, phrasing and rhythm were the areas needing great change. And according to bandleader Alberto Socarras, Gillespie accomplished just that:

Dizzy did something with the Cuban and the jazz music . . . with Chano Pozo . . . called "Manteca." . . . That was very effective. And right after that, a whole lot of

> American arrangers or orchestra leaders started having
> bongos, conga drums, [playing] the same rhythm that
> Cubans have, together with jazz. . . . I mean [making]
> improvement[s] on the rhythmically poor American
> music . . . [by] adding the best of the conga drums and
> things [which] added rhythmically to American music.[8]

This was only one of the first explicit musical fusions between
the United States and Cuba. Other Gillespie-led compositions like "Cubano Be, Cubano Bop," "A Night in Tunisia,"
and "Guarachi Guaro" became models for emulation.
Within four decades, this musical fusion had become widely
disseminated throughout the world.

The Afro-Cuban/Afro-American musical collaborations
among Bauza, Gillespie, Machito, and Pozo left an indelible
imprint on Western Europe. When Pozo was murdered,
Sabu Martinez, a Puerto Rican percussionist, was selected to
replace him. Sabu eventually relocated to Stockholm and,
with the help of Wilfredo Stephenson, established "Hot
Salsa," the first Latin Jazz band in that city. One needs only
to hear the band's fourth LP, *Hot Salsa Meets Swedish Jazz,*
to recognize the Pozo/Gillespie legacy. In 1990, Eva Svens-
son, a Swedish woman who had studied conga-drumming in
Cuba, returned to Stockholm and organized a Latin Jazz
band called "Hatuey."

Jan Hartong, a Dutch resident of Rotterdam, organized a
band in 1982, specializing in a "Latin jazz synthesis." After
playing within a salsa dance music mode for several years,
the band reverted to its former style and changed its name to
the "Nueva Manteca Latin Jazz Septet." Hartong asserted
that all of their recordings were dedicated "to the memory of
the great Cubop pioneers." This development in the Netherlands gives further proof of the impact of the early musical
collaboration that took place between Cubans and Americans in New York City, an impact variously referred to as
Cubop, Latin Jazz, and Afro-Cuban jazz.

In concluding, it can be said that although various writers
call this genre of music by different names and assert that it
is a "mix", "blending," or "fusion", what is actually being
discussed is *musical transculturation*. It has seemingly never

been compared with a well-defined musical model, an "ideal type," in order to judge its authenticity. At the moment, it is uncritically accepted as a musical fact. This uncritical acceptance lies at the heart of the Barretto-Salazar controversy. While each party to this controversy makes a strong case for his own point of view, the issue of transculturational authenticity is overlooked. Consequently, one is led to ask what indeed are the ideal parameters of an Afro-Cuban/jazz "fusion" and how well does the present-day music by that name measure up to it. When these questions are answered, we will clearly understand whether we are listening to Afro-Cuban Jazz or simply jazz. We will then be able to place a crown on either Salazar's head or that of Barretto's. Until that time, the controversy will simply remain: "Latin Jazz, Afro-Cuban Jazz, or Just Plain Ol' Jazz?"

NOTES

1. Max Salazar, "Afro-Cuban History," *Latin Beat* 2, no. 2: 20–25.
2. Fernando Ortiz, *Los Instrumentos de la Musica Afrocubano* (Havana: Ministerio de Educación, 1952–56).
3. Marshall Stearns, *The Story of Jazz* (New York: Oxford University Press, 1960), p. 173.
4. *Story of Jazz,* p. 179.
5. *Story of Jazz,* p. 182.
6. John Storm Roberts, *The Latin Tinge* (Tivoli, New York: Original Music, 1984), p. 113.
7. *Latin Tinge,* p. 126.
8. Dizzy Gillespie (with Al Fraser), *To Be or Not to Bop* (New York: Da Capo Press, 1979), p. 323.

PHOTO GALLERY:
MITCHELL SEIDEL

Mitchell Seidel began photographing jazz musicians in earnest while a student at New York University in the 1970s. A self-taught photographer, he has more than fifty magazine and album covers to his credit and is regularly published in *Down Beat, Jazz Times,* and *Swing Journal* (Japan). Many other periodicals have published his photos, including the *New York Times, Village Voice, Black Enterprise, Jazz Forum* (Poland), and *Rimshot* (Germany).

Seidel photographs in varied settings: posed portraits, live performances, and backstage or rehearsal candids. He credits a number of earlier lensmen as major influences:

> I remember looking at all those old Impulse albums and seeing Chuck Stewart's name. I was thrilled to finally meet him, and I consider it an honor every time I'm working beside him at a jazz festival.
>
> Another person I consider an influence is Raymond Ross. Self-taught photographers like me usually gain insight by picking peoples' brains, and Ray has always been generous with knowledge gleaned from years in the business.
>
> Oddly enough, my favorite book of jazz photographs was produced by Dennis Stock, a man not particularly well known for photographing musicians. However, his 1960 collaboration with Nat Hentoff, *Jazz Street,* remains the standard by which I judge all others.
>
> Among my contemporaries, I consider W. Patrick Hinely my favorite photographer. He's got a very individual style and a collection of images I wish I had shot myself.
>
> I'm also grateful to Jack Kleinsinger, a producer who generously allowed me to shoot his concerts at New York University when I was a student, and to Mark

Morganelli, with whom I've worked on countless occasions.

Seidel's photographs have appeared in many exhibits, including shows at Lincoln Center in New York City, the New Jersey State Museum, and two annual "Jazz Photo" exhibits in Europe, one of which toured Poland, the Netherlands, and Switzerland, the other Poland and Germany. His awards include a fellowship from the New Jersey State Council on the Arts; a grand prize at "Jazz Photo 1988" in Europe; and two Outstanding Service awards from the International Association of Jazz Educators.

The photographs on these pages date from the mid-1970s to the late 1980s, most of them taken in the New York area. Seidel usually uses an old model Canon F-1; for some more recent photos he has used a Pentax 645.

Top: Stan Getz
Bottom: Miles Davis

Dexter Gordon and son Benji

ORGANIZED SOUND: PITCH-CLASS RELATIONS IN THE MUSIC OF ORNETTE COLEMAN

By Steven Block

More than 30 years have passed since Ornette Coleman made his historic debut at the Five Spot night club in New York City. Coleman, along with Cecil Taylor and John Coltrane, helped to forge a new era in which the harmonic, rhythmic, and timbral freedoms that emerged changed the nature of jazz in a manner which parallels the great changes in western concert music at the turn of the century. Considering the importance of Coleman's work, however, the number of musical analyses of Coleman compositions or of other composers of "free jazz" are relatively few, and these analyses rarely transcend the initial analytical commentary made by Gunther Schuller, who sponsored Coleman in the 1960s, or by Ekkehard Jost, who in 1974 wrote the seminal work on "free jazz."[1]

The term "free jazz," comes from Ornette Coleman's landmark album of the same title,[2] in which two quartets carried out a 36-minute improvisation utilizing nontonal material with neither the benefit of a fixed meter (though there is a steady beat) nor, in all cases, fixed entries of the ensemble.[3] Unfortunately, the term has become as much a misnomer as the term "atonality" which has been used, often in a deprecatory manner, to describe twentieth century music of the formative period. It is clear that Free Jazz is *not* a music of total freedom, relying on such techniques as developing variation and the derivation of pitch material from pitch-class sets which are *not* necessarily tonal.

Using two compositions by Coleman that were written twelve years apart and in supposedly different stylistic

periods, it can be illustrated that Coleman's pitch organization is very sophisticated: an organization that cannot be
understood by simply referring to the harmonic underpin-
nings of more tonal sections or by referring to a process
whereby the performer invents motives that are independent
of a theme and develops them in a free associative manner.[4]

As in analyses of earlier twentieth century music, set-
theoretical tools prove to be very useful in the analysis of free
jazz. This is consistent with the fact that jazz evolved from a
music based primarily on chords and chord changes, while
set-theoretic analysis often involves the classification of pitch
structures which may also fall into the category of chords. In
Coleman's case, though this is not always true of all free jazz
composers, notably Cecil Taylor and Anthony Braxton, the
surface of the music is diatonic and a tonal description of the
music can sometimes be considered. This duality helped to
lead to some of the more vicious criticisms of Coleman,
which implied that Coleman could not improvise well or that
his improvisations were meaningless.[5] Since the surface of
the music contained recognizable diatonic elements which
were not functional, it was not surprising that those looking
for traditional elements would find the music incomprehen-
sible.

"Lonely Woman' and "Street Woman"[6] were both performed by Ornette Coleman, alto sax; Don Cherry, trumpet;
Charlie Haden, bass; and Billy Higgins, drums.

"STREET WOMAN"

The transcription of the theme of "Street Woman," along
with some cursory analysis, can be found in Example 1a.
(The original key is G-minor. Due to equipment problems,
the discussion and examples are in A^b minor.) The theme has
been divided into phrase units formed by Coleman's own
pauses in the piece, and these are labeled in the example.
The most obvious surface characteristic is that of the
descending three-note motive whose outside interval spans a
minor third, major third, or perfect fourth. This derives from
the initial statement where two quick ascending three-note

Example 1a: Street Woman—Theme, Shown with Melodic Pcset
Segmentation by Phrase (Originally in G-Minor; transcribed by S. Block)

motives are introduced. Except for phrases 4 through 6, which are sequential, the three-note motive is quite varied in total pitch content since of the seven remaining three-note phrases, six different trichords or three-note chord types are used.

The theme of "Street Woman" is a good example of the way Coleman mixes diatonic and chromatic elements in his music, coupled with the saturation of a few pitch-class sets.

In both this piece and "Lonely woman," larger sets which include chromatic subsets, particularly the chromatic 4-1 tetrachord, come into play.[7] The most important set of this type shown here is the 6z3 set which can be conceived of as a chromatic tetrachord and dyad a whole-tone apart (Example 1b); 6z3 has an important role as a kind of source set for this composition which cannot be found on the surface of the piece.

The total pitch content of the bass line in the theme is this 6z3 set, the main feature being the initial descent from G^b to E^b (mm. 1–4), since this is separated from the rest of the bass line by the alternation in the middle of the theme of an E^b and E-natural pedal before the final descent to C. Clearly, A^b minor is implied by both the opening and the dominant pedal, but at the same time this is undercut by the fact that the bass line descends only to the major third degree, C-natural, rather than C^b and the tonic, A^b, is not strongly enunciated.

The upper voices, alto sax and pocket trumpet, work together in strong harmonic bond. Following the phrasing as marked in the score, the first two phrases form a diatonic subset of the natural minor, scale-degrees 7 through 5, or 6–32, the "diatonic" hexachord. The third phrase features three accidentals, raised third, sixth, and seventh, but the total pitch content of this phrase is still a transposition by a minor third of the 6–32 diatonic set (Example 2a). We can thus analytically describe the first system in the upper voices as being a melodic declaration of a set (phrase 1), followed by a *verticalization* of the same pitch material (phrase 2), followed by a new arrangement of a transposition of the same pitch material (phrase 3). The important distinction here is that the third phrase does not follow directly from the previous phrase in a manner which might be expected from a superficial variation of material such as a chain-association. Its complete motivic derivation can be found only by examining pitch-class transformation, which in turn points to the use of the classic techniques of intervallic manipulation (transposition, retrogression, and inversion) by the improvisors.

While phrases 4–6 in the winds are sequential, they are

only sequential in the sense of pitch-class transposition, and not in the sense of direct pitch transposition (Example 2b). All six melodic lines form the 3–2 trichord, semitone plus whole-tone, and as a tonal unit, each phrase forms the 5-10 pentachord, a chord which is not diatonic and which is a subset of the 6z3 hexachord (the subset is literal in the fifth phrase). This is far from trivial since the exact rendering of the trichord is different from phrase to phrase (the fourth phrase is represented as descending minor second followed by descending major second; the fifth and sixth phrases are represented as descending major second followed by a descending minor second). The harmonic content of the winds in the fourth phrase, then, is a 5–10 pentachord which is followed in the fifth phrase by an inversion of that pentachord, and then a transposition down a minor third of the fifth phrase. The structure thus revealed shows that Coleman uses the same pitch-class operation on both diatonic 6–32 and chromatic 5–10 sets in contiguous passages (T9, down a mi. 3). This implies a way of thinking which is intervallically based and based on pitch-class operations (it is not significant whether the operations are intuitive or improvised). Not only is the same 5–10 set produced harmonically in the winds at each phrase, but across phrases 4–6 (see Example 1, second system), the trumpet and alto sax each form a different linear 5–10 set as well, the alto forming the set whose pitch content is that of the harmonic content of phrase 6 while the trumpet forms the set whose pitch content is that of the harmonic content of phrase 5. Thus, this single five-note chord appears in three different and related versions and saturates three phrases both linearly and harmonically. There can be no question that a choice is being made here by Coleman: if, for instance, Coleman began phrase 5 on F-natural instead of F^b, all the harmonic associations would still be present but the essential linear connection across phrases 4–6 would be destroyed.

The seventh phrase literally reiterates the diatonicism of the opening in that the three-note phrase here, while not exact, certainly implies both by rhythm and pitch, a retrogression of the first part of the second phrase, both units forming the A^b minor seventh chord.

The last three trichord motives are included as a single phrase, phrase 8, because there is an acceleration at this point, with little space between the motives. The entire phrase consists of a chromatic 7–4 set, in which the last six notes form the same 6z3 hexachord that makes up the total content of the bass material for the entire theme (Example 2c). It is important to note the chromatic content of this set because, while it could be construed as tonal in cases where the root, third, and fifth, of a minor or major triad were being chromatically decorated, this is not the case here. The hexachord's outer pitches, too, serve to bring to the ear a sense of aural condensation of the bass line since this hexachord too spans the G^b-C interval.

A brief digression is necessary in order to make one final point about the theme and this 7–4 set; the implications of the following are great for the analysis of free jazz. Henry Martin and Robert Morris[8] have shown that the most common chord progression in tonal jazz, that of the downward circle of fifths, has a function which is equivalent to a chord progression based upon a root movement of a descending chromatic scale. In particular, Morris and Martin both point out that the specific operation of mapping the two circles and transposition by the tritone describes common jazz chord substitutions. If one starts with a bass line whose root movement is a descending fifth, constructs an incomplete dominant seventh above the line, and then has each line similarly move by downward fifth motion, the result, above the bass, is the same as if one starts with a descending chromatic scale and similarly constructs a V7 above it (Example 3a). The same relationship holds true for the construction of the ^{b}9th above a descending chromatic bass or one built on descending fifths. This paradigm helps to explain why the substitution of ^{b}II7 for V7, commonly known as the tritone substitution, is so prevalent in tonal jazz. But, as Morris and Martin also point out, the example also illustrates an operation which has been expounded by Henry Weinberg, Hubert Howe, and many others, as a twelve-tone operation in addition to transposition and inversion. The *multiplicative* operation maps the circle of fifths onto the chromatic scale (or vice versa), sometimes changing the

Example 1b: Chromatic Segmentation of the 6z3 Hexachord

Example 2a: Operation on 6–32 in Phrases 1–3

Example 2b: Operation on 4–10 in Phrases 4–6

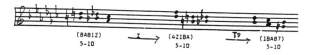

Example 2c: 7–4 Chord in Prime Form and
as Played by Coleman in Phrase 7

Example 3a: Chord Substitution: The Mapping of the Circle
of Fifths onto the Chromatic Scale

Example 3b: Multiplication Operations Mapping 7–29 Pitch Content
in Phrase 2 to 7–4 Pitch Content in Phrase 8

specific intervallic relationships while preserving contour. In tonal jazz, then, there is a specific application of this mapping, the T6MI mapping (multiplication by 7 and transposition by tritone). An additional feature of this operation, which is important in jazz, is the fact that a diatonic pitch-class set will be often be mapped onto a chromatic set.

The last phrase of the theme of Ornette Coleman's "Street Woman" forms a 7–4 chromatic set which is related by this circle-of-fifths mapping to the pitch content of the second phrase without the pickup, a phrase which forms a 7–29 chord and which is specifically related to the final phrase by the T8MI operation, which can be understood as transposition up eight semitones, followed by multiplication by 7 (Example 3b).[9] Thus, there is a neat summing up in the final measures of the theme: the last phrase is directly related to the opening in that a diatonic set is mapped onto a chromatic one, and the same final phrase includes the pitch material of the entire bass line.

The coda is included here to show that though the theme is repeated several times throughout the piece, only the final iteration moves to the clear A^b minor tonality. The final pitch, F-natural, somewhat of a spicy aural surprise, changes the pitch content of the tonic triad with added second to a 5-29 pentachord, one which is a literal subset of the 7–29 chord in the second phrase and an abstract complement (Example 3c).[10] Thus, even the final note, which is analogous to moments in many jazz pieces which end on a dissonance, provides an important structural grounding.

The first two sections of Ornette Coleman's solo in "Street Woman" are excellent examples of how important set relations may exist even within what appears to be a straightforward diatonic language (Example 4). One diffi-

Example 3c: Relationship of Coda to Phrase 2

culty with analysis of this music in the past has been the neglect of the vertical in transcriptions. The vast majority of transcriptions have followed the earlier practice of a music based upon chord changes; often only a single melodic line is transcribed. Some of Coleman's solos, as well as those of other free jazz practitioners like Coltrane, often appear with implied harmonies written above the solo in letter notation. This does a disservice to such music in which there may not be prescribed chord changes. Coleman's performance of "Street Woman," is really not so much a solo as it is two-part counterpoint with the bass. It is therefore necessary to have an entire score at one's disposal in order to understand both pitch structure and the ensemble idea which is such an important part of free jazz.[11]

Viewing the melodic line alone in the first two sections, the tonal implications are quite clear. The key is now the parallel major and no nonharmonic tones are heard in the first section in either saxophone or bass. Ornette projects a clear voice-leading background (see score, Example 4), with the first section of his improvisation centering around a third descent from the mediant to the tonic. The initial C-natural is prolonged through the beginning of the second phrase over an arpeggiation of the tonic triad, then locally descends in m. 4 to B^b when the motion of the dotted rhythmic figure speeds up, and the descent to B^b is accompanied by an octave span. B^b returns in the original register in m. 7 and this time the descent is that of a sixth to D^b, D^b in turn answered an octave above in the opening register and as an upper neighbor resolving to C in m. 10. A local descent to A^b then occurs before the final descent at the end of the chorus.

This description of a voice-leading middleground suffices to describe a simple strategy that may underly Coleman's solo. Yet here, too, important pitch-class relations can be found that are not adequately described above. Again, the sets chosen in Example 4 are sets that are enunciated by the phrasing of the music itself, the simplest rationale for segmentation. The 6z25 set that is heard in the bass in mm. 5–7, for instance, is a set that is marked off by the pauses surrounding the material. It is also true that this set accounts for all the bass's pitch material up to the final phrase. In that

Example 4: "Street Woman"—Coleman's Solo with Bass Part; Sections 1 and 2 and Opening of Section 3 (Transcribed by S. Block)

final phrase, however, while the pitch material for the bass changes, Coleman takes over the same pitch-classes of the 6z25 set which have been heard in the bass up to that moment (fourth system, Example 4). Haden's accompaniment, however, is another different 6z25 set, the only other possible set that can be derived from diatonic A^b major material.

Here is a case where the scale has been clearly segmented into these two diatonic sets of the exact same intervallic structure. There are seven possible six-note subsets of the A^b major scale, so that a clear compositional choice is being made here. 6z25 is the M-related set to 6z3, the set that had importance, among other things, as the bass line of the theme

Example 4 (continued)

which immediately precedes this first chorus. One can take the position that this is simply a fortuitous occurrence, but that position would deny the musicianship that enables Coleman and Haden to hear these strong relationships. It is clear that, earlier in the century, Schoenberg did not formulate for many years the structural concepts already present in his music. Thus, if nontonal pitch-class relations were eminently hearable by the master composer Schoenberg, we may assemble that such relations were hearable, also without being formulated, by the master improvisor Coleman.

At the beginning of the second section of Coleman's solo, there is a sense of a chromatic language, as Coleman exploits chromatic upper and lower neighbors to the tonic A^b, which is later transformed back to the diatonic realm. Nevertheless, the counterpoint features a chromatic walking bass, even when the A^b key area is returned to by Ornette in mm. 23–24. After the return to A^b, Ornette moves to a four-note figure which is permuted four times in the chorus and even in the next chorus, further developed and expanded within five-note sets. The motivic nature of the latter part of the solo is clear, but the relation between harmony and counterpoint in this section is more extraordinary. The first four notes of the descent from A^b at the return of the key in m. 24 form a diatonic 4–22 tetrachord which is related to the underlying bass notes (forming a 4–2 tetrachord), spread over the next three measures by the multiplicative operation. Likewise, when Coleman begins the development of a four-note diatonic figure in m. 26, the bass plays a whole-tone figure which is developed further into a chromatic tetrachord, which is itself related by the multiplicative operation to the motive Ornette is enunciating.

The specific operation which maps melody and counterpoint is T$_8$MI, the same operation for both sets in this passage and the same operation which mapped the final phrase of the theme to the second phrase of the theme earlier (Example 3b). While the performers were probably dealing with the idea of permuting a limited number of note choices, this cannot be construed as accidental. At m. 24–26, for instance, it would be just as logical for the bassist to incorporate G^b into the bass line. At m. 31, F^b would also be logical. Neither choice would disturb the essential nature of the bass line. Yet, neither choice produces the profound network of relationships that were chosen. Thus, we have two performers working two successive four-note permutations in which the specific pitches differ but the relationship between the two parts remains the same.

"LONELY WOMAN"

Coleman's "Lonely Woman," from his 1959 album *The Shape of Jazz to Come,* can be sectioned into the theme,

which is only slightly varied when repeated, a bridge eight
bars long, which is repeated three times, and the solo
sections which encompass Coleman's first solo (22 bars, part
1) until he is joined by Don Cherry for a variation on the
bridge (bridge 2) and a second solo (13 measures).[12] As was
the case in "Street Woman," this piece can be viewed as
tonal, firmly in D-minor (including all forms of the minor),
but this knowledge cannot contribute much to an understanding of how Coleman achieves the heights he does in this
work, though it does express his relationship to jazz's
harmonic past and to jazz's roots in the blues.

Once again, there are a significant number of abstract
relationships which can be found between three pairs of
tetrachordal sets in the theme, which are all related by the
circle-of-fifths mapping common to tonal jazz. What is
astonishing, however, is the fact that all three pairs of sets are
related by the same process, that is, mapping onto the circle
of fifths followed by transposition up a minor third (T3M).
Thus, various parts of the phrases in the theme are intimately
related to each other, even including such surprises as
Coleman's breaking out of the duet structure in m. 15
(Example 5).[13]

Example 6 shows the melodic line of the first bridge and
Coleman's solo, part one, with a segmentation by tetrachord.
In most circumstances, Coleman's own phrasing has been
followed in choosing the segmentation, going beyond phrase
boundaries only when a pitch is needed to complete a
tetrachord within the previous phrase. Once more, the small
number of sets utilized helps project the tautness of the
passage.

In Example 7, the same material has been rearranged to
show the network of relationships that exist between the sets
in this passage. The organization is expressed by operation
first, and then the sets which are related by the operation are
shown in their musical context. Two sets are omitted, 4–10
and 4–3, because they are not reiterated by Coleman in these
two passages.

What emerges from this type of examination is that a small
number of operations can explain how pitches are derived
and often have great musical import. Taking the first case,

Example 5: "Lonely Woman"—Segmentation of Theme (Parentheses
indicate m-related pairs, asterisks indicate T₃M-related sets)

T$_A$MI, one sees and hears a very interesting relationship in
the music where two sets, 4–24 and 4–2, are successively
sounded in the passage (and here the sets are separated by
the phrasing); then later, the order of the set succession is
reversed, and their M-related counterparts are sounded
instead. The aural relationship is particularly keen in this
passage both because of the relationships detailed above and
because of the clear whole-tone elements which make up
4–24.

The T$_3$ relationship comes into play in several places in this
piece as well as operations which may preceed transposition
by a minor third, such as T$_3$M and T$_3$MI. One interesting
passage here based upon this relation features the juxtaposition of two 4–12 sets. This can be seen in the third section of

Example 6: "Lonely Woman"—Segmentation of the Melodic Line of
Bridge and Solo (Part 1) (Paretheses indicate m-related sets)

Example 7. In the music itself, the sound is that of a fragment
which is announced in the first phrase, followed by the
completion of the fragment as it moves to its highest point in
the second phrase. One of the reasons the sound of the two
phrases seems so right here is that both phrases, as they are
being developed within a larger context, are additionally
pitch-class transpositions, and therefore directly related on a
lower hierarchical level as well.

Two notations in part 4 of Example 7 are given which
detail relationships at the moment in the theme when
Coleman and Cherry split the line at a cadence (mm. 13–14,
Example 5). The transposition up or down a perfect fourth or
fifth also is important in this passage, and one striking T_5
relation is formed by the rounding off of the opening of the
first bridge and closing of the first part of Coleman's solo by
two such T_5-related 4–14 sets.

Lastly, this example shows some of the T_0 relations, i.e.,
relations where the same pitch-classes are utilized. These are

Example 7: Some Pitch-Class Relations in Bridge and Solo (Part 1)

Example 7 (continued)

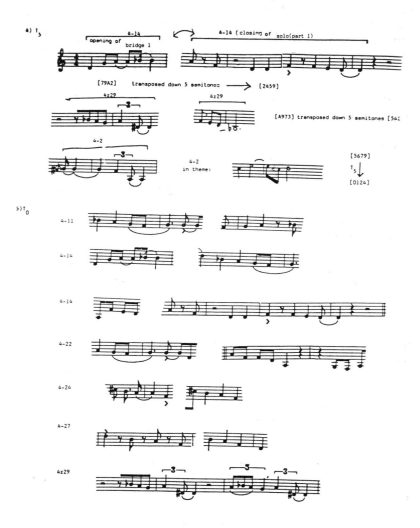

not trivial, since they reaffirm the pitch-class content but not the contour of the music. After all, it is a given that much improvisation will naturally feature reinterpretation and variation of the same pitch material on a clear surface level. In "Street Woman," the permutation was on the surface of the piece at the end of the second part and the opening of the third part of Coleman's solo since this involved successive variations based on four primary pitches. In "Lonely Woman," however, the pitch-class permutations are more subtle, since various sets of pitches, as shown in the fifth part of Example 7, are being permuted at nonadjacent sections of the bridge and opening of Coleman's solo. While it is true that these pitch-classes represent different arrangements of what can be construed as scalar material (save for the flat second) related to d-minor, it is still Coleman's genius which groups some of these tetrachordal segments in the manner that produces the rich relationships detailed above. A random breakdown of the d-minor modes into tetrachords will not produce the same tetrachordal sets with the same frequency or intensity of relationship.

It is fruitful to think about larger pitch-class collections that are formed in this work. Example 8 shows a segmentation of the second bridge and second solo melodic line into larger sets, primarily hexachords.[14] Five of the eight melodic segmentations shown form or include one of the two z-related sets, 6z3 and 6z36.[15] *None of these five sets are duplications, a very clear indication that Coleman must be thinking intervallically as he improvises the line.* If one considers only the diatonic scale (7–35) or the natural minor mode, these hexachords are not included. If one considers d-minor with raised sixth and seventh scale degrees (9–7), there are 42 hexachords, other than 6z3 and 6z36, which are included in this larger set. Many of these have greater odds of occurring randomly than 6z3 or 6z36. In fact, for any such given scale, only one possible 6z3 set would be derivable (three possible 6z36 chords). Thus, given all the modes of the d-minor tonality, Coleman has such a wide number of choices to make, if he is utilizing phrases containing six pitch-classes, that the aural relationships presented here in this improvisation must be considered phenomenal.

Example 8: Segmentation of Melodic Line for Bridge 2 and Solo 2
(Slashes [/] indicate z-related sets (sets with the same intervallic structure);
parentheses indicate m-related sets)

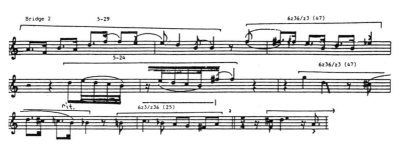

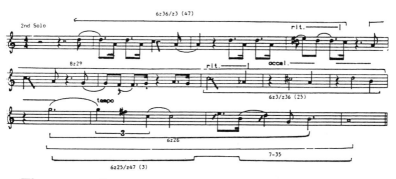

The reason these sets occur here spontaneously is that all three 6z36 sets are related by whole-tone transposition or T_2 (naturally one pair is related by T_4) and the 6z3 pair is also related by T_2. The first 6z3 set which emerges in the fifth segmentation in the third system shown here is related to the 6z25 set shown in the segmentation in the last phrase by T_0M and, in fact, 6z25 can also be considered a superset for the initial five notes. In this section, a pattern of relationships based upon whole-tone transpositions begins to emerge.

The two five-note sets formed here are included in larger sets that have some prominence in the second bridge and second solo material. The first 5–29 set, for instance, is abstractly included in 6z47, a set which is related by the circle of fifths mapping, M, to 6z36. Even more to the point, if F# is added to the 5–29 (it occurs in the next phrase) at the opening of the section, the 6z47 formed would be related to T0MI to the following phrase's 6z36 and T_AMI to the last 6z36 shown in the example. The second pentachord, 5–24, is included in the set 6z26, a set formed by the six notes which precedes the final cadence on A. Specifically, if the pitch-class G is added to the 5–24 shown, and here G is available as the first note of the next phrase, it will form the same pitch-classes sounded at the end of the chorus.

The relationships that are unfolded in this second solo are even more impressive when the harmonic considerations are viewed as has been shown in an earlier article.[16] In the same way that 6z3 and 6z36 sets account for much of the linear structure of Coleman's solo, another pair of related sets, 6z26 and 6z48 (introduced linearly by Coleman at the end of this solo) account for much of the vertical exchange. These relationships are the result of a spontaneous counterpoint where the bass is clearly an independent voice.

SUMMARY

It is important to understand that pitch-class set analysis has been used solely as a tool for understanding some of the relationships that exist in two works by Ornette Coleman, one of which is an acknowledged classic. No assertion has been made that Coleman or any member of his group understood these intervallic relationships in any manner beyond natural and ingenious intuitive construction (although, it is likely that some calculated intellectual understanding existed as well). Set-theoretical analysis has been shown to reveal important new ideas and to model Coleman's compositions in ways which increase our understanding of these works.[17]

In determining that such pitch-class relationships exist in these two compositions of Ornette Coleman's, it has been shown that, while these occur naturally as a result of intervallic transformation, they do not occur by chance. The art of free jazz requires that the improvisors think less in terms of chord changes and more in terms of transforming motives (or chords) which are understood as intervallic events. In Coleman's music, this is harder to grasp because it occurs within a distinctly tonal context. Yet the center of Coleman's genius is not that he simply created a freer rhythmic context for his compositions or sometimes abandoned chord changes in the traditional sense, but that, in eschewing the use of chord changes as a primary basis for improvisation, he applied his considerable improvisational talents to a new manner of variation style based on motivic transformation. This meant that while the listener was hearing such standard chords as a minor seventh, the minor seventh was instead being utilized as an abstract object, not necessarily contextual. The intervallic relationships expressed by such chords as the minor seventh (not its tonal function) became the subject for a Coleman improvisation.[18]

As has also been shown, Coleman went beyond this as well since long-range connections, over the course of a solo or even an entire piece, became an additional concern. Thus, Coleman and other modern giants were hearing pitch-class relationships within the context of their own musical style and history which early 20th century composers, faced with the demise of functional tonality, sought to construct. There is no doubt that Ornette Coleman's entrance into the limelight in 1959 was a singular event in the history of jazz. The deep musical relationships and structures shown here are further testimony to Coleman's highly original and innovative genius.

NOTES

1. Gunther Schuller, *A Collection of the Compositions of Ornette Coleman* (New York: MJQ Music, 1961). Ekkehard Jost, *Free Jazz* (Vienna, Universal, 1974; reprinted by Da Capo.)
2. Ornette Coleman, *Free Jazz* (Atlantic 1364). An alternate take was issued on *Twins*.
3. The term "nontonal" is used here in its strictest sense, referring to common-practice tonality or jazz tonality built on chord changes (though these musics are not equivalent with respect to harmony or voice leading). Thus, the composition "Free Jazz," which is *not* based on chord changes, uses diatonic elements which are developed primarily as motivic

units without harmonic reference and thus would not be considered tonal.

4. The latter process basically defines the term invented by Jost, "motivic chain association," to describe Coleman's music, though Schuller had discussed this earlier.

5. See Schuller's introduction to *A Collection . . .* (cited above), p. 4.

6. Lonely Woman is transcribed from *The Shape of Jazz to Come* (Atlantic 1317), and Street Woman is transcribed from *Science Fiction* (Columbia 31061).

7. The designation "4–1" indicates any transposition of an unordered collection of four pitches, in any octave, with any number of (in this case) successive repetitions which form a chromatic tetrachord. All pitch-class set labeling in this paper utilizes the nomenclature from Robert Morris's *Composition with Pitch Classes: A Theory of Compositional Design* (New Haven: Yale University Press, 1987). Individual pitch classes will be represented by a numeric notation whereby pitch-class "C" = 0, "C#" = 1, "D" = 2. . . ."A" = 9, "A#" = A, and "B" = B. The standard pitch and pitch-class operations of Transposition (T), Inversion (I), Retrogression (R), and Retrogression and Inversion (RI) will be referred to as well as Multiplication (M). Many of the set-theoretic concepts discussed in this paper can be found in Morris's work and in Allen Forte's earlier and seminal work, *The Structure of Atonal Music* (New Haven: Yale University Press, 1973). For a rare use of set-theoretic methodology with jazz, see Jeff Pressing, "Pitch Class Set Structures in Contemporary Jazz" (*Jazzforschung/Jazz Research,* 14, 1983).

8. Robert Morris, review of John Rahn, *Basic Atonal Theory, In Music Theory Spectrum 4* (1982): 152–154. Henry Martin, "Jazz Harmony: A Syntactic Background," *Annual Review of Jazz Studies 4* (1988): 9–30.

9. With the operations performed in this way, MI being equivalent to multiplication by 7, transposition and multiplication can be performed in any order (they are commutative). However, it should be understood that when the operations are separated out, the logical order of operations would be inversion followed by multiplication (by 5) followed by transposition.

10. In dealing with the nomenclature of pitch class sets, the complement of any set (the remaining notes of the twelve-note universe which are not included in the original set), contains the same place in the respective list of sets by that cardinality.

Thus, a seven-note chromatic set, 7–1, would be complemented by the remaining five chromatic notes, which would be named 5–1 since it is a complete five-note chromatic set. Literal complementation exists when the specific remaining notes are present. Thus, a chromatic set, 7–1, whose pitch-classes spanned C–F#, would be a literal complement of the five remaining notes spanning G–B (5–1). An *abstract* complementation would exist, for instance, in a case where a five note-chromatic set (5–1) was included in the original set of seven chromatic notes (7–1). Thus, the notes spanning C–E, C#–F, or D–F# would all represent instances of the set 5–1, an abstract complementation with respect to the 7-note chromatic set spanning all the pitches from C–F#.

11. Regrettably, this paper deals only with pitch relations. However, there are unquestionably important rhythmic-motivic considerations to be examined in this music as well, some of which would likely shed even more light on Coleman's "free" improvisational process. In the author's transcriptions of compositions by Cecil Taylor, for instance, percussion parts are likewise transcribed. For the purposes of this narrow focus, however, the drums have not been included.

12. The form of "Lonely Woman" was enunciated differently in a previous paper (see note 13, below). I am indebted to Lewis Porter, for pointing out a conflict in terms used in that article and thus clarifying the form which is more appropriately explained here.

13. For a further discussion of the theme of "Lonely Woman" and other sections of the composition not included in this paper, see Steven Block, "Pitch-Class Transformation in Free Jazz," *Music Theory Spectrum*, 12/2 (Fall 1990): 181–202. There is wonderful detail present in the theme and elsewhere in the composition.

14. Since the rationale for segmentation has been to stick closely to Coleman's phrasing, in the last two systems of the example, where the phrasing does not break well into hexachordal units, the phrases have been segmented into the sets 8z29, the complement of the very important 4z29 set in this work, and 7–35, which is equivalent to a diatonic scale. Here some of the included hexachords formed by successive pitches are also shown.

15. Z-related sets are pitch-class collections which have the identical interval-class content but which, when reduced to their most compact state within the octave, will not form the same representative pitch classes.

16. See Block, "Pitch-Class Transformation. . . ," p. 200–202.
17. One historical precedent for an analytical tool which does not reflect the composer's manner of composition but is useful in examining vertical sonorities is the use of roman numeral designations, an idea that didn't come to the fore until the "classical" period of music was almost spent. Thus, we can examine a verticality in a composition by Bach as a V6 chord knowing full well that Bach did not think of that sonority as a V6 chord.
18. This, of course, is similar to the manner in which Stravinsky led the neoclassic movement in the earlier part of the century, in which tonality is treated as a static object rather than functional harmonic system.

WORDS AND MUSIC
BY ARTHUR TAYLOR

By Bonnie L. Johnson

On Saturday August 4, 1990 alto saxophonist Jackie McLean took center stage at Alice Tully Hall in New York City. The program that evening honored his immense talent as a composer as well as an intrumentalist and presented his music in a variety of settings. A quartet with Arthur Taylor on drums backed a series of guest musicians, including Curtis Fuller, Benny Golson, Wynton Marsalis, and Wallace Roney. On the following Tuesday, Peter Watrous's glowing review of the concert appeared in the New York Times. A portion of it read:

> . . . But as well as the guests played, it was Mr. Taylor who defined this section of the concert. Mr. Taylor is among jazz's finest drummers, and he made every soloist better, making sure they arrived at logical peaks during their improvisations, urging them on, dictating the form of the pieces, . . . creating a narrative that constantly unfolded. It was the sort of virtuosic performance that seemed heroic, and the concert achieved an intensity it never recaptured and probably couldn't have sustained.

On three separate occasions,[1] I had the opportunity to conduct interviews with Arthur Taylor in an attempt to glean insights more personal and substantial and therefore more meaningful than those found in previous articles about him. It isn't that abridged versions of biographical information abound and need fleshing out. Quite the contrary and more to the point, his achievements have been diminished by nonrecognition. That he spent 17 years away from the U.S. may account for some of this neglect. Perhaps being younger than Max Roach, Art Blakey, and Philly Joe Jones pushed him out of the limelight. Or maybe the importance of his style in the historical scheme of jazz drumming has yet to be borne out. Whatever the reason, surely any musician whose playing can be heard on nearly three hundred recordings[2]— many of them classics and made in the heyday of the bebop movement and with the leading contributors of the idiom— deserves more.

I consider myself privileged and fortunate to have come to know Arthur Taylor. A lesson I took with him at the suggestion of Jackie McLean three summers ago provided me with a first-hand glimpse of his approach to playing the drums. The telephone conversations we had in preparation for this article were illuminating.

What I have attempted to present here is a two-dimensional view of Arthur Taylor: first, a biographical montage drawn from more than four hours of taped conversation; second, musical examples of two contrasting solos— one a blues at a moderate tempo, the other an extended introduction played considerably faster, both representative of his style when recording with John Coltrane in the late fifties.

THE FORMATIVE YEARS

Arthur Taylor was born on April 6, 1929, in the Sugar Hill section of Harlem, a veritable breeding ground for jazz players. Although he was always an avid music fan, his early life does not reveal those oft-heard stories of the prodigious child who beats on pots and pans in a desperate effort to express himself. Instead, Arthur showed considerable athletic prowess and possessed what he and family members felt were "razor sharp reflexes" on which he had hoped to capitalize.

> I loved track and basketball but what I really loved most was baseball. I had hoped for a career as a professional baseball player but my father said "No, that's no livelihood." Because at that time there were no teams that allowed blacks.

Becoming a jazz musician may not have been the preferred career for Arthur but his father (who is from Belize, then British Honduras) had an interest in music that influenced the young boy.

> My father used to take me to the Apollo Theatre to see people like Billie Holiday, John Kirby, and Duke Ellington. And then I started going downtown to the Paramount to see people like Tommy Dorsey and Charlie Barnet, Sinatra, and groups like that. On Wednesday the show changed at the Paramount and on Friday the show changed at the Apollo. So on Wednesday and Friday I didn't go to school. Nobody would.

Arthur took up playing the drums at the age of 18 or 19, considered late by most standards and admittedly so by Arthur.

> I started very, very late but I always loved music, *always*. I just wanted to learn and I got a practice pad and started going for lessons in the Bronx. I took lessons from a man by the name of Aubrey Brooks, who was really a taskmaster. He couldn't stand me because I wasn't as conscientious as he would like his students to be. He started me out first of all singing. I had to sing notes and so forth. He was getting me into reading, which I really didn't want to be bothered with. I wanted to *play*. Like he was always saying, "You're putting the cart before the horse. You learn this, then you'll be able to do that," which is correct, but when you're young, you cast it aside because you have your own method which you think is right.

Obviously, this teacher/student relationship was not a match made in heaven.

> I didn't study with him long. He got bored with me. He was quite a disciplinarian, which didn't work. Our manners were a little different. It was interesting, though, because later on, when I became professional and started doing gigs and became a little well known, I would meet him and he was amazed that I was able to do it without doing that study.

Taylor was almost 21 years old when he received his first drumset and began performing shortly thereafter.

> My mother bought me a drum set in 1949. That was for Christmas, and in January I started working. We started out in a Catholic church. We used to play on Friday evenings for the kids to dance. That was the St. Charles Church which is in the neighborhood more or less where I live now—140th or 141st near Lenox Ave. We were playing with Sonny [Rollins] and Jackie [McLean], and others would alternate on that job.

It was a stellar beginning for Arthur Taylor, cutting his teeth with neighborhood chums like Jackie McLean, Sonny Rollins and Kenny Drew. As he puts it, "These guys were geniuses. Even when they were young their talents were highly developed."

Arthur cites several drummers as early influences. Some were on the scene at the time, such as Max Roach, Art Blakey, and Philly Joe Jones. Some were from his Apollo Theatre/Paramount days, such as Gene Krupa, Chick Webb, and Buddy Rich. Imbued with a strong sense of "swing" even at this seminal stage of his career, he corroborates the high regard held by all drummers for Buddy Rich.

> The only white bands that could play the Apollo Theatre—because the audiences were really hard— were Buddy Rich and Charlie Barnet, who had a big hit with "Redskin Rhumba" that everyone liked. When I saw Buddy Rich, I can still visualize it in my mind. He had a broken arm, one arm in a cast and a sling, and he played the *whole* show. I mean, you know, with dancers and comedians, and he's got to make these cues and these accents and everything. It was *unbelievable*. He played the whole show and then played a big solo that broke the place down . . . with just his right hand. I said "Yeah, I think I'd like to try that."

But it was J.C. Heard, the drummer for John Kirby, who affected Arthur's playing the most profoundly.

> After seeing Buddy and Krupa, then I heard J.C. Heard. He was really my idol. I fell in love when I saw

him. He was the one who really inspired me, starting
out that is. It was the way he played the cymbals. The
way he could swing. You know, he could swing so
much. He had a really beautiful beat.

CAREER HIGHLIGHTS: 1950–1963

Almost all successful musicians tell of turning points in life
which acted as a catalyst in their careers. Often sounding like
fairy tales, with immediate and rewarding results, these tales
can be misleading. Taylor's episode illustrates this well. In
1950, Oscar Pettiford, arguably the most important and
influential bassist after Jimmy Blanton, gave Arthur his first
real opportunity by hiring him to be part of his trio along with
pianist Wynton Kelly.

> The first break I really got was in 1950 when I went with
> Oscar Pettiford, the great bassist, to Chicago. It was
> also with him that I made my first record date. We went
> into the studio and we made 36 takes of "Love for
> Sale." If somebody calls "Love For Sale" today, I
> cringe. There was a part I couldn't get, I just couldn't
> get it. There was some certain rhythm that was going on
> that I couldn't grasp at the time. It was tricky and I
> didn't have enough experience. I was so nervous and
> getting worse. I was in a state of shock. And every time
> I played it, it got worse and worse and worse. We made
> 36 takes and then got in the car and drove to Chicago.
> So that's about 10 hours in the studio and then off to
> Chicago. It was traumatic.[3]

It was during this three-week engagement in Chicago that
Arthur met for the first time many of the musicians who
would later become his colleagues.

> We went to the South Central Hotel [in Chicago] where
> Dizzy Gillespie's band was staying. Coltrane and
> Jimmy Heath and Specs Wright and Milt Jackson and
> all those people were in Dizzy's band and I met them
> right then and there. I can't remember where Dizzy was
> playing, but my last set was over before his, so I'd run

and catch about a half hour of his last show. It was very exciting. That's where I met Coltrane.

He also got a glimpse of a remarkable drummer whose name not many people will recognize and I suspect only a few ever heard.

> Sonny Rollins was there at the time too, and that's when I heard the great drummer Ike Day, who was working in the trio with Sonny Rollins and the piano player, Vernon Bivel. Ike Day is the baddest in the history. Art Blakey and Max Roach used to tell me about him. He was the heaviest of any of the drummers. He was a terrible dope fiend and he just died young. Unbelievable! When I heard him, I had to revamp my thinking. I thought about giving up music right then and there. He sounded like Buddy Rich, Tony Williams, Art Blakey, Max Roach, and Kenny Clarke, and all of them rolled into one. I'm telling you, I never heard anything like that in the history of music. In my experience I never heard anyone play that much drums. He could *swing*—he could swing you into bad health and he could solo like Buddy Rich and Tony Williams or Philly Joe and do all kinds of things—unbelievable. It was shocking.

Through most of 1950 and into 1951 Arthur worked with the Pettiford Trio. The young drummer was in awe of Pettiford and attests to his greatness.

> He could play the bass like Charlie Parker could play the saxophone, with that beautiful tone. The first record I ever made was with Oscar Pettiford playing cello. The way he sounded on cello is the way bass players sound today. I swear it's true. You'll hear the record and you'll know what I'm talking about, ting, ting, ting, ting, instead of boom, boom, boom, boom.[4]

After his stint with Pettiford, Taylor performed and recorded with Coleman Hawkins and his quintet which included Harry "Sweets" Edison, Tommy Potter, and Kenny Drew. He stayed with Hawkins through 1951, garnering a lot of road experience touring the Northeast, Midwest, and Canada.

> I was with Coleman Hawkins all of '51—the end of '50 through all of '51. Then Max Roach got me the job with Bud Powell, which is what I always wanted. I replaced Max. He was working a lot with Charlie Parker, and he was ready to form his own group so he recommended me to Bud.

As a youngster, Taylor had tagged along with Jackie McLean. They used to hang out at Bud's house and the pianist "took us under his wing . . . we were his protégés . . . he used to stick up for us if people teased us." Taylor considered Powell his mentor—even more than he did any drummer. The single most important musical event in Arthur Taylor's life was his association with the piano genius.

> The main ambition of my whole life was to play with Bud Powell. I stayed with him for three years straight—longer than I've ever stayed with anybody. Bud was *IT*—drummers and all. I adored him. I admired his music. I use his rhythmic patterns to this day. I base my rhythm off Bud Powell. I don't tell everybody this—but anyway, everybody wouldn't even know how to figure it out, you know. I still will listen to him: I'll put on one of his old records and hear some of those rhythms, and I'll use them just to see how I can duplicate them on the drum. It's very interesting. It's a different type of study.

Taylor spent the remainder of the fifties in a whirlwind of recording activity, playing on over two hundred albums. To say he was in demand is an understatement. By his own accounts, he often felt overworked and expresses incredulity at the thought of ever being able to have accomplished so much: "I may be 62 but I feel like 128. I could *never, would never* do that again."

A partial list of the artists that retained his services includes Charlie Parker, Thelonious Monk, Gene Ammons, Jackie McLean, Miles Davis, Sonny Rollins, John Coltrane, Donald Byrd, Red Garland, Gigi Gryce, J.J. Johnson, and

Mal Waldron. Taylor confesses that he was disturbed with the animosity directed towards him by certain musicians who complained about his doing "the bulk of the record dates." He went to Coltrane, who told him plainly, "I use you because you don't get in the way."

With so many excellent cuts to chose from it is the track "A Glass Enclosure"[5] made with Bud Powell that is Taylor's personal favorite ("It's almost more a classical piece than jazz.")[6] Also making Taylor's top ten list are those dates he made with Jackie McLean—*456* especially; *Hope Meets Foster* with Elmo Hope and Frank Foster; and several with Coltrane, in particular *Soultrane*, *Traneing-In*, and *Bahia*. Ironically, *Giant Steps* is one of his least favorites, not so much because of his playing, but because of the poor sound quality.

> I can hardly stand to listen to it. The sound is so high and tinny. This was at Atlantic and they ruined my sound. Not like for Prestige at Rudy Van Gelder's, where it was basically a live sound with only one or two mikes. I like recording live. *You* have control over your sound. With all those mikes, the engineer can fool with and mess up your balance.

Two albums with Miles Davis make his list as well: *Milt and Miles* with vibist Milt Jackson, bassist Percy Heath, pianist Ray Bryant, and alto saxophonist Jackie McLean, and the great orchestral album Gil Evans arranged, *Miles Ahead*. An intimidated Taylor wished he had studied harder as a youngster.

> When you get into large orchestras it [reading] is necessary. But even so, like when I was making that record with Miles Davis, *Miles Ahead*, Gil Evans had this music that had to have *three* music stands to hold it up. I saw that thing when I walked in the studio and I said 'Oh my God, how am I going to deal with this?' Miles looked at it, walked over and took the music and threw it on the floor. He said "I just want you to play what you feel." I was relieved. At the time he had all those great studio musicians there—people like Bernie

Glow and Ernie Royal and the heavy guy, Lee
Konitz—oh so many excellent musicians.

Miles had a special regard for Taylor and on more than one
occasion in his recent autobiography he comments on the
drummer's sensitivity.[7] Although they had their differences,
their relationship was one of great mutual respect and
admiration—and protected egos.

This is Taylor's account of the night he walked out on
Davis:

> I got angry. We were playing at the Bohemia Club and
> the place was packed—lines around the block and all
> my friends from Uptown were there. And even though
> I played with Bud Powell and Charlie Parker—Miles
> has another kind of charisma you know. He used to
> make me nervous anyway because he would stand there
> and watch me all the time when he finished his solo.
> And I said "Man, why don't you take a walk or
> something, you're making me nervous." He would
> stand there, and he would make comments. He made
> one comment and I said "Yeah." I cursed him out and
> walked off the bandstand, and I say it's the only time I
> saw Red Garland when he couldn't figure out what was
> happening. But the beautiful thing about it—there was
> never anything ever said about it—it never changed
> *anything* about anything. *Miles* never mentioned it
> again; *I* never mentioned it. Other people talk about it.

They certainly do. Drummer Keith Copeland quipped that it
was the only time that anybody ever out-Milesed Miles.

The collaboration of percussionists on Art Blakey's *Orgy
in Rhythm* albums has a special place in Arthur's heart
because of the mutual respect among these drummers.

> It was very exciting doing the *Orgy in Rhythm* albums.
> A series of maybe three albums with Art Blakey where
> he had Philly Joe Jones and old Jo Jones and a host of
> great musicians. We just went into the studio. I had just
> come back from Europe one night before. And the
> phone rings and who is it but Art, and he says "I got a
> record date tonight, get your drums and get down

here." Blue Note records had hired an enormous ballroom on the upper West Side. And I guess Art went to Spanish Harlem and picked guys up off the street; guys were banging on books or bongos, whatever. They had the tympani, and it was a very thrilling setting because Art was in the center of this enormous hall, and they had all of us around him—Philly Joe and Jo Jones and Specs Wright and they had the tympani, the gongs, and the congas. That's one record that I like because it's not dated; it could have been made yesterday, maybe because it's all percussion. They are outstanding records and I enjoyed them. I can put them on and I still enjoy them. That was really a great experience.

So great in fact that it inspired Taylor to organize an annual drumfest.

I used to do Gretsch Night at Birdland. Once every year. And that was with the guys that were using Gretsch: Max Roach, Philly Joe Jones, Charli Persip, Elvin Jones, who else? Well, that's enough right there. But there used to be six of us on the stage. Good God almighty! That was really too much. Can you imagine playing on the same stage with Elvin and Max and Art Blakey and Philly Joe and Charlie Persip? That's too heavy. Just the drums.

EUROPEAN INTERLUDE: 1963–1980

In 1963, Taylor went on a European tour with Johnny Griffin. ("I left for a three-week engagement and ended up staying for 17 years!") As the civil rights movement gained momentum and was giving way to major sociological and cultural changes, an increasing number of African-American artists were making Europe their home.

The same thing exists all over the planet you know. But it's a little more moderate over there. The people are not as—well, they've been through wars and they've suffered quite a bit, so they have a little more compassion, a little human compassion. They told me, especially the older people, what they went through during Hitler's occupation in Paris and so forth. It was really horrible. People here don't know about those things. They'd act in a different manner if they had experienced them.

For ten years he lived in France and for seven years in Belgium. Bop may have had its last hurrah in the U.S. but it was thriving in Paris, and Taylor performed frequently with Dexter Gordon and Johnny Griffin, as well as with touring American musicians.

Europe offered more than just a release from heightened racial tensions and the security of performing for appreciative audiences; it provided a respite from the frenetic pace Taylor kept up in the States. Thus, he had an opportunity to do a few things he probably would not have done had he never left New York. First and foremost, he continued to develop as a drummer.

> J.C. Heard came down to the club one night. And I was so nervous because he was my idol, you know, and naturally I wanted to play my best. He told me that the best thing I ever did was to go to Europe because I came into my own as a drummer there.

> When I look back on it and think about it, when you live in a place like Europe you don't hear anybody, so there's nobody to influence you. Everything you get you're getting from yourself. Like here, I'm in New York, I can go downtown and hear somebody right now if I want to hear somebody play. They may play something I could like and I might try to do it, but in Europe that's out. Well, okay, maybe I could go hear Kenny Clarke or Philly Joe, but I've been hearing them all my life anyway, and it's not on a regular basis either.

Kenny Clarke was one of the first musicians to relocate to Europe; he had been living in Paris since 1956. A very special student-teacher relationship developed between him and Taylor.

> I studied for the first time in my life. Kenny Clarke insisted that I study with him when he opened his

school. He told me that if I didn't study with him I'd
have to fight him, so it was easier to study. I found out
what I was doing all those years, and I was able to
improve on it and do it with more control.

Ironically, as an up-and-coming player, Taylor had neither
been impressed nor influenced by Clarke, who has been
recognized indisputably as the pivotal drummer in the
development of bebop as it evolved from swing.

I listened to Max of course and Blakey. They used to
talk about Kenny Clarke; they had such a great respect
for him. I had listened to him, and I wasn't impressed.
He was a little different; he wasn't into the same type of
thing as Art and Max. His cymbal beat was different,
into another kind of thing. And then I heard him when
he returned to the U.S., because he had lived in Europe
even way back then. So naturally he was around all his
old friends. I heard him, and I still wasn't impressed.
Then one night, I heard him play. I said, "Oh my
goodness, this is something *different*. I should check this
out." It wasn't your regular type of thing. He had
another kind of timing and everything—little offbeats.
It wasn't the same basic cymbal beat that he used.
There were intricate rhythms in his cymbal work.

Another major accomplishment during his stay in Europe
was Taylor's first—and quite successful—attempt at journalism. He collected a remarkable set of interviews that he
conducted with musicians either living in or traveling through
Europe and it resulted in the publication of a critically
acclaimed book entitled *Notes and Tones* (New York:
Putnam, 1977). Subtitled "Musician-to-Musician Interviews," it contains controversial statements concerning the
role of the African-American jazz artist in the mainstream of
American culture. Stitched together by a continuum of
similar questions, the book's value lies in its utter candor and
uniqueness for this genre. A partial list of those interviewed
includes Art Blakey, Miles Davis, Dizzy Gillespie, Sonny
Rollins, Erroll Garner, Carmen McRae, and Freddie Hub-
bard. It is compelling reading.
Family matters, specifically an aging mother, required that

Taylor return to the States and for several years he straddled the two continents. In 1984, he made the U.S. his permanent home again.

BACK IN THE U.S.A.

There are no regrets on Taylor's part about living in the States again. He has maintained a viable performing schedule that takes him to Europe regularly for concerts, festivals, and recordings. Back home, a cultural awakening has finally resulted in a burgeoning recognition of jazz as American art. This, combined with a resurgent interest in bebop specifically, is adding fuel to Taylor's career. He continues to play with his "friends from the neighborhood," Jackie McLean and Sonny Rollins, and others from that era like Jimmy Heath, in addition to artists he had never performed with before the years in Europe, such as the great bassist Ray Brown.

He has resumed performing with his group "Taylor's Wailer's"[8] and now, a full 25 years later, has released his second recording as a leader; it is entitled *Mr. A.T.* (December 9, 1991, Enja Records, R2 79677). He has nearly completed work on an additional volume of *Notes and Tones*[9] and has been approached by a film company in Europe to produce a documentary using videotapes he recorded of Art Blakey, Ron Carter, and Randy Weston.

He is more than a little concerned about the current state of jazz expression, attributing what he feels is a lack of passion to the times in which we live.

> In this life you have to be aware of what happened before you. I guess you have to listen. The times are so different. These people came in different times; when I started out with Jackie and Sonny Rollins, we were twenty years old too, but they were geniuses even then. I was talking to Sonny Rollins about this the other day. We had more opportunities to develop than these people today. They go and develop in the school. We were going into night clubs and beer and gin mills and playing all night long. So you get a chance to really hone

your craft like that. When you're sitting up in some school you come out sounding like a school. So it's a different time and different era, which is why these people sound like that.

He is particularly hard on the current crop of drummers and, after a lively exchange as we ran through my list, he considered his responses and requested that I omit specific names—at least for the time being. ("After I die, you may print them—I *want* you to print them.")

I don't like any of them. They all play on the same volume level; they never go up or down. They sound like they come out of school or something like that. I was never one to advocate a young person using drugs or anything, but at least in the Charlie Parker era there was some excitement. Would he show up? Would he fall out? Is he drunk or is he doped up or something? Always an excitement. Today it's just like [makes a droning sound]; it's just a bore. And I tell them, I tell a lot of them—I say, "I'm going to get you a box of Wheaties or something," They're trying but they're not on the right track. Last one I heard was Tony Williams, who could really play, I mean really make some contribution. And they all copy, they all sound alike, you can't tell one from the other.

HIS MUSIC

If I were given only one word to best describe Arthur Taylor's playing it would be "swinging." He is blessed with instincts and good judgment that always keep the music flowing. And he possesses a powerful right hand that, with all its energy and drive, creates sheer beauty on the ride cymbal. That, more than anything else, defines his style of drumming and is his claim to fame.

Other hallmarks of his style include his rock-solid sense of the beat which, underlying everything else, is implied by a light quarter-note pulse on the bass drum that is felt more than heard, and a strong 2-and-4 on the hi-hat. He has, as well, a blazing fast right foot that has a mind of its own and can interplay with his left hand at will. In playing fills, he displays technical finesse with tightly controlled double strokes.

Since Taylor is known less for his solos than for his generous comping abilities, his comping will merit future study. After all, that's what a jazz drummer is supposed to do best. Taylor agrees.

> Soloing is not something that ever really interested me. Even when I go on a gig right now . . . when I walk in, everybody's smiling and saying "Oh boy we're gonna have some fun" because I'm going to swing and give everything I have. But with the reputation I have, it is necessary for me to play a solo. It's *necessary*. So I had a devise some things about solos even though I never had a big thing about them. That is not my forte; my forte is swinging. Sometimes I like soloing; sometimes I don't. I really prefer to be playing with the rhythm section. I like the collective thing.

The two solos appended to this article, "Countdown" and "SlowTrane," are representative of Taylor's soloing style during the late fifties. Both were recorded on dates with John Coltrane within two years of each other. The former appeared on *Giant Steps* (Atlantic 1311), recorded in August 1959; the latter can be found on two separate issues, *Lush Life* (Prestige 7581) and *The Last Trane* (Prestige 7378), and was recorded in May 1957.

The "Countdown" solo is an extended introduction. It is 36 bars long, and its form can be viewed as AABA plus a four-bar coda.[10] The coda is Taylor's signature. Snippets of it can be heard on other records, either within the context of a drum solo or as an entire or partial exchange in a "trading-fours" situation. It is a series of rhythmic figures voiced in a manner unique unto Taylor.[11] When he plays the form of the tune up front, please note Taylor's consistency in the final A section. The first measure is exactly that of the first A, and the following three measures are either a clever displacement of the rhythmic figure by one quarter note or a muffed execution of an attempt to reiterate exactly. I suspect the latter because the next four measures comprise the stock "George of the Jungle" riff which provides a graceful recovery. In any event, we can't help but be completely gratified by that wonderful signature coda.

"SlowTrane" is a standard slow blues that was recorded using only bass, drums, and tenor. ("Red [Garland] forgot to show up.") It is another good example of Taylor's sense of the form. After six tenor choruses, bassist Earl May takes two. Midway through May's last chorus, Taylor employs the hi-hat in double time to create a feeling of a faster tempo without speeding up. This enables the drummer to solo in a more comfortable setting. It is very difficult and definitely not preferred by drummers to solo in a slow tempo. Taylor plays four choruses, each of which has its own theme; one can follow the blues changes throughout as he punctuates those measures accordingly. Please notice the relentless hi-hat on beats 2 and 4 that, except for four counts between the fourth and fifth measure of the final chorus, is ever-present.

NOTES

1. The first interview took place in April 1988, the other two in May of 1991, one week apart.
2. Jeff Potter, "Taylor, Art(hur S., Jr.)" in *The New Grove Dictionary of Jazz,* ed. Barry Kernfeld (London: Macmillan, 1988), vol. 2, pp. 520–21.
3. The session was done in New York City on April 28, 1951. Pettiford never used Taylor again on a record date and the track, "Love For Sale," went unissued. Bruyninckx, W., *Sixty Years of Recorded Jazz, 1917–1977* (issued in looseleaf form), "Pettiford," p. P–211.
4. See note 3. Of the four tracks recorded that day, two were issued (Mercer 1966). Taylor is probably not referring to these specifically, but instead to any recording on which Pettiford plays cello.
5. On the album, *The Amazing Bud Powell, Vol. 2* (Blue Note 1504).
6. Leonard Feather's liner notes bear this out. He analyzes the tune as containing four movements.
7. *Miles: The Autobiography,* (with Quincy Troupe) (New York: Simon and Schuster, 1989) pp. 194, 216.

8. "Taylor's Wailers" recorded once. The album *A.T.'s Delight* (Blue Note 4047) was issued in 1957.
9. A German translation of the book is soon to be published.
10. Taylor remembers playing only 32 bars ("I did a chorus.") and was genuinely surprised when I informed him of the additional four measures.
11. The track "Goldsboro Express" on Coltrane's album *Bahia* (Prestige 7353) recorded three months earlier (December 26, 1958), contains several examples of this coda figure, as does Taylor's extended solo on the cut "Sweet Sapphire Blues" on Coltrane's *Black Pearls* (Prestige 7316), also recorded in 1958.

BIBLIOGRAPHY

Bruyninckx, W. *Sixty Years of Recorded Jazz, 1917–1977.* Issued in looseleaf form. Belgium: various dates.

Chambers, Jack. *Milestones I: The Music and Times of Miles Davis to 1960.* Toronto: University of Toronto Press, 1988.

Davis, Miles, with Quincy Troupe. *Miles, The Autobiography.* New York: Simon and Schuster, 1989.

Mintz, Billy. *Different Drummers.* New York: Amsco Music Publishing Co., 1977.

Potter, Jeff. "Taylor, Art(thur S., Jr.)." In Barry Kernfeld, ed., *The New Grove Dictionary of Jazz.* London: Macmillan, 1988.

Taylor, Arthur. *Notes and Tones.* New York: Perigee Books, 1977.

Thomas, J.C. *Coltrane: Chasin' the Trane.* New York: DaCapo Press, 1976.

KEY TO TRANSCRIPTIONS OF DRUM SOLOS

Key:

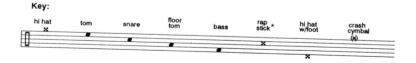

* With the left stick positioned normally on the snare drum, the right stick strikes the left stick's shaft.

MELODIC NOTATION IN JAZZ TRANSCRIPTION

By Mark S. Haywood

Jazz transcriptions often oversimplify or otherwise blur what actually happens in performance, and this can manifest itself in several ways. This paper attempts to define some of the problems which arise and to suggest some solutions. It deals specifically with transcription of melodic line and addresses separately the two issues of pitch and timing.

PITCH

Example A illustrates an inadequate transcription of bent pitches. No standard musical notation exists to express a bend in a note, let alone a particular bend such as an even rise of 1/5 of a tone over the first 1/4 of a note, then a more gradual drop of 1/5 of a tone over the remaining 3/4. Various imprecise attempts have been made to capture effects of this kind on paper, often using arrows

and verbal explanations of the sound by way of footnotes. For many jazz solos, this technique would probably involve writing a book! Such a set of explanations could never convey the sound of the melody as it runs along.

I propose the following solution: a 'pitch chart' can be placed above the melody note in question in order to show how the note varies from normal pitch. Such charts should only be added to notes which do actually vary from what is actually written. The pitch chart is a box in which duration is shown horizontally and pitch vertically. Hence a box for ♩ .

Example A

will be three times wider than one for ♩ ; the height of the
pitch chart can follow a standard whereby a central horizontal line shows the written pitch, the top of the box one
semitone higher, the bottom one semitone lower. Hence we
might have Example B.

Example B

Of course, since the width of the chart is determined by the
note value, the notes themselves must be spaced accordingly
in order that they appear beneath their respective charts. A
key at the top of the transcription should give details, e.g.:

Pitch chart. Vertical range : +/- one semitone.
Horizontal scale : ♪ = 3mm.

The vertical range should be the same for all charts in the
transcription. Once the chart is set up in this way, a line is
drawn within it from left to right, showing as accurately as
possible the pitch envelope of the note as performed. Hence
it is possible to show clearly how a note is affected by pitch
nuance, as in Example C.

Example C

The example now shows how the initial C was bent upwards then downwards, reaching its highest point, almost a semitone above C, about 2/3 of its way through. 2/3 of a whole-note cannot otherwise be easily expressed, nor can the extent of the bend, other than diagrammatically. The A^b is shown to have a downward bend which is at its most pronounced early in the quarter-note. The final G is played as written and therefore requires no pitch chart.

TIMING

Example D

The transcription in Example D illustrates a totally inadequate representation of the timing of a performed melodic phrase. An accurate notation might be represented by Example E.

Example E

This example shows precisely that the notes originally represented as straight quarter- or eighth-notes are in reality delayed or anticipated as follows:

Bar 1: E On the beat   Bar 2: E Delayed by ♪≣

C Delayed by ♪≣   C On the beat

B Delayed by ♪≣   A Anticipated by ♪≣

A Delayed by ♪═   B Anticipated by ♪≣

G# Delayed by ♪═   G Anticipated by ♪═

B Delayed by ♪═   F Anticipated by ♪═

D Delayed by ♪≣   G Anticipated by ♪═

F Delayed by ♪≣ Bar 3: E Anticipated by ♪═

Even this notation cannot be absolutely precise, but it may be as near to the truth as is audibly possible. But is it readable? Does it mean anything? This kind of notation does not clearly show how the various anticipations and delays vary with respect to each other, for example whether a dragging tempo gradually develops but then is swiftly compensated. This notation is no better than the original version using straight quarter- and eighth-notes for someone wishing to see clearly on paper the nuances and nuance relationships in the melody as played.

I propose a solution as follows: slight anticipations or delays to melodic notes can be indicated by adding an arrow beneath the notes in question. To show increased degrees of anticipation or delay the arrow's horizontal stroke can be doubled or trebled. Our passage now appears as in Example F.

Example F

The notation is once again simple and easy to read, as in the original version, but the arrows now show visibly how a dragging tempo gradually develops and is then gradually compensated (bar 1) and how the timing of the notes then increasingly races ahead of the beat (bars 2–3). The arrows should define solely the time relationship between the notes as played and the beat on which they appear in the written transcription. Thus in our example all the notes in the first bar except the initial E are behind the beat and therefore require left-pointing arrows, even though the sixth and seventh eighth-notes actually make up time on their predecessors.

As was the case with the melodic pitch chart, a key should be set up at the beginning of the transcription, showing the full range of arrow symbols to be used (a standard could be those introduced here) plus a note as to how much anticipation or delay is denoted by the most extreme case, for example:

$$\Rightarrow = \flat$$

This paper has tried to illustrate some of the difficulties inherent in much jazz transcription today, and to suggest that some standards be set. Two types of musical misrepresentation have been discussed, in order to attempt a broadening of the scope of transcription so as to accommodate the audible language of jazz.

BOOK REVIEWS

Bill Crow, *From Birdland to Broadway: Scenes from a Jazz Life* (New York: Oxford University Press, 1992, 273 pp., $24.00)

Ross Firestone, *Swing, Swing, Swing: The Life and Times of Benny Goodman* (New York: W.W. Norton, 1993, 522 pp., $29.95)

Reviewed by Loren Schoenberg

In his second book, Bill Crow has managed to capture the flavor and vibrancy of one of jazz's golden ages. A skilled observer of his fellow man's attributes and foibles, Crow vividly brings to life many of the fabled, and—perhaps more significantly—under-appreciated, musicians (and selected others) of the last half-century.

This book is an effective antidote to jazz histories peopled with "innovators" only and with musical schools which exist in a vacuum. The author, a skilled (and here thoroughly self-effacing) bassist, has worked over the last 40 years with an astonishing list of musicians from virtually every corner of the large and varied jazz family. Entering the profession at a time when the first generation of jazz musicians were still in their fifties, Crow learned much from hanging around an array of jazz giants, ranging from Sidney Bechet, Hot Lips Page (with whom he met Bunk Johnson!), and Pee Wee Russell to Lennie Tristano, Kenny Clarke, and Duke Ellington. While many musicians of his generation were caught up in immature prejudices against the older players, Crow never let mere chronology stand in the way of a musical experience.

Crow writes in an unassuming, almost journalistic prose. At first, the succession of short sentences is a little jarring, as is the paucity of rhythm within the paragraphs. This is quickly remedied as Crow expands on an early influence and friend, Dave Lambert. The words are driven by Crow's reactions to the person he is writing about; obvious as that sounds, it is not always the case, especially with more "professional" writers. Therefore, he is at his best when recounting special moments. His recollections and anecdotes are always refreshingly to the point. When he stretches out, as he does with a lovely and perceptive reminiscence of the great singer Ivie Anderson, the results are magical.

Friendships and/or encounters with Marian McPartland, Charlie Parker, Gerry Mulligan, Jo Jones, Claude Thornhill (one of the book's greatest joys), Benny Goodman (the 1962 Russian tour), Slim Gaillard, and Mike ("The Music Goes 'Round and 'Round") Riley are recounted with a remarkable clarity and depth of perception. Time and time again, Crow paints a telling portrait with a minimum of keystrokes, in a fashion that would be the envy of many a writer.

At times, Crow's work seems more than tangentially related to that of the great paragon of New York storytelling, Joseph Mitchell. The chapter on Al the Waiter (a fixture at the old Half Note) would have fit right in Mitchell's *McSorley's Wonderful Saloon*. Indeed, the subject of one of Mitchell's greatest essays, Joe Gould (Professor Seagull), shows up in Crow's book.

Crow's warm but unsentimental picture of Birdland and its environs is one of the best portraits of that legendary domain. This in turn magical and seedy area just about a dozen blocks north of Times Square had more great jazz talent per square inch for a while than any other place. Through his depiction of the interiors of these nightclubs and the seemingly unending flow of musicians in their vicinity, Crow gives the reader a real feeling for what it meant to be on the scene at the time. This may be the greatest gift this book can bestow on subsequent generations. It is a written corollary to the famous 1958 Harlem photo that appeared in *Esquire* magazine.

That this jazz world was a living, breathing place where

musicians as diverse as Charles Mingus, Miff Mole, Rex Stewart, Thelonious Monk, Scoville Brown, Art Blakey, and, for that matter, Bill Crow exchanged ideas is well worth keeping in mind these days, when some would have us believe that any time two disparate musicians happened upon the same little phrase it was due to an assiduous copying of a recorded solo. While this undoubtedly did happen occasionally, it was far from the rule. Read Crow's chapters on whom he ran into during his various musical peregrinations, and you'll get a feeling for how the jazz vocabulary evolved. Due to the vagaries of popular taste, the real estate market in New York City, and many other intangibles, those days and the music that came from them are gone forever—except, that is, in these pages.

Himself a gifted raconteur, Crow the author has adhered to the Shakespearian adage "brevity is the soul of wit." Many of the anecdotes get even better on reflection. In a passage about his first New York jam session, we get an indelible portrait of the legendary Brew Moore. Crow encountered him

> lying on the floor with his head propped against the wall. Brew had his tenor sax laying beside him where he could play it without having to hold it up. His florid complexion and the nearly empty half-gallon of wine in the crook of his arm indicated the reason for his supine position. Brew was drunk, but he still sounded good. He hadn't removed the cigarette from the corner of his mouth when he began playing, and as he blew into the mouthpiece, sparks flew from the end of the cigarette. I stood there, saucer-eyed, thinking, "Wow! This is really far out!"

Crow combines a sharp eye with a good ear for dialects, which is used to great advantage in his chapter on Pee Wee Marquette, the major domo at Birdland.

> William Clayton Marquette, three feet nine inches tall, was usually nattily dressed in a brown pin-stripe vested suit and a floral tie, or a dark green velvet suit with a large bow tie. On special occasions he wore tails. His

miniature suits were fairly zoot. His belt line was at his armpits, his trousers were heavily pleated and tightly cuffed, and his box-back jackets featured extra-wide lapels.

Pee-Wee's voice was high-pitched and brassy. Though he did his best to enunciate carefully, he frequently slipped into the dialect of Montgomery, Alabama, his birthplace. He would climb laboriously onto the Birdland bandstand, pull the microphone down to chin and shout officiously:

"AND NOW, LAYDUHS AND GENTLEMEN, BIRDLAND, THE JAZZ CORNAH OF THE WORLD, IS PROUD TO PRESENT, THE ONE AND ONLAH. . . ."

After laboriously naming the bandleader and all the musicians and asking for a "large round of applaw" for the band, he would climb back down to floor level and admonish piercingly "All right, now, fellas, let's get right UP heah! We don't want no LULLS 'roun' heah! no LULLS!"

One of the book's most refreshing aspects is its total lack of pretense. While telling his story with confidence, humor and honesty, Crow goes out of his way to place his own presence in whatever event he is describing in the proper context. He also subtly and sympathetically gauges the differences in temperament from generation to generation. His Henry "Red" Allen story comes to mind on this score. There are also many instances where one can read between the lines—an option seldom granted us in this age of tell-all and ultimately tell-nothing-significant autobiographies.

Crow saves his warmest prose for the lovely and elegant portrait of his long-time friend, John Haley "Zoot" Sims, which closes the book, but Crow manages to convey the essence of Zoot's personality throughout. (I don't want to spoil the reader's opportunity for encountering it for the first time by quoting it here.)

In the course of preparing this review, I began to skim the book; I'd read it completely a few months earlier. As is always the case with the best ones, I wound up reading the whole thing again, and with even more admiration for the many facets of Bill Crow.

Oddly enough, one emerges with a similar feeling of admiration, although of a far more grudging type, for the subject of Ross Firestone's biography of Benny Goodman. While the stories of Goodman's personal eccentricities are legion, Firestone has dug deeply into the personal and social background of this still controversial figure, and has emerged with a balanced and honest portrait.

Never before have Benny's early years been explored in such depth. The lasting effect of a childhood that included occasional days without food, and the sudden and early death of his much-revered father, are here considered seriously for the first time. While misfortunes were by no means unique to Goodman among the early generations of jazzmen, they did have a significant impact on Goodman's almost inhuman quest for instrumental perfection. What makes this book so valuable is Firestone's ability to convey, weigh, and place this material in its proper perspective without becoming an amateur psychoanalyst. His method is clean and transparent when dealing with these matters, and he makes his case convincingly.

Early chapters are rightly devoted at length to a detailed but always interesting study of life in Chicago during Goodman's childhood. After reading about the rise in juvenile lawlessness that overtook the Windy City after World War I, you will appreciate Goodman's comment that if it hadn't been for the clarinet, he might well have wound up as a gangster.

The story moves seamlessly from city to city and decade to decade with a wealth of interesting and, in many cases, new details about Goodman's life. These are all supported, thankfully, in an extensive source list in the back of the book. James T. Maher, whose extensive knowledge of both the music and the music business was an invaluable resource, is prominently credited in the acknowledgements; Firestone has used this living Rosetta stone of American music to its best advantage.

There are many revelations about Goodman's private life, including an early and ill-fated romance with the singer Helen Ward, and his varied medical problems. These are all handled with taste as Firestone respectfully recedes into the distance, letting the participants tell their own stories. This is just one of the many aspects that make this book so far superior to J.L. Collier's myopic and ultimately condescending Goodman book of recent vintage. While Collier went in for misguided musical analysis, Firestone wisely refrains from getting technical. This is not to say that an informed Goodmanophile will agree with all of Firestone's opinions, but they are not tied in some odd way to the author's own musical abilities, or lack thereof (there is no clarinet envy here).

Time after time, eyewitnesses capitivatingly recount their experiences in and around Goodman's world, and, through expert editing of these reminiscences, Firestone has created an engaging tapestry to illustrate Goodman's life and times. Particularly valuable are the quotes from the still unheralded Helen Oakley (not yet Dance) about the winter of 1935–6, when she produced a series of jazz concerts in Chicago that were the first of their kind. Featuring both the Goodman and Fletcher Henderson bands, along with the best Chicago musicians, these events had repercussions for decades. One was the hiring of Teddy Wilson as a permanent part of the Goodman entourage, striking the first of many blows against racial segregation.

Firestone never gets bogged down in speculation about Benny's motives in this or other controversial areas. He gives us first-hand narration whenever possible, sometimes adding a few paragraphs of interpretation, and picks up the story. This is a wonderful way of dealing with a life that spanned more than seven and a half decades, without the telescoping frequently characteristic of Collier's jazz biographies. Firestone deals admirably with the fact that the final decades of Goodman's life were spent far removed from the musical curiosity that he had shown so often before the 1950s. His musical priorities had changed, and this is reflected in the shift to a slight fast-forward that occurs from page 337 on.

Throughout the book, Goodman's occasional episodes of pettiness and financial chicanery are juxtaposed with sincere testimonials to another and better side of this complicated personality. Because he never mentioned it, few knew the degree to which he suffered for decades from chronic back pain, or how he never looked back after a particularly devastating bout with cancer. His friends come off sympathetically as protective of him, and this is another major strength of the book. The reader gleans a feeling for a complete man, not just a clarinet virtuoso, pop idol, or elder statesman. And Goodman's final heroic days are perfectly set down through the recollections of his companion, Carol Phillips.

There is one link, however, between not just Collier and Firestone, but also with the ultimate Goodman chronicler, D. Russ Connor. Each has one major photo misidentification in his book. In Collier, it's Jack Bregman, not Fletcher Henderson; in Connor, it's Harry Sosnick, not George Gershwin; now, in Firestone, it's not Eddie Sauter (perhaps Fud Livingston?). The other photos in *Swing, Swing, Swing,* mostly from the Ken Whitten collection, are fine, and in many instances, relatively rare.

Gene Lees, photographs by John Reeves, *Jazz Lives: 100 Portraits in Jazz* (New York: Firefly Books, 1992, 216 pp., $39.95)

Robert O'Meally, *Lady Day: The Many Faces of Billie Holiday* (New York: Arcade Publishing, 1991, 207 pp., $29.95)

Reviewed by Edward Berger

Jazz Lives is a collaboration between a noted jazz writer, Gene Lees, and an equally distinguished photographer, John Reeves. As its subtitle implies, *Jazz Lives* contains a brief essay and a corresponding full-page black-and-white photo (or in some cases several smaller photos) of some 100 jazz artists, ranging from famous to comparatively unknown. There is no indication of how this selection was made. These verbal and visual portraits appear in order by age of the subjects, an effective departure from the usual alphabetical arrangement. The book begins with the venerable trombonist Spiegle Willcox (b. 1903) and concludes with bass wunderkind Christian McBride (b. 1972). Watching the faces gradually grow younger as one flips the pages does convey a sense of the continuity of the art form. Given the credentials of both writer and photographer, however, the overall results are disappointing, particularly Lees's contribution.

In seeking a new approach to jazz photography, Reeves settled on what he calls the "big face" portrait idea. As he explains, "I thought that straight intimate portraiture might yield viewers useful—and different—information that had not been provided in quite as much quantity as the other photographic approaches to jazz." Thus, Reeves's work for the most part consists of full-page, ultra-close-up, black-and-white head shots which, while often striking and technically impressive, tend to lose their effectiveness due to lack of

variety. Furthermore, many of the portraits are so clinically
stark that they cross the line between insight and invasion of
privacy. Nevertheless, there are some real gems here: Doc
Cheatham with cigar, soulful shots of Benny Carter and
Oscar Peterson, and pensive ones of Clark Terry and Hank
Jones. Some of the best images capture musicians in
somewhat lighter moments, for example Herb Ellis and Ray
Brown together, the Candoli brothers, Kenny Washington,
and Roy Hargrove.

Lees's text gives the impression of having been written in
great haste, with numerous factual errors and occasional
syntactical lapses and misspellings. Among the more glaring
inaccuracies is a reference in the Doc Cheatham entry to the
McKinney's Cotton Pickers. In an aside, Lees asserts that
"there was no one named McKinney" (p. 6). It is well
documented that drummer Bill McKinney organized that
legendary orchestra and remained with it in various capacities for virtually its entire tenure.

Cheatham's colleague and fellow McKinney alumnus
Benny Carter fares particularly badly in *Jazz Lives*. Lee trots
out the old canard about Carter having studied theology at
Wilberforce University, a myth which Carter himself has
dispelled countless times. Lees has Carter in London in the
1930s leading "a BBC staff band of American and British
musicians," which, if only because of British musicians'
union regulations, would have been impossible. (He is
confusing Carter's *arranging* for the BBC Dance Orchestra
with Carter's own international orchestra which played in
Holland in the summer of 1937.) He further claims that, after
penetrating the Hollywood studios, Carter wrote arrangements "usually for black singers such as Lena Horne
appearing in white movies." Such assignments represented a
very small part of Carter's film writing. Finally, we are told
that "in the mid-1940s he [Carter] returned to playing and
travel . . ." This was precisely when Carter disbanded his
orchestra and devoted more and more time to work as a
composer and arranger in Hollywood. All of these blunders
(and a couple of others) occur in the space of four
paragraphs. This treatment is even more disappointing since

Lees lists Carter as "one of my early idols." Indeed, he has written most perceptively and eloquently about Carter in his *Jazzletter*.

Granted that this is one of the worst entries, but such inaccuracies are commonplace. Writing about Marian McPartland, Lees states that the pianist asked him if she and her ex-husband, cornetist Jimmy McPartland (who was gravely ill at the time), should remarry. "Without a second thought I said 'Yes,' " writes Lees, "but there wasn't time." (P. 26) One would think that Lees would have bothered to find out that the McPartlands *were* remarried, particularly since he claims to have been consulted. While this is not a reference book, a writer of Lees's experience and skill should be a bit less cavalier with facts.

As a talented lyricist and respected writer on jazz and popular music, Lees has formed close relationships with many of the figures about whom he writes. His past work has often reflected the deep personal insights such relationships can yield. Here, however, it results in little more than incessant name-dropping and a propensity to inject himself onto almost every page, even when this serves no useful purpose. We are constantly reminded who wrote songs with Lees, who recorded them, who influenced him, and whom he influenced. Even the most inconsequential connections between author and subject are scrupulously pointed out: who once gave him a ride, who called him on the phone, whom he met at Henry Mancini's house, who shares a near-birthday with him, etc.

Occasionally, Lees claims a less modest role: "Kenny [Wheeler] has often said in interviews that he moved to England (in 1952) at my suggestion. . . . Had he (and I) been able to get visas to the United States, we'd have gone there. Thus I, quite inadvertently, influenced jazz in England and on the Continent, because Kenny became one of the major European jazz figures." (P. 102)

On the positive side, it is good to see something written about some deserving but often overlooked artists such as Bill Challis, Jimmy Rowles, Lou Levy, and Bill Kirchner. In addition, there are approximately twenty profiles of musicians under forty, about whom there is relatively little in print. But this is hardly enough to justify this beautifully produced but strangely self-indulgent volume.

Photographs also are a central component of *Lady Day: The Many Faces of Billie Holiday,* but the photos here are historical in nature. Taking advantage of a treasure-trove of photos, interviews and other research assembled by Linda Kuehl, a Holiday devotee who died in 1973 before she could complete her own Holiday study, Robert O'Meally has constructed a fascinating aural and visual picture of the singer. The illustrations include dozens of previously unpublished photos of Holiday—from age two right up until her death in 1959. There are also many wonderful shots of the singer's illustrious musical associates and effective background photographs depicting places where she lived and venues in which she worked. In addition to the photos, there are reproductions of all sorts of memorabilia: newspaper clippings, letters, a baptismal certificate, a passport, even a room service check.

O'Meally modestly calls his accompanying text a biographical essay, not a full biography. Nevertheless, in an entertaining way he sheds new light on Holiday's early years, corrects a number of factual errors, and debunks many oft-repeated myths about the singer and her music. Although he by no means glosses over the seamier aspects of Holiday's personal life, O'Meally admirably focuses on Billie Holiday, the artist:

> We have been so mesmerized by the recital of this singer's private woes that at times we have lost sight of the real reason that history cares about her at all: the lure and spiritedness of her voice, her way of turning bad songs into good or even great songs, and her way of transforming already great songs into music and poetry that will last forever." (P. 10)

O'Meally writes with sympathy and understanding about Holiday's singing style and recordings—the perfect antidote to Michael Brooks's often perverse annotations to the Columbia Jazz Masterpieces *Quintessential Billie Holiday* series. One of the hoary myths tackled by O'Meally is the claim that Holiday had no say in the material foisted upon her by insidious music publishers and crass record company executives—particular bêtes noires of Brooks. Revealing remarks by Teddy Wilson show that she exerted far more control over the selection process than previously assumed: "I would get together with Billie first, and we would take a stack of music, maybe thirty, forty songs, and go through them, and pick out the ones that would appeal to her—the lyric, the melody." (P. 111) O'Meally adds:

> It is important to know that Holiday was not just singing whatever songs she was given, as most accounts report. While it is clear that she sometimes was stuck at the last moment with a song that Columbia insisted she do to honor an obligation to a publisher or song plugger, she usually had some choice in these matters. According to Wilson, the two of them rejected 90 percent of the material they reviewed. (Pp. 111–12)

The Wilson quote is one of dozens of valuable observations by musicians, many published here for the first time. Unfortunately, none of the sources are cited. One presumes that they derive from original interviews conducted by Kuehl or O'Meally, but this fact is not made clear. Similarly, O'Meally includes many insightful but uncited observations by such writers as Gunther Schuller, Stanley Crouch, Leonard Feather, Martin Williams, Albert Murray, and Ralph Ellison. These are presumably from the works by these authors listed in the book's bibliography but, again, even in a nonscholarly work such as this, some more precise method of identifying sources is needed. A more serious citation problem occurs when O'Meally uses a description and attributes it only to "one writer," without even naming the source.

O'Meally's enthusiastic prose sometimes leads to hyperbole: "Between 1935 and 1942 . . . Holiday cut hundreds of titles for Columbia" (p. 114); it was actually around 125. The author cites John Hammond's portentous visit to Monette's in Harlem in 1933, when he first heard Billie Holiday, as "an event for the jazz history book, though so far, aside from [Humphrey] Lyttelton, no jazz historian has noticed it." (P. 55) Virtually every major survey of Holiday's career mentions this event.

Despite these lapses, along with frequent repetition and the absence of an index, the text is a fine complement to the stunning illustrations. Returning to the photos, O'Meally opens Part Three with an astute observation (once again uncredited—it is from Melvin Maddocks's booklet accompanying the Time-Life *Giants of Jazz* series Billie Holiday set), which underscores the book's fitting subtitle, *The Many Faces of Billie Holiday:* " 'No camera,' one writer said, 'could ever contrive to capture once and for all the elusive essence of Billy Holiday . . . [seven] pictures taken in her twenties and thirties are so strikingly dissimilar that they might pass for portraits of seven different women.' " (p. 91)

REVIEW ESSAY

The Hal Leonard Artist Transcription Series

By Lewis Porter

Charlie Christian: The Art of Jazz Guitar
Edited by Dan Fox (Goodman Group, 1964; reprinted and
distributed by Hal Leonard, 1988, 32 pp., $5.95)

The Music of John Coltrane
No editor listed; Alice Coltrane mentioned as a collaborator
(Hal Leonard, 1991, 125 pp., $17.95)

Charles Mingus: More Than a Fake Book
Compiled by Sue Mingus, Andrews Homzy, and Don Sickler
(Jazz Workshop, 1991; distributed by Hal Leonard, joint
publication, 160 pp., $19.95)

Wes Montgomery
Transcribed by Fred Sokolow (Third Earth and Hal Leonard, joint publication, 1988, 96 pp., $14.95)

James Newton: The Improvising Flute
By James Newton (Third Earth and Hal Leonard, joint
publication, 1989, 69 pp., $14.95)

Wayne Shorter
Transcribed by Sanford Marten (Third Earth and Hal
Leonard, joint publication, 1990, 110 pp., $14.95)

Hal Leonard has put together an impressive series of jazz
leadsheets and transcribed solos that musicians and educators will find indispensable. While some collections have

their shortcomings, as noted below, they are all a great place to start, and the collections of Coltrane, Mingus, and Shorter are the first authorized editions for these important artists.

Each book has a unique format. Some offer leadsheets only, some provide transcribed solos, some give both. Most have commentary for each piece, and a few offer technical advice for improvisers. Taking them in the order listed above, the Christian book is the only one that has been issued before. The short biography gives 1919 as Christian's birth year, even though we now know that he was born in 1916, but otherwise this reissue has not become obsolete. The twelve solos are all taken from Christian's studio recordings with Benny Goodman. Most are from originals by Goodman such as "Six Appeal," "Wholly Cats," and "Breakfast Feud," but Christian is represented as coauthor on "Airmail Special," "Solo Flight," "Seven Come Eleven," and "Shivers." The transcriptions are fairly accurate, but ghosted notes are often omitted. Themes and background riffs are usually indicated, although it would have been nice to have shown the guitar part for the theme of "Airmail Special"—he is not playing in unison with the winds, as implied here. The chords provided on "Wholly Cats" are more complicated than the simple blues changes that are actually played. Finally, users should be warned that the versions transcribed of "Breakfast Feud" and "Airmail Special" are the ones once issued on Columbia 652 that spliced together Christian solos from several takes. One will have to compare these aurally when using more recent CD issues. (An article by Clive G. Downs elsewhere in this *Annual Review* details the available Christian transcriptions and their sources.)

Over one hundred compositions are represented in the Coltrane book. Any Coltrane original you are looking for is likely to be there, from "Nita," which was in 1956 among his first originals to be recorded, to the four parts of "A Love Supreme," to the titles on his last album, *Expression.* One can study Coltrane's fascinating and challenging reworkings of "Confirmation" ("26-2," which he begins on tenor and ends on soprano saxophone) and "I Can't Get Started" ("Exotica," also known as "Untitled Original"). Among the few missing items are "Straight Street" from 1957 and "Trane's Blues," also known as "John Paul Jones." The sources are the lead sheets compiled mostly in the 1970s for copyright purposes, and they are for the most part quite accurate. In some cases bass lines and countermelodies are given, and Alice Coltrane has suggested alternate chords for some of the later items. The pieces are in alphabetical order, and a discography at the back gives the album title on which each one may be found. The album numbers are of course mostly out of date, but luckily the titles have mostly remained the same on the CD releases. The dates given in the discography are an odd mix of recording dates (mostly) and release dates.

Many of Coltrane's recordings have no real theme, since he often soloed over the chords or, from 1965 on, worked freely from a set of thematic motives, and here things get interesting. For "Ascension" we get a sketch that amounts to a drastically simplified but useful reduction of the group sound actually heard. For the titles from *Expression* and *Interstellar Space* we essentially get the first page of Coltrane's solo transcribed, although on "Venus" it appears to be the last page. By the way, "Equinox" is given here in the usual key of C-sharp minor, but Coltrane's handwritten version (reproduced on p. 283 of *Coltrane: A Biography,* by C.O. Simpkins, reissued in 1989 by Black Classic Press) shows he wrote it in D-flat minor.

There is quite a bit of confusion here about Coltrane's version of "I Can't Get Started" mentioned above. It was recorded for Roulette on September 8, 1960, as "Exotica," then for Atlantic on October 24, 1960, in a version originally unreleased. In 1970, Atlantic issued its version as "Untitled Original." In this book, for "Exotica" one gets the first A section of Coltrane's solo on the Roulette version and the date is given as 10/24/64 (apparently a typo for 1960, but still incorrect). Under "Untitled Original" one finds the first A section of Coltrane's solo from the Atlantic version, marked with a repeat, than a transcription of Coltrane's solo on the bridge of the last chorus and the last A and coda of the recording. For the date, both 10/24 and 10/26/60 are given.

The Mingus collection is the most authoritative of the batch, due to the active involvement of Mingus's wife Sue, musician Don Sickler, and scholar Andrew Homzy. It includes commentary on each piece by Homzy and is interspersed with photographs and with pages of Mingus's own manuscripts. Two of Mingus's provocative essays are reprinted. For the music, numerous details of the arrangements are provided, including some of the many variations Mingus would throw in at different performances. While these charts may represent what Mingus wrote, one will occasionally spot slight differences in the theme or chords from what was actually recorded. For example, on "Fables of Faubus" the four sixteenths in the second measure should read b-natural, c, b-flat (not b-natural again, as given), a-flat; every occurrence of this pattern—it is found starting on d-flat also—should be corrected accordingly.

There have been previous volumes devoted to Wes Montgomery, compiled by guitarists Steve Khan (Gopam Enterprises, 1978) and Jimmy Stewart (Robbins Music, 1968), and certain favorite tunes show up in this new book by Sokolow that have been available before, among them "Boss City," "Bumpin' On Sunset," "Tear It Down," and "West Coast Blues." Sokolow's transcriptions seem fine— Montgomery's marvelous clarity of phrasing seems to make him an ideal subject—although Stewart's versions also showed the arrangements and bass lines. Sokolow gives an informative introduction that breaks down some of the trademarks of Montgomery's style. All three volumes to date are disappointing in their choice of repertoire. They focus on the Verve and A&M recordings, on which the guitarist sometimes solos entirely in octaves, and sometimes only paraphrases the theme. Out of fifteen solos in Sokolow's book, only one is from the early records with the Mastersounds and only one, the delightful "West Coast Blues," is from the Riverside albums that are generally considered (and I agree) his best jazz work.

James Newton's book will be of great interest because there are few books for jazz flutists and because Newton's own attractive and varied compositions are featured throughout, along with his version of Ellington's "Heaven." The book is for jazz and classical flutists, who already are fairly competent. For each piece, Newton provides guidelines for study. For example, the lead sheet of his tribute to Mingus,

"Forever Charles," is followed by two pages of exercises based on the chords of the piece, then by a transcription of Newton's solo on the piece. Newton provides notes on each piece, in general recommending this procedure of studying the chords first and then mastering one or more solos (transcribed from the recording or written out by the student) on the way to developing one's own improvisations. One piece, "Crystal Texts," is a duet for flute and piano, with the piano part provided. A discography and biography of Newton complete this book.

Because Wayne Shorter is one of the most admired and influential of saxophonists—and composers—the final volume reviewed here has been much awaited. It includes a generous sampling of Shorter's written pieces and saxophone solos, each introduced by an interview with Shorter conducted by Ronny Schiff. The twenty-five pieces include "Lester Left Town," "E.S.P.," "Footprints" (as recorded on Shorter's album *Adam's Apple*), "Ana Maria," "Nefertiti" (only the theme is given for this one because Shorter took no solo on the Miles Davis recording), "Speak No Evil," and other celebrated recordings. The transcriptions are of high quality, with attention to such details as articulation. (One obvious typo will be caught by most musicians: the last two notes at the end of the first line of "Footprints" should of course be e and d, not d and d.)

The Hal Leonard series also includes volumes devoted to Chick Corea's written themes, a David Sanborn book, and a number of guitar books devoted to Al Di Meola, John Scofield, Pat Metheny, and others.

ABOUT THE EDITORS

EDWARD BERGER, assistant director of the Institute of Jazz Studies, is coauthor of the two-volume biodiscography, *Benny Carter: A Life in American Music,* and the autobiography of Teddy Reig, *Reminiscing in Tempo.* His biodiscography of bassist George Duvivier, *Basically Speaking,* will be published by Scarecrow Press this year. He has frequently served as road manager for Benny Carter, has produced and annotated a number of Carter's recent recordings (including the Grammy-winning *Benny Carter: Harlem Renaissance*), and has recently issued, on his own Evening Star label, a CD featuring trumpeter Joe Wilder, *Alone With Just My Dreams.*

DAVID A. CAYER was a founding coeditor of *Journal of Jazz Studies,* the predecessor of *Annual Review of Jazz Studies,* in 1973 and has been affiliated with the Institute of Jazz Studies since 1965. In 1991 he retired from Rutgers University as Associate Vice President for Academic Affairs.

DAN MORGENSTERN, Director of the Institute of Jazz Studies, is a jazz historian and former editor of *Down Beat.* His many publications include *Jazz People,* and he has won five Grammy awards for album notes. He has been a vice president of the National Academy of Recording Arts and Sciences, a jazz panelist for the Music Program of the National Endowment for the Arts, and a teacher of jazz history at Brooklyn College, New York University, the Peabody Institute, and Rutgers.

LEWIS PORTER, associate professor of music at the Newark Campus of Rutgers, is coauthor (with Michael Ullman) of *Jazz: From Its Origins to the Present* (Prentice-

Hall), author of *Lester Young,* and editor of *The Lester Young Reader.* He has been jazz editor and a regular contributor to *Black Perspective in Music.* Other writings have appeared in *The New Grove Dictionary of Music in the United States, The Grove Dictionary of Jazz,* and *Journal of the American Musicological Society.* He performs as pianist, drummer, and vocalist.

ABOUT THE CONTRIBUTORS

WILLIAM BAUER lives in Piermont, New York, with his wife Marjorie and twin sons, Conrad and Isaac. He is currently pursuing a doctorate in composition at the Ph.D. program in music at the Graduate Center of the City University of New York. He teaches choral and elementary music at the Hackley School in Tarrytown and theory at the Hoff-Barthelson Music School in Scarsdale, in addition to conducting workshops nationwide on the Dalcroze approach.

STEVEN BLOCK is assistant professor of composition and theory at the University of New Mexico. His article on free jazz in *Music Theory Spectrum* was the first jazz article ever published in that journal. He has written on contemporary classical music for *Perspectives in New Music, Integrales, High Fidelity/Musical America,* and other publications.

VERNON W. BOGGS, Ph.D., is assistant professor of sociology at the City University of New York and conducts studies of crime and deviance in the U.S. and Scandinavia at CUNY's Center for Social Research. He recently published *Salsiology: Afro-Cuban Music and the Evolution of Salsa in New York City* (New York: Excelsior, 1992). His current musical research is on Cuban influences on doowop and early rhythm and blues.

CLIVE G. DOWNS devotes most of his research to applying Q-analysis (a mathematical methodology) in psychology and is nearing completion of a Ph.D. concerned with applications in representing the structure of knowledge and skills needed in jobs. His musical articles have appeared in *Saxophone Journal* and *Jazz Journal International.* He is currently working also in implementing computer systems in local authorities.

JONATHAN FINKELMAN is a guitarist and is currently pursuing a Ph.D. in composition in the music program at the Graduate Center of the City University of New York. He has freelanced as a jazz and rock musician and conducted research on Frank Zappa and Aaron Copland.

KRIN GABBARD, associate professor of comparative literature at the State University of New York at Stony Brook, is coauthor of *Psychiatry and the Cinema* (Chicago: University of Chicago Press, 1987) and has published widely on film, music, art, and literature. He is currently writing a book, tentatively titled *Jamming at the Margins: Jazz and the American Cinema,* and is editor of two forthcoming anthologies, *Representing Jazz* and *Jazz Among the Discourses.*

MARK S. HAYWOOD works for the British National Health Service and holds a Ph.D. in classics from Liverpool University. A lifelong student of music, he has gained accreditation on several instruments and in music theory from the Associated Board of the Royal Schools of Music.

BONNIE L. JOHNSON is a professional drummer currently performing and teaching in the New York area. She has recorded and toured internationally and has a B.A. in Anthropology from the University of California at Berkeley, a B.M. in Percussion from the Hartt School of Music, and an M.A. in Jazz Performance from Queens College in Flushing, NY. She cites as her mentors Jackie Mclean, Jimmy Heath, Art Taylor, Bernard Purdie, and Sharon Russell.

LOREN SCHOENBERG, a tenor saxophonist and pianist, leads his own big band, and has played and recorded with Benny Carter, Jimmy Heath, and David Murray. He is now associated with the Smithsonian Jazz Masterworks Orchestra (under Gunther Schuller and David Baker) and conducted the American Jazz Orchestra (with John Lewis). He teaches aesthetics at the New School in New York City.

CHARLES H. WATERS, JR., is a practicing lawyer in Houston, Texas. He has a longstanding interest in the life and music of Duke Ellington and is a regular presenter at the annual Ellington Study Group Conferences. An abstract of this essay was presented at the Eighth Annual Ellington Study Group Conference in Ottawa, Ontario, in May 1990.

ABOUT THE INSTITUTE
OF JAZZ STUDIES

The Institute of Jazz Studies of Rutgers, the State University of New Jersey, is a unique research facility and archival collection, the foremost of its kind. IJS was founded in 1952 by Marshall Stearns (1908–1966), a pioneer jazz scholar, professor of medieval English literature at Hunter College, and the author of two essential jazz books: *The Story of Jazz* and *Jazz Dance.* In 1966, Rutgers was chosen as the collection's permanent academic home. IJS is located on the Newark campus of Rutgers and is a branch of the John Cotton Dana Library of the Rutgers University Libraries.

IJS carries on a comprehensive program to preserve and further jazz in all its facets. The archival collection, which has quadrupled its holdings since coming to Rutgers, as of 1991 consists of more than 100,000 sound recordings in all formats, from phonograph cylinders and piano rolls to video cassettes and laser discs; more than 5,000 books on jazz and related subjects, including discographies, bibliographies, and dissertations; and comprehensive holdings in jazz periodicals from throughout the world. In addition, there are extensive vertical files on individuals and selected topics, a large collection of photographs, sheet music, big band arrangements, realia, and memorabilia.

IJS serves a broad range of users, from students to seasoned scholars, authors, and collectors. The facilities are open to the public on weekdays by appointment. In order to allow the widest possible access, there is no charge for routine use of reference materials. Researchers requiring extensive staff assistance, however, are assessed a charge. Due to limited audio facilities, as well as to preserve the record collection, listening and taping are limited to serious research projects.

In addition to students, scholars, and other researchers, IJS routinely assists teachers, musicians, the media, record companies and producers, libraries and archives, arts agencies, and jazz organizations.

For further information on IJS programs and activities, write to:

Institute of Jazz Studies
135 Bradley Hall
Rutgers, The State University
Newark, NJ 07102